Beyond Time

by Isabella Clarence

This book is a work of non-fiction based on the life, experiences and recollections of the author. Some names have been changed in this book to protect the privacy of the individuals involved.

No part of this book may be reproduced, stored in a retrieval system, or transmitted in any form or by any means, electronic, mechanical, photocopying, recording or otherwise, without express written permission of the author.

www.isabellaclarence.co.uk

Copyright © 2018 Isabella Clarence

All rights reserved.

ISBN-10: 1983875945
ISBN-13: 978-1983875946

DEDICATION

To my family with love.

CONTENTS

CONTENTS i
ACKNOWLEDGMENTS iii
FOREWORD viii
INTRODUCTION x

CHAPTER ONE 12
CHAPTER TWO 17
CHAPTER THREE 30
CHAPTER FOUR 36
CHAPTER FIVE 41
CHAPTER SIX 55
CHAPTER SEVEN 68
CHAPTER EIGHT 80
CHAPTER NINE 84
CHAPTER TEN 92
CHAPTER ELEVEN 101
CHAPTER TWELVE 110
CHAPTER THIRTEEN 125
CHAPTER FOURTEEN 137
CHAPTER FIFTEEN 157
CHAPTER SIXTEEN 168
CHAPTER SEVENTEEN 180
CHAPTER EIGHTEEN 187

CHAPTER NINETEEN 198
CHAPTER TWENTY 204
CHAPTER TWENTY-ONE 214
CHAPTER TWENTY-TWO 226
CHAPTER TWENTY-THREE 234
CHAPTER TWENTY-FOUR 249
CHAPTER TWENTY-FIVE 265

ACKNOWLEDGMENTS

The stories are written, the book is finished, edited and proofread, all ready to be published. So it's time now for me to sit and write my thank you list and place the page or pages in the front of my completed manuscript. Apparently, this is where in my book I'm supposed to put them and I've never quite understood why because, until my book was finished, I had no idea who I would need to thank. So that's why I have had to leave the writing of this until last and I still think it should be placed at the end of the book.

Protocol. It's all double-dutch to me.

I've lost track over the years of some people and I regret this. This not only applies to people that were personal friends, it also applies to some patients I haven't seen for many years and that's very relevant for now.

One or two of the stories you are about to read are about people I've lost touch with and, consequently, I was unable to contact them to get their permission to use their stories. However, I have changed nearly all the names in this book to protect the privacy of those involved, so I'm sure everyone is safe and their privacy is still well protected. If I have used an actual name it's because I have that person's permission. By any chance you read this book and you think one of the stories is about you, the chances of it being you are very very remote.

My first thank you absolutely must go to my beautiful daughter. She somehow managed to find the time in her busy schedule to edit this book for me. Thank you, my precious girl, for giving of your time. Thank you for all the hours you gave me, thank you for loving me enough to find them. You've done a fantastic job.

If any of you reading this are thinking that getting a family member to do my editing for me was going to make my life easier, forget it. Trust me, I couldn't have had a tougher, stricter or better editor if I'd tried. She has done an amazing job. Unless you've written a book yourself you will not realise that my writing the book was the easy part. The hard work began when I had finished it.

Picture the scene. Firstly the book was written. Then the book was read by my editor. The edited book then came back to me with comments written all over it. I then sat and read through them one at a time, making the adjustments that I was asked for (if I agreed), from changing the odd word here and there, to the addition of pages and pages of extra information and the moving around of words, paragraphs and sentences. I have a tendency to write things backwards. Somehow I start at the end of a sentence and finish at the beginning. Then my edits were re-edited (driving us both crazy) and then the process was repeated. Each time this was done there were fewer and fewer adjustments to make. A lot of the time my daughter was asking me for more information, or better explanations. She actually got me to take a whole chapter out because she felt I needed to say so much more, so much more it would have turned that particular chapter into another book, so I'm leaving the subject for another time. So perhaps now you can see how important the job of an editor is, and she was the best. I often fell about laughing (or crying) at the comments she wrote or scribbled at the side of the page as she instructed me as to what additions or subtractions she wanted me to make. By and large I agreed with them. Let's have a few of her actual comments that I had to contend with so that you can get a clearer picture:

"What is this?...wrong word...all to be rewritten!...what do you mean?...you have no proof...you've got this backwards...reword...expand...relevance?...more detail...who cares...omit...explain...follow up." You get the picture, there were several swear words too that I'll save you from, but with all the edits that were made, I've got lots to come back to in another book.

I didn't make all the changes she asked me to do (almost but not quite). I left in a funny story even though she was right; it wasn't relevant but it was funny and we all need a good giggle from time to time. But on the whole I agreed with her. I ended up writing at least another ten thousand words, so she got her 'I want more'. So thank you my precious girl, your mum is very grateful that you gave of your time.

And time to me is precious. Once it's gone, it's gone. You can never repeat or replace it. You can't ever have it back, not even by having all the money in the world to try and buy it back, it's so precious it is priceless. As each and every second of each and every day ticks away we can never get the time back and we need to give that a bit of thought!

Time, when a person gives me some of their time I'm so grateful. So for me it's very important that I thank them. I know they have given me something they can never replace and that's special. So it's time for me to say a few more very heartfelt thank you's.

Equally as important as the editor, is the proofreader so the next huge thank you goes to Eileen Burrell, again. Dear Eileen proofread my first book for me, and if you've read that book you will know what a fantastic job she did. I'm grateful beyond words that she was prepared to proofread book two. Friendship is a wonderful thing. I don't know if you remember but I first met Eileen when Nansi (book one) asked me to see one of her patients as she herself felt she couldn't help her any further, but she thought that perhaps I could, and twenty-odd years ago, I did. That story is still to be written and it's a good one. Eileen and I have remained friends to this day even though she and her family moved hundreds of miles away some twenty years ago. We have kept in touch and we have even managed to see each other a few times over the years. I have been blessed to make some very good close friends through the work I do and Eileen is one of the oldest and closest. Not in her years, but in the time we've known each other. She was the very first person outside of my own family that I was asked to see and heal before I set up my healing practice. Thank you for giving me of your precious time. I dare not even begin to try and work out how many hours it must have taken you. One day this kindness you have shown me will, without doubt, come back to you tenfold. Thank you for doing another fantastic job.

A second thank you must also go to Eileen for the wonderful forward she has written for my book. I knew she would be very honest with her words. She questioned me as to why I wanted her to write the forward and I had a very simple answer for her. She was the very first patient I had outside of my own family unit and this book is the very first book I have written with lots of different healing stories, so she was the perfect choice. First patient, first book of healing stories. Thank you my precious friend, I love you.

Now to another trusted friend, who started out as a patient a few years ago, Angela H.

Angela very kindly edited book one for me (along with one of her friends) and did a fantastic job. I felt at the time that she didn't actually need her friend's help (a confidence thing I think). I'm sure she would have done an equally good job left to her own devices. This time around, I asked Angela if she would please read (without her friend) the finished book. This was to enable her to cast her very observant and critical eye over what I had written and give me her honest opinion. And guess what, she enjoyed reading it but she spotted a rather large error of judgment which now, thanks to her vigilance, has been put right. So a huge thank you Angela, you will never know how much I value your expertise. Thank you for being there for me.

Almost last but not quite, I must thank the patients I was able to contact. I sent them each a draft copy of their own story and, without exception, they were pleased with my storytelling.

So my love and grateful thanks go to Jean, Anne and Becky, Jane (Colin's daughter), Linda and Geoff, Jane and her mother (Hannah's mother and grandmother), Sophie and a special thank you to Michelle who I managed to contact after many years. I had written her very sad story down before I eventually managed to track her down, and also thank you to Alice. To all the patients I didn't mention by name, my love and blessings go out to you all.

My love as always must also go to my husband, David. I didn't burn his tea during the writing of this book so I'm definitely getting better at being able to put my writing down. But, of course, this book is not about me; it's lots of separate individual stories with one or two of my own adventures thrown in. Thank you, David, for your patience and always being there for me in so many ways that even I don't see.

And last, but most certainly not least, my son. He's last because he was the very last cog in the fantastic wheel of love that has produced this book.

Firstly, I must thank him for doing the final read-through before publication. This was done in case there were things he felt needed to be taken out or changed. Fresh eyes and a fresh approach is always a good idea. Thank you for then producing the final PDF file of my book, all ready for print and publication. And thank you for another wonderful book cover, what a very special eye you have. And lastly yet another thank you for finding the title of this my second book. You found it once again in the words written down. Thank you my precious boy.

What a very fortunate mother I am. Blessed with two wonderful children, both having given me of their precious time. So to my family and friends and anyone I may have unwittingly forgotten: love, light and blessings to each and every one of you.

FOREWORD

by Eileen Burrell

I met Isabella 25 years ago and we became close friends but the strange thing is that, if given the choice at that time in my life, I would have emphatically refused to meet her! Yet how glad I am that I did meet her, as she has been such an important influence in my life.

Let me explain. I had a worsening condition for which I was receiving conventional medical treatment. When the proposal was made by my specialist to bring in a pioneering surgeon from America to carry out drastic surgery not yet carried out in Britain, I panicked and searched for alternatives.

I was lucky enough to find Nansi, the naturopath who just happened to be Isabella's trusted friend and mentor. Nansi helped me as far as she could, then recommended that I needed further treatment so suggested I transfer to Isabella.

Mistakenly, I assumed she too was a naturopath, as nothing had been said to the contrary. So, when Isabella asked me to sit in a chair and then explained how she would help me by using healing energy channeled through her from the Spirit world, all I wanted to do was get up and flee. I wanted nothing to do with spiritualism in any shape or form. In fact, I thought it was something to fear, something not to be dabbled with! It was only once Isabella reassured me that she would not tell me anything I was not ready to hear, that I 'allowed' her to finish my treatment that day, privately resolving not to book another appointment.

Well, as they say, the rest is history, a quarter of a century's worth. I did choose to see Isabella again, who did bring about significant improvements in my health and, as she predicted, when I was ready, I began to ask questions. I grew fascinated by the concepts she explained to me and avidly read books she lent me which were enlightening. Other ways of looking at life opened up for me, for which I was, and still am, grateful. I became deeply curious about how the Spirit guides worked with Isabella to help so many of her patients, myself included. On a personal level, I welcomed messages from the Spirit world, especially from my dad who died far too early when I was only fourteen and who I missed desperately. There was great comfort in having that connection with Dad through Isabella and in his more personal messages to me, sharing special memories and expressing his love for me and our family. Not all messages were on an emotional level, however. Some were downright mundane, like asking us to fix Mum's leaking tap as it was getting on her nerves! We did as we were told and the tap was duly fixed.

I have learned so much from Isabella and believe I am a more receptive and open-minded person because of her influence and friendship. Not only has she offered me specific advice and treatment to help me cope with some of the real challenges our family have had to cope with over the years, she has brought out an inner strength in me that I did not know I had when faced with certain dark times. She has known when I needed her most, contacting me 'out of the blue' when I was at my most vulnerable. She has loyally looked out for me, my husband and children over all these years, always there when we need her, making us feel safer and more optimistic. Helping with this book, merely as a proof reader, is a chance to offer something back, even in a small way.

Valuable lessons have been learned. I have been fortunate to learn them personally through years of conversation with Isabella but, with the publication of this book and her first book, *'Different,...You Have Always Been Different'*, her invaluable teaching and insight can reach a much wider audience.

Isabella is generous with her time, her advice and her love and I feel lucky and privileged to have met her and to have her as my friend. She does say people come into our lives for a reason – thank goodness I changed my mind and did not refuse to have another appointment with her. Isabella has been blessed with the special gift of being a healer but her most special gift is simply being herself.

INTRODUCTION

As you flick through the opening pages of this book you're probably asking yourself, "Who is this woman, why is she writing this and what's this book all about?"

So let me explain.

I am a wife, mother and grandmother, and I love my life. I've been married to my husband for 43 years and we are just beginning to get to know each other and have some fun. We have two wonderful children and two adorable grandchildren.

Life has thrown many difficulties my way, from serious illness to divorce due to mental and physical abuse, loss of loved ones, loss of home and so much more. All these stories and many more are written down and explained in my first book *'Different?...You Have Always Been Different'*.

I have been working (and I hate using the word *working* but I don't know what other word to use) as a registered Spiritual healer for the past 27 years. In other words it's been my full time job for 27 years, but I've actually been healing all my life. Because of this I have managed to accumulate a wealth of useful and helpful information that we can all benefit from, if I pass it on. I never set out to be a healer, I never set out to write books, but that's what my higher-self chose as my mission for this time around, and many years ago my guidance clearly pointed me in the direction of both and thankfully I knew I needed to comply, so comply I did.

I did however have a choice as we all have choices in this life, just as you now have a choice as to whether to read on, or put my book back on the shelf.

This book is full of different healing stories taken from my own patient's files. It also includes some of my own life experiences and some of my own spiritual insights thrown in where appropriate. Nothing you will read has been taken from other people's work. I have either experienced for myself, or I have seen or heard it on one of my many out of this world journeys. I have been blessed with the ability to recall information that might otherwise have been locked away from my conscious mind.

Now I'm not going to say to you, "Don't ask me why," because I now know why. It's to enable me to be able to pass on or teach, or I would rather say to enable me to give people the reassurance or assurance that nearly everyone needs and yearns for, at some time in their lives.

Perhaps the open and honest approach in the way that I tell my stories, and my simplistic way of telling them, makes them that much more powerful. Perhaps that's why so many people are beginning to benefit from my written words. That's what gives me hope, that's what gives me joy, being able to help people.

We are all living in a vast multidimensional universe, full of adventures, and hardly anyone realises or understands that they are all within our grasp.

You might ask me, "What the heck are you talking about?"

Well if you read my book you may begin to understand.

If you travel with me through the coming pages you will read stories of past-life healings, ghostly encounters, spirit encounters and all the explanations that go with them and many healing stories and experiences from my own memory files from the past fifty-odd years of this life; along with many of what I have called my insights and I may, if I find the courage, relate to you an adventure that I had many years ago that changed my way of thinking and my life, on every level, for eternity.

But please begin the journey with me and I'm sure you will begin to appreciate what an amazing spiritual library of information and knowledge both you and I have.

CHAPTER ONE

"My choices are so many they completely overwhelm me, and I love it."

Me

Have you ever stopped to think how amazing our minds are? Our minds hold everything that we have seen, heard and experienced from the day that we were born into this life, and they will keep on recording until the day that we pass into the next and it doesn't stop there. In fact, our memory banks actually started recording data from the very first life each of us ever experienced and also each and every time we travel back into the Spirit world. In other words, our minds are a storehouse of accumulated information, our very own vast library of knowledge, our memories. So please stop for a few moments and really think about this. Some people will say that our mind is in our brain, but is it? Or could it be that our minds are part of the real us? That part of us that lives on forever. Our Soul.

Remembering that everything is connected, perhaps the wealth of knowledge that we all have is being constantly recorded and transferred into our Souls' memory banks and that's the library that we bring back into each life with us. The truth is I have no idea where our mind actually is or how it all works and I'm not in the least bit bothered; I just know that it does. It's truly amazing when you think about it. An unknown number of pieces of information stored for all time, and most people in the world have never given this a thought and that, to me, is a shame.

There are ways to access information from past lives and I will explain this to you somewhere in the following pages, but when I do I will be making it very clear that the most important life for everyone is this life. (But my thoughts are jumping ahead of myself.)

Just for now I would like to share with you a happy memory of my own from this life and, with a bit of luck, you will also have a similar memory stored away somewhere in your own vast library.

Remember back to your childhood to the very first time you were allowed to go into a sweetie shop on your own with your pocket money held tightly in your hand? If the memory of that day is anything like mine, as your eyes scanned the shelves and counter with the amazing selection in front of you, all crying out to be picked and put into a small paper bag, it would have seemed as if you had just stepped into your very own sweetie wonderland. The choices completely overwhelmed me at the time and, that's exactly how I'm feeling now. I'm standing in my very own shop of accumulated knowledge and I'm so overwhelmed by the choices that I have in front of me I don't know what to choose first. So many healing stories to share with you, including some past-life healings and the lessons that I have learned from them, insights that I have been given, knowledge of this life and others. Out of body adventures to other worlds and other times and Spirit and angel encounters and so much more, and that is why I feel like that little girl in the sweetie shop all over again, and I'm sure that's why the memory of that sweetie shop all those years ago came flooding back to me as I tried (unsuccessfully) to unscramble my thoughts.

As we get older we are supposed to grow up but I guess a part of me never has because I spend so much of my time in a world that most people don't even know exists. My family often say to me, "Mum, you live in your own world but it's a nice place for you to be." An amazing world of things not of this world and I'm so very thankful that I've never lost the childlike awe that I have always had for the things that I see here and experience in my work and in my life, and I pray that I never do.

Please don't get me wrong, I'm not childish; I'm childlike and there's a huge difference. A child simply trusts. Trusts that the people who are looking after them will love them and keep them safe and that's me. I simply trust. I trust that God or the Universal energy will always be there by my side, loving me and keeping me safe and well and if it wasn't for that trust, quite simply, I wouldn't be here now.

I'm going to follow my instincts, let my hand and my 'voice' take me and wait and see where we end up. And I'm going to enjoy every minute of my journey.

So where do I begin?

I'm smiling to myself as I write this because the first memory that my mind has gone to happens to be a story about Multiple Sclerosis and I think you might be able to guess why.

Having told you in my first book how and why I developed MS at a very young age, I also told you that I had my own theory as to why people develop MS and that I would explain myself sometime in the future. My theory started to form in my mind when my own healer, Nansi, helped me find the traumatic event in my own life that had triggered me to develop MS, along with her explanations to me at the time. That was the starting point and after years of meeting with and listening to, talking with and helping people with MS myself, my theory has become set. So now is the time for me to explain it to you.

If you are anything like me when it comes to reading any author's work, I get a bit frustrated when I realise that I have already read the story on the page in front of me in a prior work of the author's so, with this thought in my mind, the last thing I want to do is repeat anything I have already said so now what should I do? But as I am scanning through my memory files to the words I wrote down in my first book there were one or two points that I made that are very relevant to the following true stories that I am going to tell you, so I feel that I do need to repeat one or two points for the sake of clarity. Just like at the beginning of any TV series you get a little bit about what occurred in the first episode before the second episode gets into full swing.

So as briefly as I can.

I believe that every disease known to man has its own trigger. Anything that happens to us in our lives (be it this life or a past life) that upsets us, makes us angry, jealous or frightened, and the list goes on, and we keep our feelings locked away inside our mind (our memory banks), will subsequently eventually cause our aura to become unbalanced. And if this is ignored, and left, the unbalance will transfer into our physical body and a disease will follow. Anything that knocks the balance out in our lives and in our aura and is left to fester will cause us a problem in the months and years that follow and, if we don't manage to clear and heal it in this life, we will end up carrying it forward into our next.

Just to remind you:

To me, the word disease is made up of two words 'dis' and 'ease'.

We become out of ease with ourselves.

We become out of balance.

We become ill just like me.

I also need to mention something of my own story but if I try and tell you a shortened version I know I will lose the impact it had on me at the time. So guess what, I'm not going to repeat myself even in a shortened version, other than say that at twelve years of age I experienced something I would not wish to happen to anyone and, at the time, I kept my fear and hurt buried deep, so deep in fact that in the years that followed I forgot the whole episode ever happened.

Personal experiences of any kind are very important for all of us because we can learn from them if we share what we have learned, and that's what I'm going to do now. I'm going to share. Quite simply, my own experience and then the following true stories will help you to understand that each and every disease *does* have its own trigger.

This is my theory (and to the best of my knowledge no one else has ever written or explained what I'm about to say in the way that I am going to explain it). It's not proven. It's not scientific and I would expect the medical profession would tell me that I am wrong, but in every case of Multiple Sclerosis I have dealt with over the past thirty years (including myself) it has applied one hundred per cent. The trigger that will cause a human being to develop Multiple Sclerosis is by being involved in an event that has traumatised you (be it physical or emotional trauma) and you have kept your fear and hurt to yourself, you have kept your true feelings hidden and locked away deep inside you, you have locked it away inside your mind. The important word here is *deep*. Our central nervous system is buried deep within us to protect it. MS affects the central nervous system. If the fear and trauma (or emotional hurt) is left untreated and hidden it will unbalance the whole of you to such an extent that you will develop a disease and the dis-ease in my humble opinion is very likely to be Multiple Sclerosis.

I have already explained my own experience to you in my first book and now I am going to give you more examples, lots more healing stories, not just about MS but also examples of lots of other health problems that we as human beings suffer from, to help clarify my reasoning.

I'm excited because I have no worries about keeping the stories I'm about to tell you in the correct timeline or sequence like I did in my first book. I'm going to let my mind wander more freely when I need to, so let's start wandering.

CHAPTER TWO

"You can lead a horse to water, but you can't make it drink"
Proverb recorded in 1175 in 'Old English Homilies'

About twenty years ago I was asked to see a young lady who had been diagnosed with Multiple Sclerosis a few months earlier. Because she lived a three-hour drive away from my home, she arrived for her first and subsequent treatments accompanied by her father. He had taken the time to go to her home the previous evening and stay overnight with her to enable him to drive her to her appointment with me and then take her back home again. He was obviously very concerned about her; she was his only child and he was going to do everything he could to help her. She was very pale and nervous when she and her father entered the room I was working in. Her father asked me if he could stay in the room with her.

"Of course you can," was my reply.

I invited them both to sit down as I wanted to have a chat with Helen before any healing work began. She explained to me that she had been unwell for a couple of years, having problems with her legs and balance but because her symptoms were intermittent it had taken time before she eventually received her diagnosis.

Because the symptoms of MS are very diverse it is often missed or misdiagnosed by the medical profession. If you would like to know more, please refer to the back pages of my first book where I have listed all of the symptoms I myself experienced. Or see the list on my web page.

As we were talking, Helen began to relax. I did explain to her that if she didn't feel comfortable with me or she didn't like me this was not to put her off trying healing. There would be a healer somewhere out there that she could respond to. She smiled at me and said, "No, I feel fine with you."

It's important for any healer to remember that when we see new patients they actually may not like us and may not feel at ease with us so, for years now, I have said to new patients, and I still do sometimes, that if they would like to try another healer I would and will completely understand. But in twenty-five years no one has asked to leave and try someone else. I must be doing something right.

After explaining to her as simply as I could what Spiritual Healing is all about, I then asked her to sit on a stool so that I (me and the healing energy *we*) could work in the energy around her. She quickly became very relaxed. I then asked her to climb up onto my healing bed and lie down as I was going to work in the aura around her. She almost fell asleep during that first healing session and by the time I had finished her treatment her father was fast asleep on the chair he had sat himself down on. When he opened his eyes a little while later and looked across the room at his daughter he said, "My God, you've got rosy cheeks. You'd think you'd been given a blood transfusion, you look so well."

And she did. She arose from my healing bed smiling and said she was tingling all over, especially her legs.

Her father explained to me that he had been very worried about bringing her to me because he and Helen's mum had no idea what Spiritual Healing was all about. He said to me, "I thought you would be much older and dressed in black from head to toe. You're not what I expected."

I just laughed and made a joke of his words because this was not the first time I had been told the very same thing and it wasn't to be the last. He said they had been given my name and telephone number by a friend of their family who had recommended me. He then explained to me that he felt it was worth a try; anything was worth a try if it would help her, as the family were in the process of arranging Helen's wedding. The wedding was being organised for the following year and her father said he was concerned in case she would not be able to walk down the aisle unaided on her wedding day. But now that he knew she was in safe hands he would be more than happy to bring her to me again. With what I can only describe as a very bewildered look on his face, he then said, "I'm feeling so relaxed I think some of the healing energy must have flown across the room to me. I can't believe I fell asleep in a strange house with a strange woman in the room!"

We all laughed.

Helen said she would love to come for some more treatments just as her father piped up, "And me too."

We arranged some more appointment times and, with smiles on their faces, they left.

Because this all happened over twenty years ago I can't be exact in the timing but it would have been about three sessions into her treatments (allowing Helen and her father time to feel at ease and comfortable with me) when I explained to them that I would like us to try and find the trigger, the event in her life that had caused Helen to develop M.S. If we could find the trigger she would then have the chance to be able to clear it from her aura and rebalance, with a lot of help, love and forgiveness. I sat and explained my own theory to them and some of my own healing story and that's when Helen became visibly upset. She looked at me with a horrified expression on her face as she looked across the room at her father who gave her a reassuring nod of his head and then she said, "I think I know what it was. I think I know what the trigger was."

"Do you think you can explain to me what happened?"

"I'll try."

Her story started to come out in such a torrent of muddled words that I was having great difficulty trying to piece together what she was saying to me.

"Please take a breath, Helen, and slow down. It's not your fault but I'm not grasping what you are trying to tell me."

She did and, to the best of my memory, this is the story as she relayed it to me.

"I was very close to my grandfather. He meant the world to me and when he died I was heartbroken and I still am. I didn't get the chance to say goodbye to him. There was such a lot I wanted to tell him. I desperately wanted to go and see him in the mortuary to be able to talk to him and say my goodbyes."

She looked across the room at her father at this point and

said, "But both my mother and father didn't want me to see him. They said I would be too upset seeing Grandad dead, but I was insistent. I so desperately wanted to say goodbye to him."

Her father spoke at this point saying, "We thought she was too young to be able to cope seeing him dead. We thought she was much too young to see a dead body. But she got her way."

"When I went with my parents into the little room that my grandad was being kept in he was lying on a table with a sheet up to his chin. I walked towards the table, took one look at his face and turned to my parents and said, "That's not my grandad." But both Mum and Dad said, "Of course it is." I said, "No it's not, that's not my grandfather." Oh Isabella, this was horrible. I was insistent. I kept saying to them both that it wasn't him, but my parents said I was wrong, of course it's Grandad. My mother became very upset. She kept saying to me, "Don't be silly. It's my father and I should know."

And I kept saying to her, "No it's not. It's not your dad." It was horrible for me and for my parents, but they wouldn't listen to me. Mum tried to explain to me that when someone is dead their body changes a bit. I said to her, "A dead person might change a bit Mum but they don't become a different person. This doesn't even look like Grandad, Mum. Surely you can see that. My father was so annoyed with me that he went to find a member of staff that worked in the mortuary to explain to me that this was most definitely my grandfather, and that was that. My grandfather wanted to be buried. He told me before he died that he didn't like crematoriums and he didn't want to be cremated. He had even put it in his will that he wanted to be buried. We had the funeral but, the day after, the coroner's office got in touch with my parents and asked them to go to a meeting with them.

You're not going to believe this, Isabella, you're just not going to believe it.

They cremated my grandad by mistake and we buried someone else's grandad who wanted to be cremated, thinking he was ours, but I knew he wasn't. I just knew. But no one would listen to me."

Dear Lord, I just stood beside Helen speechless.

Apparently there had been a huge mistake made (the understatement of the century) and the bodies had been wrongly labelled. It had come to light when a family member from the other family had commented on the fact that their father didn't look like him. Someone in the mortuary had passed both Helen's comments and the other family's comments on to someone in authority and an investigation quickly followed, showing that an error had been made in the paperwork but all too late to stop the burial and the cremation.

Apparently, both the deceased gentlemen had died at the same time and had been about the same age. The wrong body was buried. That gentleman had wanted to be cremated and Helen's grandfather was cremated, when he had wanted to be buried. And God bless Helen, she had known they had the wrong person, but no one would listen to her.

"Grandad must be so cross with me because I couldn't get anyone to listen to me. The man in the mortuary told me I was being silly and Mum and Dad said it was because I was upset.

I was screaming inside.

I wanted to scream at my parents.

It's horrible, Isabella, when you know you are right and no one will take any notice of you. I never got the chance to say goodbye to him. I didn't say goodbye to the body on the table that day. I refused because I knew it wasn't Grandad. All through the funeral service I kept thinking to myself, "That's not my Grandad in the coffin. Where's my Grandad? What have they done with him? Perhaps he's not dead?"

She was crying her eyes out by the time the story was told and I had a few tears myself.

"Do you think that was the trigger, Isabella?"

"I should say so, phew!"

When I looked across the room at her father he had his head down. It was obvious he didn't want to hear another word about it.

It's not often I'm lost for words but I struggled for a few moments before I came out with, "I'm so sorry this happened to you," completely inadequate for what I had just been told, but I was a bit shocked myself. I gave her a cuddle and tried to reassure her on many levels that it wasn't her fault. Her grandfather would not be annoyed with her because she did everything she could to alert her parents and the staff in the mortuary that a mistake had been made. The fact no one took any notice of her was most definitely not her fault.

I learned a very valuable lesson that day.

Sometimes it's nice for a patient to have someone in the room with them, especially for their first appointment if they are apprehensive or nervous, but Helen was not a child; she was in her late twenties. She had needed to tell me her own story without anyone else listening to her. It didn't take a genius to realise that a lot of her anger was directed towards her parents and by having her father in the room with her she was not able to fully express herself, although what she had said certainly told her story.

I felt there was still more to come out.

I should have known this myself.

I should have made sure Helen was able to talk to me on her own without anyone else in the room with her. But I'm human and sometimes I forget things but, more importantly, learning through experience is a very valuable lesson and this one certainly was for me. I promised myself after they left that afternoon that I would never again put someone else in the same position and to the best of my knowledge I haven't.

I did try and get her father to leave her alone with me when she came for further treatments, suggesting he might like to go for a walk but it wasn't to be. He enjoyed being in the room with her too much. As he told me, he always had a very restful sleep as Helen had her treatment and he didn't want to miss it.

I've got to be honest here and say I can still remember thinking at the time that he didn't want to leave her alone with me because he knew there was more she wanted to tell me and all he wanted her to do was to forget the whole episode ever happened. That was a great shame and as this story unfolds you will see why.

If my memory is correct, Helen came to see me on a regular basis for about eight treatments, the first four or five on a weekly basis and then once a fortnight for a few more weeks (along with her Dad), and it was wonderful to see her becoming so much stronger with lots more energy.

Then the day came when she told me that she would like to take a break from her treatments as I lived such a long way from her home, which of course was true.

About three months passed by and then Helen rang me and made another appointment. When she came into my room (with her father) I couldn't believe the change in her; she looked grey and she was having difficulty walking.

They both sat down and before I had a chance to say a word her father said, "Go on, tell her. Tell her what you did."

And before I could blink Helen said to me, "I went to see another healer who lives close by me."

I said, "That's alright, Helen. I perfectly understand."

"It's not alright. I've not been right since."

"Go on, tell her what happened." (That was her father.)

And this is what she told me.

"When the lady opened her front door to me she directed me straight into the little room she was working in and, without giving me a chance to say anything or react in any way, she told me to take my coat off and lie down on her healing bed. I was feeling very uneasy. My stomach was beginning to churn because nothing about this lady or her house 'felt right'. She was dressed in black from head to toe and the room she worked in was dark, with lots of strange objects about the place. I wanted to say to her, "I'm sorry but I don't like this." I wanted to say, "I'm not stopping," but I didn't. I thought she would think I was being rude or something. I could feel myself shaking inside, but I kept quiet. I had no sooner lain down on her bed when she starting waving her arms in the air and at the same time she started chanting.

Let's face it, Isabella, this was not what I was used to experiencing. You never chanted at me. You never made me feel uneasy or afraid. I just wanted to get up and run away. But again I didn't. When she started to work around me in my aura, chanting out loud to herself at the same time, I began to feel sick. I just lay there on her bed shaking, with my eyes tight shut so I couldn't see what she was doing. By the time she told me the treatment had finished I felt ill. I got up from her bed feeling awful, put my coat on, paid her and left her house without saying a word. Then I walked across the road to meet dad. I was feeling stupid and cross with myself for not leaving her house before the treatment had started, when every part of me was telling me to get out, but she didn't give me the chance to say anything and I wasn't brave enough to speak out."

Her father spoke then and said, "Because this lady only lived a mile or so away from Helen's house I said I would meet her for a coffee when she had had her treatment but when she came out of the lady's house and walked towards me I took one look at her and said, 'We better go straight home because I can see you don't look well,' and she's not been right since."

Helen was in tears by this time and said to me, "I'm sorry, Isabella, I'm so sorry. I was stupid and I shouldn't have let that lady give me a treatment."

Then her father said, "We had to come back to you. Can you put her right again, please? Can you undo the harm that lady seems to have done?"

Giving Helen a reassuring hug, I explained to them both that her aura was all over the place but I was fairly sure that *we* could put it right (that's me and the Universal healing energy *we*) but I did say to her, "The sad thing is, Helen, we are back to square one with you but, not to worry, we'll get you back on track. But please, Helen, this has been a very valuable lesson for you. You need to learn from this and try and follow your instincts in the future." By the time her treatment with me/*us* was finished, Helen had pink cheeks again, much to her father's delight.

This should not have happened to Helen, (or anyone

else) but everyone knows no matter what professional help we seek we will find good and we will find bad. Be it accountants, plumbers or electricians, priests or builders, doctors or dentists, teachers or chimney sweeps, we are going to find good ones and we will find bad ones and the same unfortunately applies to healers. So if you are thinking of making an appointment to have a treatment from a therapist of any kind, the best advice I can give you is to ask your family, friends and colleagues if they know of a good one and even then, above everything else, follow your own instincts. So even if the therapist was recommended to you but you don't feel completely at ease with the person just politely say I'm sorry and explain to them how you are feeling. If they are worth their salt they will completely understand.

I wouldn't dream of criticising Helen for not following and acting on her instincts that day when she knew she should have asked to leave the lady's house. Let's face it, she should have run like the wind and not looked back but that's dead easy for me to say because I wasn't there. I think I can be very honest here and say at twenty-eight years of age (the same age as Helen) I would probably have done exactly the same as Helen. I would have recognised what my instincts were telling me, just as Helen had, but I don't think I would have had the confidence to act and follow them, just like Helen. We have all ignored our own instincts at some time or another for a multitude of different reasons. It takes courage to follow our instincts. Sometimes we don't follow them because we don't want to look foolish or stupid. That, unfortunately, is human nature.

In my first book I explained that if we follow our instincts they will keep us safe and they won't let us down, but if we ignore them we do so at our peril and this was most definitely one of those times for Helen and a very good lesson and example for all of us to remember.

Helen came for more treatments over the next few months and it didn't take long for her to start feeling much better. She even managed to drive to one appointment with me on her own. This was the only time during this period in her life that I was given the chance to be able to talk to her about her grandfather without her father being present in the room with us, and I've got to be honest and say I was very disappointed for her by her response. Apparently, her parents were refusing to discuss the event with her. She told me that each time she had asked them to sit down and talk about it with her they had said, "No, leave it alone." They had told her that as far as they were concerned it happened and it was past and gone, so she was to forget about it. But, of course, it could never be 'past and gone' for Helen (or her parents for that matter). She needed to be able to talk to her parents about what happened, she needed to be able to let go of the hurt and anger she felt and she needed to be able to forgive and then, and only then, would she be able to move her life forward, let go and rebalance herself completely. Not even her parents, no matter how hard they tried, would ever be able to forget what happened. How could they? The tragic event happened and was firmly logged in their memory banks. They may have been able to push it into a filing cabinet at the back of their minds in the hope it would stay locked away but, of course, the memory of that day years earlier would always be there. Try as they might they will never be able to wipe their memory banks clean. (None of us can, we're not meant to forget, but we are meant to learn from the things that happen to us.)

    I can't remember exactly how many treatments Helen had with me in total but on her wedding day not only was she able to walk down the aisle with ease, she was also able to dance the night away with her new husband. I know because my husband and I were there, joining in the celebrations.

    Sadly, I lost track of Helen when my family and I moved house and out of the area we were living in which meant we were much further away from Helen, making it almost impossible for her to come to me for treatments but that's not quite the end of this story.

    About nine years after we moved house I received a most unexpected phone call from Helen asking if she could make an appointment for a treatment. She said she was going to be holidaying with her parents within a manageable drive of our home and she wanted to come and see me. She said she was going to be staying with her parents during the school holidays along with her daughter (I didn't know she had a daughter). Helen duly arrived with her family. It was lovely for me to see them all again plus Helen's lovely eight-year-old child. Because it was such a beautiful summer's afternoon Helen's parents decided they would take their granddaughter for a walk while Helen had her treatment (which was just what I had hoped would happen).

After I had put the phone down from Helen a few weeks earlier when she made the appointment with me, I had asked the Universe to allow me to see her on her own so that I could talk to her but, more importantly, so that she could talk to me without her father listening to our conversation and thankfully my prayer was answered.

I was a bit taken aback by the way Helen was walking. It reminded me of myself many years earlier when I struggled to walk on my wobbly legs with the aid of a stick. Helen was now also using a walking stick to aid her.

There was so much catching up to do between the two of us that her treatment was almost over before I got the chance to talk to her about her 'letting go' of the hurt she had experienced many years earlier and this is where in our conversation she astounded me.

"Oh I don't think my grandfather's death was the problem. I only wish I could find the cause of my imbalance."

You could have knocked me down with a feather.

"But Helen your grandfather's death and everything that happened afterwards to his body was so upsetting it would cause the strongest of us to crumble. Don't you remember how you felt? Don't you remember how you were screaming inside your head to be heard at the time?"

She was quiet for a little while and then she said, "You don't understand, Isabella. There are so many secrets in our family, there is so much that needs to be said and sorted. But my father will not allow my mother or myself to talk about anything. He gets upset and angry with Mum and me if we try and talk about things. My mother has a very difficult life with him. She has tried to get him to seek help because he has issues but he refuses and won't accept the fact that he needs to talk. Mum and I do love him but I'm just pleased I don't live at home anymore. Over the last eleven years since I last saw you I have pushed my memory of Grandad away because I've not been allowed to talk about what happened with either Mum or Dad. I was never able to talk about it, so over the years I decided I must forget about it. I kept thinking if I can forget it will go away."

"You need to think about this again, Helen. You desperately need to think about your grandfather and what happened. You need to clear and let go of the hurt and anger you have buried. If you can't talk to your parents talk to you husband, talk to friends, because until you can let go of the hurt and anger you have locked away you will never be able to rebalance yourself and become healed."

What more could I say?

Helen did, however, get up from my healing bed with a smile on her face because, much to her delight, she was tingling all over. She loved the feeling of the healing energy as it flowed through her, leaving her body tingling and, of course, she hadn't felt that for a long time.

Was Helen eventually able to clear and let go of the trauma she experienced surrounding her grandfather's passing? I honestly don't know because I only saw her once more a week later and I've never seen her since.

There were other issues at play within her family unit. There were other family members that desperately needed healing but they have never to my knowledge asked for help. If only they would then perhaps Helen will finally get the chance to let go of the hurt and trauma she experienced.

All I can do is send Helen and all her family love and blessing over the airwaves.

You must be wondering how on earth I can remember

everything that was said to me in such detail?

It is amazing that I can remember not only what was said to me but also how a person looked at the time and sometimes even the clothes they had on. My own simple explanation is that my mind holds a file on each and every person I have ever seen for a treatment over the years. As I meet them for the first time a file is opened. Each treatment is recorded in their own personal file (in my memory) and as the person leaves my home after their treatment the file is closed and stored away ready for their next appointment and, no matter how many years pass by, the file is kept safe. It might be a bit dusty but all the files in my vast 'library' are still in perfect condition. That's how I have been able to relay Helen's story to you.

The sad thing is, to the best of my knowledge, Helen has not been able to free herself from the trauma she experienced when her grandfather was cremated by mistake. I'm feeling very sad because I know that until she can forgive and let go, she will never be able to be healed. And I guess the lesson here for me was to learn that no matter how hard I try and explain things to some people, they will go their own way and not take on board the lessons and knowledge I try and teach them and that has to be fine because, after all, I'm not responsible for anyone other than myself. So all I can do is try and help in whatever way I can, when I can, and always send everyone my love.

CHAPTER THREE

"People need to learn that their actions do affect other people. So be careful what you say and do, it's not always about you"
Unknown

Over the many years I have been healing, I often receive phone calls from new patients asking to book two appointments together. This could be for a variety of different reasons. They may want to come together because they are driving a long way and they want to share the cost of the fuel or it might be that they each would like some company on the car journey or one of them may not be well and unable to drive a car themselves. When this happens I always ask to see the driver of the car first so that they can relax for an hour while I give their friend their treatment. By my doing this, the driver of the car can sit quietly and chill before having to drive them both back home. This then sets the scene for the next two ladies I was about to meet.

I will call the lady who rang me and made the appointment for them both Claire and the friend she would be bringing with her was Jackie. To cut a long story short, Claire did tell me over the telephone that she had a minor problem that she needed help with but the real reason she was making the appointments with me was to bring her friend Jackie. Claire explained to me she was about to give up on her and she was feeling badly about the way she was feeling.

The following story will not only give you another example of my own theory, it will also explain Claire's frustration.

After I welcomed them into our home and showed them both into the room they could sit and relax in, Claire (who was driving the car) then followed me into my healing room that I affectionately call my office, amongst many other things. I asked Claire to sit down for a few minutes so that we could have a chat together before her first treatment began. I needed to take down her personal details and the problem she had come to me with, thinking she would then tell me a little bit about herself and the way she was feeling about the problem she had, but she immediately started to talk about Jackie. She told me that Jackie had been diagnosed with Multiple Sclerosis twenty-four years ago and that she was living in her own home on her own but she was struggling to cope with her everyday chores and, because of this, some of her family and a lot of her friends were helping and supporting her as much as they could. Then she explained to me that over the past nine years she had taken Jackie to see numerous therapists in the hope she could find someone to help her. This had opened Claire's eyes to most if not all the alternative therapies available for everyone to use. She had a very good understanding of what they were all about and how they worked. Her knowledge was vast. Then she told me that she had taken Jackie to see every alternative therapist she could find in the phone book that were in a reasonable travelling distance to them and also the ones that had been recommended to her, in the hope Jackie would respond to one of them. But she said after only one or two treatments Jackie would tell her that they were not helping and she didn't want to see the therapist again. Crystal healing, reflexology, aromatherapy, faith healing, the Alexander technique and many more had been tried, all to no avail. Claire said she was now at her wits' end as to what to do next. That's when she told me that she was about to turn her back on her friend and walk away from her. I reassured Claire that I wouldn't say a word to Jackie about what she had just said to me; anything that is said in my 'office' has to remain confidential. That is why all names, places, times and anything else that could identify a person have been changed in my book but the stories are all true and need to be told. Experiences are what we all learn from and if I didn't tell my stories none of us would learn and my memory files and my insights would lie dormant and never be used.

 Claire did tell me that every treatment Jackie had received had helped her in some small way but no one had been able to get through to her and she was praying I would. Talk about putting pressure on someone! She did relax and enjoy her first treatment with me/*us* after she had been able to empty her mind and feelings onto me. It's a good job I've got big shoulders (metaphysically speaking) to lean on. When her treatment was over she said she would go and get Jackie and bring her into my room. She felt it would be better if she helped Jackie relay all the information I needed to record as she had done this numerous times over the past few years, as Jackie had problems with her speech, and then she would leave us and go and have a quiet sit. So that's what we did.

To be honest with you, after I had welcomed Jackie into my room and I had taken down her personal information with Claire's help I was very quiet during the time the treatment was in progress. I'm often aware that part of me is not in my room as the healing energy is working its magic. I didn't ask Jackie any questions during that first treatment. Not because Jackie might have struggled with her speech but because I was lost in my own thoughts. I was beyond time, thinking to myself that this so easily could have been me. Not walking or talking very well, needing lots of help from family and friends and really not managing life at all. The treatment was over before I felt I had had time to blink. When Jackie got up from my healing bed she looked so different, she had colour in her cheeks and a smile on her face. Much to my amazement, she walked out of my room holding but not using her stick and I can still see her doing this even now. I went to retrieve Claire from in front of the fire in our spare room. She took one look at Jackie and said, "I've never seen you look so glowing. My God, you look so different."

And she did.

They made another appointment to come back in two weeks time. They both gave me a hug and left. As I was watching them walk to their car Claire turned to Jackie and said, "I've never seen such a change in you in just one treatment."

When they both came back two weeks later for their appointments there was a marked improvement in the way Jackie was walking and talking (it never ceases to amaze me what a difference just one treatment can make to a patient's aura and the energy flowing through them).

Just as before, I gave Claire her treatment first while Jackie sat by the fire in our spare room. She told me that she was thrilled by the way Jackie had responded to her first treatment with me two weeks earlier and she was praying that her friend would keep coming to me. Then it was Jackie's turn. She came into my room and sat herself down on my settee, which was perfect for me because I wanted to ask her a few questions before her second treatment started. Did she feel that the healing energy had helped her? And how had she been over the past two weeks? She told me that she had noticed a difference. She was sleeping better, her speech wasn't as slurred and she was managing to walk a bit better, so yes the healing energy was helping her. It's all very well for a friend to notice a difference in a person, but I always ask the patients themselves how they think the healing is helping. Before I realised what I was doing I started to question Jackie. If I had had time to think I would have left the questions for a later appointment but my mouth had opened and the words were pouring out of me before I had a chance to stop myself. When I realised what I was doing I knew there would be a reason. I found myself explaining to her that she had developed MS because somewhere in her past she had been traumatised (I would normally have explained all this to her after a few treatments, giving her more time to get comfortable with me, but I guess my higher self knew I would not be seeing her again and this would be my only chance). As I was talking, the expression on her face began to change as tears started to run slowly down her face. (My voice in my ear had already told me that her trauma had been caused during her young teenage years.) I explained to her that if she could find the trigger in her life, the traumatic event that had set the wheels in motion, then it would allow her to let go of whatever happened, move her life forward and rebalance herself and heal.

"I can't," she said.

My response was instant. "Why not?"

"Because I can't. I've never told anyone what happened to me, it's so horrible."

The tears were now streaming down her face. I gave her a handful of paper hankies to allow her to dry her face and eyes as she was speaking.

"It was horrible. He would abuse me whenever he could and I spent my life in constant fear. I told no one what was happening to me because he told me that no one would believe me. There was no way my family would believe me. It was all too horrible."

She did tell me a little of her story.

She even told me who the abuser was.

Her story was without doubt something that you would watch in a horror film. During her treatment she repeatedly asked me not tell her friend what she had confided in me. I promised her; her secret would remain with me but would she please think about telling her friend (or someone else)?

"No," she said. "Because she knows nearly everyone involved and I don't want anyone else to know in case my family finds out. That's why I can't tell her."

I knew after they both left that day that I would not be seeing Jackie again and I was right. She had confided in me and as far as she was concerned that was the nail in my coffin, so to speak. It was the last time I ever saw her. If only she could have found the courage to tell someone, her doctor, one of her friends or even another therapist. The abuse had stopped years ago but the fear and hurt she was carrying was just getting worse and so was her MS. Her mental torture hadn't stopped just because the actual physical abuse had stopped. There was no way she could let go of this period in her life, move forward and heal and I have an awful feeling she never will in this lifetime. I don't think she will ever tell anyone what happened to her and that is sad beyond words.

Claire, however, did come back for one or two more treatments but I never saw Jackie again and, of course, Claire couldn't understand why Jackie wasn't coming to see me, because the two treatments she had had been so positive for her and, of course, I couldn't say a word. Claire was angry with Jackie because she felt Jackie had given up yet again. How I wish Jackie could have told Claire what had happened to her. 'The truth will set you free' comes to mind when I think about this story.

If Jackie had been able to tell Claire the truth then Claire would have understood why Jackie was so reluctant to see therapists. She was so frightened in case her story came out. I had obviously got far too close. The fact she told me what happened was a miracle in itself. I can only pray one day she does tell someone else and I can only hope and pray that Claire doesn't give up on her friend in the meantime.

The only person in this life that any of us is responsible for is ourselves. There is only one exception to this rule, our precious children. All children need to be loved, looked after and nurtured for them to blossom and grow into caring, loving adults. But we must remember that when they are fully grown they then become responsible for themselves. I am assuming we all have the sense to realise that if an adult is incapable of looking after themselves because of a problem of the body or mind then, of course, they could be forty years old but still have the mental age of a child. Bless them all, they are still our children. I've seen and listened to far too many people over the years taking on responsibilities for their parents, loved ones and friends, trying to take control of a life that they are not responsible for and, in turn, they make themselves ill or they fall out with their loved ones for all time. When will we all learn? Help if asked, care always. But think before you try and take responsibility for someone else and interfere in their life because that's not what we are meant to do. I will come back to this later on in my storytelling as my father gave me some words of wisdom on this subject and I will share them with you all but not at the moment.

CHAPTER FOUR

"Time decides who you meet in this life, your heart decides who you want in your life, and your behaviour decides who stays in your life."
Ziad K. Abdelnour

This next chapter is going to be relatively short because I only saw this particular gentleman once and I've got to be honest and say that I think it was probably my fault that he never came back for a second treatment from me.

I think I frightened him.

To the best of my knowledge this is the one and only time that I know of that I have frightened someone.

This gentleman had been recommended to me by another one of my patients. I will call him Colin, for the sake of his story. Colin was a man in his mid-fifties and yet he had only just been diagnosed with Multiple Sclerosis which, to me, was very unusual. MS is usually diagnosed in the late twenties to early thirties so for Colin to have just been diagnosed was almost unheard of. He was a tall man and quite well built. To look at him, you would not have known there was anything wrong. He was walking fine and his speech was also fine. After I had invited him into our home I asked him to sit down so that we could have a chat and I could take a few of his details down. He explained to me that he would be fine for a few weeks then he would start to have problems with his eyesight and his legs. Without thinking what I was saying, I asked him what had happened to him two and a half years earlier. I found myself saying, "Something terrible happened to you. What was it?" As I was speaking to him his face turned white, the colour just drained away from him as I asked him the question.

"How did you know? How the heck did you know? You couldn't possibly know. Who told you?"

"Who told me what?"

"Someone must have told you."

"Sorry, Colin. I have no idea what you are talking

about."

"But how could you possibly know something terrible happened to me exactly two and a half years ago?"

"Colin, I didn't know. A voice in my ear told me."

It was at this point by the look on his face he was ready to run for the door but, give him his due, he didn't. I told him I was sorry if I had given him a bit of a start but could he perhaps tell me what happened because I honestly believed that whatever it was had been the trigger to cause him to develop Multiple Sclerosis.

And this is what he told me.

"It was a lovely summer's afternoon when I decided to take my girls for a walk. My girls were my two beautiful Alsatian dogs. They loved nothing better than to run free in the fields about half a mile from our home. I didn't give much thought to the black clouds in the sky to the north of our home that day as we set off on our walk because there was far more blue sky than storm clouds. I walked the short distance to the fields with the girls on their leads as I always did until we were well clear of the paths where other people walked. I was almost to the point of unleashing them when I heard the distant rumble of thunder. The rain clouds still looked miles away so I was very confident that we could have our walk and get back home before any rain would fall. We were walking up a small hill, just as I was about to unclip their leads, when I heard the most horrendous cracking noise and at the same time I saw a massive flash of lightning hit the tree on the top of the hill that we were walking towards. Then I watched in awe and dread as the lightning rushed down the outside of the tree trunk. It was a streak of bright blue light moving at an incredible speed. Then, to my horror, with a hissing, fizzling noise the lightning started to race across the ground straight towards us. I was frozen to the spot, not believing what I was seeing. It all happened so quickly. I don't think I could have run away from it if I'd tried, I wouldn't have had time. A split second later the leads in both my hands were ripped from me with an incredible force as I watched in horror as both my girls were hurled into the air, right in front of me, just as I was lifted off my feet and forcefully thrown backwards into the air myself, just like a rag doll, and then I blacked out. When I came to and opened my eyes it took me a few moments to realise where I was and what had happened. I looked around me and there on the ground, about twenty yards away from me, lay both my girls and I knew in an instant that they were both dead. I was hysterical and I don't mind admitting it. I was physically sick on the ground where I lay. I somehow got myself up onto my feet and I went over to them. I desperately wanted to pick them both up and take them home with me. I didn't want to leave them alone even for a moment but there was no way I could carry them both back home on my own because they were both very heavy. I needed help. Isabella, I felt as if I had stepped into a nightmare but what had just happened was very real and horrific. They were my babies, they were dead and it was my fault. Why didn't I run when I saw the lightning strike the tree? How could the lightning throw me not just inches but tens of feet both high into the air and tens of feet back from where I had been standing and my girls high into the air, ripping them from my grasp as I held their leads, killing them both? I still keep playing it back over and over in my mind, those split seconds that changed my life. I watched the blue streak coming straight for us and I froze. I should have tried to run with my girls. It was as if time stood still and I couldn't move. I should have tried to save us, but I didn't."

    He had tears in his eyes as he was relating all of this to me but, by the time the story was finished, he was visibly upset (and so was I). I obviously tried to comfort him in some small way and I also tried to explain to him that he needed to forgive himself as I was sure his girls would not want him to spend years blaming and punishing himself. I also tried to explain to him that the shock of the event had caused the imbalance in his whole being and that, in turn, it had triggered the MS.

    After his treatment was over he was relaxed and he did thank me for that but I never did see him again. I'm so sorry I gave him a bit of a fright so to speak. I most certainly hadn't intended to, but sometimes my mouth just opens and I come out with things without thinking.

The fear as he watched the lightning coming across the ground at them at great speed. The shock, the fear and the horror as he watched his beloved girls being flung into the air. The shock of being thrown into the air himself and being knocked out, and his beloved girls being killed, was without doubt the trigger to cause a serious imbalance in his aura and his emotions which, in turn, caused him to develop a disease and the dis-ease that it caused him was MS (cause and effect). And before Colin left me that day he agreed with me.

For every cause there is an effect.

Fear, fright or trauma, without a shadow of doubt, will trigger an imbalance in a person's aura and a physical problem will ensure. Because of my personal belief, it's my humble opinion the problem/dis-ease that will be triggered will be Multiple Sclerosis. The above true story is just one of many examples I have showing the reason why I formed my theory many years ago.

I don't want to upset or antagonise anyone so please forgive me for using the words 'will cause' and not 'may cause'. Obviously I have no way of knowing if I am correct in my theory and I did say when I started writing this book that the medical profession would not agree with me. But I have learnt, seen and experienced such a lot over the past 50 years of me having MS that, like everyone in the world, I have my own beliefs and opinions. I guess this is the time for me to be brave enough to voice them. It's most definitely not fact, but it's the rock I've built my life on. So if I have antagonised you with what I have said please forgive me. Someone once told me to 'practise what I preach' and I was also told to 'stand up and be counted' so I guess this is my way of doing both of those things. I would just like everyone to think about the things I am saying and if that's what I manage to achieve, then I will be a happy girl.

And here's one more very short simple example of exactly what I have been saying.

While on holiday a couple of years ago, a lady (a complete stranger) started talking to me. I don't know how the conversation got around to my first book but she was very interested to know what it was about. When I had given her a very brief description she told me that her mother had just been diagnosed with MS at eighty-two years of age. I told her I was amazed that a lady of that age should be just displaying the symptoms so late in life. Had she perhaps been in an accident of some sort? The lady smiled at me and said, "Yes, my mother fell and broke her hip a few months ago and I knew as soon as she was told she had MS that her fall had been the cause."

She told me she'd even tried to tell her mother's doctor that she was sure the shock of her mother's accident had caused her to develop MS but she said the doctor was having none of it. She said to me, "Do you know what, I know it was her accident and I don't care what her doctor says. I know I'm right and my mother also says the same thing when anyone asks her."

I said to her, "I'm sure you are both right. In fact, I know you are."

I hope somehow that the lady is directed to one of my books so that she can read about how her mother's fall was most definitely the cause, and her diagnosis of MS was the effect, having had MS for over 50 years myself.

CHAPTER FIVE

"Surely the immutable laws of the Universe can teach more impressive and exalted lessons than the holy books of all the religions on earth."
Elizabeth Cady Stanton

A word has been niggling away at me since I wrote Helen's story and I know I need to stop my flow for a minute and explain something to you here before I move on. The niggling word was mistake and it has sent me travelling off through my mind. I used it when I said her grandfather was cremated by mistake. I personally believe there are no mistakes in this life, only lessons to be learnt, so I'm not even sure why I wrote the word down. I would like to try and find the right analogy and the right words for me to use to explain myself.

Imagine yourself flying in an aircraft high above a river. As your plane winds its way down through the countryside you will pass over hills and valleys until you eventually reach the sea. From your vantage point in the sky you will be able to see the river for miles. You will be able to see where the river came from (its source) and you will be able to see where it's going to. Now try and picture yourself walking the same riverbank. Your perspective has now been completely changed. As you begin to walk along the banks of the river through the undergrowth you will pass through woodland forests and valleys as the turns in the river take you through the countryside and you will completely lose sight of where you have been. You won't be able to see what's behind you anymore and you won't be able to see around the bend in front of you to see where you and the river are going. If you stop for a few moments and think about this you will realise that that's what our lives are like.

But I'm not just talking about this life, I'm talking about all our lives over the centuries of time.

For the sake of the next bit of my story I'm going to have to assume something. I'm going to assume that we can't remember what happened to us in our previous lives and we obviously don't know for sure the path or the way that our lives are going to go in the future. But using the analogy of our aeroplane journey, if we were in our plane up in the sky (looking over our life) we would be able to see both where we have come from and where we are going. Just like the river we all have our source. We came from the source of all life and one day we will be going back to it again. Please also think about this, everything in the Universe is connected. We are all connected and have been through the eons of time. We are especially connected to the people closest to us, from our family, loved ones and friends. I can say, with almost certainty, that you will have been with and around most of them many times before. Not necessarily all together or even in the same lifetime and the reason you are with them now is because there is some karma for you all to work through and work out. It could be you have a kindness you need to pass on to one or more of them. It might be that one of them needs to be able to make amends for something they did to you, or you to them, lifetimes ago.

It may be that you do know what happened to you in one or more of your previous lives because you have been able to access them yourself through meditations, or someone has given you a past-life reading so you will know a little bit about where you have come from, but none of us knows for sure the way our lives are going as we journey into our futures. I will come back to accessing your past lives later on in my storytelling or perhaps even another book.

Now I mentioned the word karma a few sentences ago and maybe the word is new to you? But even if you have heard the word before it would be wrong of me to surmise that everyone reading this knows what the word actually means so, for those of you that are a bit unsure, here's some information. And for those of you that know exactly what I'm talking about, reinforcing our beliefs and knowledge is always a good thing.

If you look the word up on a popular reference site you may see that it says karma is the Sanskrit word for action. If you would like more information please research this yourself.

There are some great explanations of the word and some really good quotes to be found. I rather liked this one.

"How people treat you is their karma; how you react is yours." Wayne Dyer.

Karma also refers to the Spiritual principal of cause and effect.

So, in other words, it's almost the equivalent of Newton's Third Law of Motion. "For every action, there is an equal and opposite reaction."

Basically, the law of cause and effect tells us that for every movement of energy, whether it's physical, emotional, mental or Spiritual, there is a corresponding effect. The law of cause and effect affects every aspect of our lives.

I was simply taught as a child that we all reap what we sow in this life. This teaching came from my father's Bible, the authorised King James version to be precise, and the exact quote came from part of Galatians 6:7 –"for whatsoever a man soweth, that shall he also reap". In my case, this was from my family's Western religion, Methodist. Buddhists and Hindus (Eastern religions) believe that whatever you do comes back to you e.g. if you do something good, something good will come back to you and vice versa. They call this 'karma'. So both Western and Eastern religions and philosophies are saying exactly the same thing, only they are using different words.

But there is one fundamental difference between the two viewpoints and that is in Eastern religions they teach that the law of karma 'we reap what we sow' is over many lifetimes, not just this one. Eastern religions recognise that we have all been here before whereas our Western religions do not.

Quite simply, that is one of the reasons why I moved away from the confines of my religious upbringing many years ago. Because I had felt from being a child and I had seen and heard things from the Spirit world (and I will come back to this) that made me realise, as young as I was, that I had been here before. But as a child and young adult I kept those thoughts to myself.

Now I think I can leave these spiritual insights and

continue from where I left off.

Back to the word mistake.
Was the mix-up over Helen's grandfather's funeral a mistake? Not for me it wasn't, it was a lesson. Lessons and yet more lessons. That's why I am sure we are all here, to learn and rebalance the scales and also to clear some of our karmic debts.
Is there such a thing as a mistake?
And you're all going to shout at me at once and say, "Yes, of course there is."
I'm not so sure.
I would have been the first one to agree with you and say, "Yes, of course we all make mistakes," but that was before I sat and gave it some serious thought.
I honestly believe that Helen's grandfather's mix-up should not be seen as or termed a mistake so I used the word wrongly. My understanding of that event would be to call it a lesson. Who the lesson was for at the time, I'm not sure and I never will be because it wasn't my lesson. But, for me, it wasn't a mistake so I should not have used that word. But let's face it, by me using the word wrongly has allowed me to meander on and explain one or two things to you that might otherwise have been passed over. So, I guess in a way I was meant to use the word mistake, if only for the sake of my storytelling.
Again, please let me continue to meander for a little while.
Here's a simple example of what we all would term a mistake and it was me who made it a few months ago. And I'll bet I'm not the only one that's done this and I won't be the last. I started to fill my car up with petrol at the pumps when I should have been putting diesel into my tank. I had only put in a small amount when I realised what I was doing. I stopped immediately, feeling slightly panicky and ran into the garage to tell the person on the till what I'd done. I stood in front of him, not quite sure whether to laugh or cry. Okay, so he laughed at me (I was smiling with embarrassment) and not without cause. He explained that because I'd only put a little bit of petrol into

my tank, if I filled it up with diesel it would dilute the petrol and the car would run and it should get me home safely. So that's what I did. I filled the tank with diesel and, yes he was right, I got home without any trouble. But I don't think I'll be doing that again any time soon.

Now that was my mistake.

Sorry folks, no it wasn't.

I learned from what happened, so actually it wasn't a mistake; it was a lesson.

So what did I learn?

I learnt the very simple lesson of remembering to focus on what I am doing at the time and to stop my mind from wandering all over the place (easier said than done) when I am performing even the simplest of tasks. In other words I learned the lesson of being more in the moment or, the new way of saying focus, I learned a lesson in mindfulness. If I had been concentrating on what I was actually doing i.e. filling my car with fuel and not gazing into space and daydreaming like I do most of the time, I wouldn't have put the wrong fuel in my car. So focus girl focus. Or as my parents used to tell me as a child, "For heaven's sake, Isabella, just do one thing at a time and concentrate." In actual fact, when I sat and thought about it, and after casting my mind back to all the so-called mistakes I have made throughout my life well all the ones I could remember, they weren't mistakes at all. Without exception they were all lessons.

So I'm clearly back to where I started at the beginning of this chapter.

Because of my beliefs, to me, there are no mistakes in this life, only lessons.

You, of course, may have a completely different point of view. Choices again, we all have them, thank goodness.

And here's yet another expression that we all use in our daily lives that I don't personally believe to be true. Again, please remember these are my beliefs. They may not be yours and they certainly aren't fact. 'We choose our friends but we don't choose our family.' Please let me explain my reasons why I don't think this saying is correct.

We all have choices in this life and I believe we all have choices not only when we are here on earth but also when we are in Heaven, or if you would prefer to call it the Spirit world. I believe that before we come back into our next life here on earth we choose the lessons we want to learn. I also believe that we choose who will become our parents and in choosing them we know that they will enable us to learn the lessons we have chosen to learn. And we also know who our siblings will be and that they, in turn, will also allow us to learn and clear some of our karmic debts that we will have all built up between us in our previous lives together.

I really do believe that we choose our families.

We wouldn't be able to clear our karmic debts if we didn't come back with people we had been here with before. Our friends, family, loved ones and the people we fell out with, yes, even our archenemies. I'll bet some of them turned out to be people we have been very close to. We need to come back with them all to clear things up and once we do clear the debts we have created we can then move on to a different group of people. I don't think any of us can fully appreciate or understand just how big and how spread out across the world some of our connections are.

I also believe we don't always come back into the same lifetime as other members of our family and, just to confuse the issue even further, I believe we will have had many different families over the last few thousand years. In other words we will have been with different groups of people, creating different family units, over a vast geographical area.

The picture is actually so vast it's almost enough to blow your mind.

How many times do we meet people that we speak to for only a few minutes each month or each year? Or we are introduced to someone at a party or gathering we have never met before. They might have been visiting from abroad but hey presto a karmic connection has just been formed. Or a family member brings a friend home for the weekend and we sit and talk to them and they happen to live abroad. Hey presto, again, yet another karmic connection. The connections that pull us towards a group of people or an individual person can also be very small. The stranger you speak to for three minutes at the bus stop that likes the same dogs or cats that you like. Or the person you sit next to on the train or tube starts talking to you about horses or even a certain book or the designer shoes that you have on your feet that you both like. You have just become connected and that stranger could be connected to people from the other side of the world. But that very brief encounter could pull you back into another life on another continent for a lifetime away from the family unit that you think of as yours. But if this was another life you might be living it with one of your other families.

Then think about every person you have ever met and spoken to for perhaps just one minute in time. In other words, every person you have come into contact with up to now in your life from you being a child and everyone you will meet in the future until the day you pass from this life. There will be a reason you will have met them and interacted with them. And there will be a reason they met you and interacted with you.

If you think about it, it's a bit like the roots of a tree as they spread out underground, touching other tree roots as they, in turn, touch hundreds and then thousands more.

Then take the seeds from the trees as they are eaten by birds who then fly to another continent and deposit them. Those seeds then take root and grow. A jigsaw puzzle so vast it covers the whole of the globe.

I'm sure you have heard the expression 'the six degrees of separation'. Well perhaps now you can see the picture a little bit clearer.

Now let's leave my spiritual insight on the connections between us and move onto the laws of karma properly because they are both very much connected. I have said before that every living thing is connected and far more connected than most people have ever dreamed of and this next spiritual insight might help to put the pieces of our world jigsaw puzzle together.

I used the expression 'you reap what you sow' a few minutes ago when I was explaining the word karma to you and again, for more clarity, karma simply means if you do something good something good will be done to you. Do something bad and something bad will happen to you. 'What goes around comes around' and how many times do we all use that one? It's as simple as that.

But it's not just what we all do that causes us to create ourselves a karmic debt; it's also what we say and also what we think. Yes, our words and our thoughts are all very powerful. Think bad thoughts and the energy of those bad thoughts will go out into the Universe and by the law of cause and effect, by the law of you reap what you sow, by the law of karma, our thoughts, words and deeds will come back to us, without a shadow of doubt.

Someone asked me the other week, "What's happening with time, Isabella. What is it doing? Do you feel it is quickening?"

And this was my reply.

Time is and always has been a very strange thing for me. When I'm meditating or remote viewing or travelling outside of myself (covered in later chapters) either on this plane of existence or another, time is non-existent. I'm out of time, away from it, beyond time. But I did say to this person, to me, time seems to be doing two things. Firstly, it seems to be slowing down because last Christmas feels like a lifetime ago; so much seems to have happened this year and it seems like an age since our Christmas tree was last up. But, on the other hand, time seems to be quickening. I am aware that that's a huge contradiction. The thing I have noticed most this past year, much more than in previous years, is that the law of karma, the law of cause and effect, the law of we reap what we sow is most definitely quickening. If you had asked me ten years ago how fast the law of karma was operating I would have told you it can take years and sometimes even another lifetime for the law to come into force, but not now.

If you do a good deed it will come back to you now in a matter of weeks, not months or years like before and, in some cases, even days. And remember if you do a bad deed or even a bad thought that is also going to come back at you very quickly and I have a fantastic example of my own to illustrate this to you.

About a month ago, I was having a really bad week. All sorts of things had gone wrong. I've got to be honest with you a few people had annoyed and upset me. You know how it goes, we lose the plot and start feeling very sorry for ourselves because people seem not to care about us. Here's us trying our best to help everyone but who the heck is bothering to help us? I guess I was having a bad week, feeling ultra-sorry for myself. I don't often get angry because I know it's a waste of time and energy but by the end of this particular week, oh boy, I got mad. I felt as if I had been walked and trampled on and then run over by a truck and left in a heap in a muddy puddle. And at the end of the week I gave myself a really good talking to.

Now I'm normally quite a mild-mannered person but, on that particular day, I turned the air and the energy around me blue with my thoughts (just for a few minutes). But that's all it took.

Yes, my thoughts.

You get the picture. Talk about letting off steam.

And what was the outcome of all of my angry thoughts?

The following week, yes, just one week later I received the most horrendous book review for my first book. All of my friends, patients and family members that read it were upset by it. Two of my patients were actually in tears when they read the review. They were so upset and hurt by what it said.

My daughter said to me, "Mum, it's not a book review. It's a personal attack against you."

She was very upset by what had been written and that, of course, upset me. I myself obviously didn't like what I read, but I was okay with what had been written because I realised almost instantaneously what had happened. The reviewer was fully entitled to their opinion but this was not a book review. It was, as my daughter had said, a personal attack against me.

That was my anger coming right back at me.

This was the perfect law of karma in action.

This was the law of the Universe giving me a good slap on the backside.

But what the reviewer hadn't stopped to think about before their comments were made public was the hurt and upset the reviewer would cause other people. This reviewer most definitely doesn't understand the simplicity of the law of karma and I happily leave that person in the safe hands of the Universe.

'What goes around comes around.'

I would like to explain to you at this point what I believe happens to all our thoughts, words and actions as we spill them out, each and every day of our lives, into the ether all around us.

I honestly believe all our thoughts, words and deeds cause ripples in the fabric of time.

Now I know that that sounds very theatrical and way over the top, but actually that's exactly what I believe happens each and every day of our lives.

When we perform a bad deed and yes, of course, when we perform a good deed, it triggers a ripple of energy that travels right through the Universe, just like the ripples on a pond when we throw in a stone and watch them as they seem to go on forever, because actually they do, wow!

A disturbance in the fabric of time, yes, a disturbance in the Force. Okay, so I love Star Wars, but those words describe what I believe happens, perfectly.

Bad deeds of any kind will disturb the 'force', not quite as strongly as some of the natural things that happen here on earth, like earthquakes, tornadoes and tidal waves, but a ripple definitely.

I put my anger out into the Universe and caused a ripple and someone else sent it right back to me and caused another ripple, and now we all know and understand what goes around

comes around, without a shadow of doubt.
To me, God's wonderful law of karma.

Now let's go back to that huge jigsaw puzzle, the jigsaw puzzle that covers the world and our connections. All of the connections we all have through the eons of time with everyone we have met and are still to meet. We will all create karmic debts good and bad. The only thing that we can all hope for is that we recognise the opportunities that will be given to us during this lifetime to allow us to rebalance the scales.

For me there are no mistakes in this life, only lessons and a myriad of different opportunities for us to be able to rebalance our own scales which can also, in turn, allow other people to be able to rebalance theirs and that's actually very important. You see, it's not always our own karma that we clear each and every day; everything we do, and everything we say, affects everyone around us and what we do and say often allows other people the opportunity to be able to clear some of their own karmic debt. What an amazing jigsaw of connection this beautiful planet of ours actually allows us all to join in!

If you have understood all of the above, that's great. I can move on with my stories.

But what if you didn't?

I have been merrily writing away without stopping, lost in my own thoughts, allowing the words that are coming into my head to flow with ease but something (or someone) has just put the brakes on me.

I must apologise to you if I have made too many assumptions.

I am expecting you to understand the concept of past lives, that we have all been here many times before and that you agree with me on this. But I haven't even stopped to ask you the question. So I guess there's nothing for it. I'm just going to have to be a bit blunt and ask you the question.

Do you think you have had a life before this life?
Do you think you have lived before?
Give yourself a minute to think about this before you

keep on reading.

If you do, that's great. You will have understood most if not everything I have been talking about. But if you don't believe or you haven't given it any thought and you haven't followed me so far, then please forgive me.

I myself had a very strong Christian upbringing. My father was a Methodist lay preacher. But that doesn't stop or hinder me from my belief. Actually, 'belief' is not the right word for me to use. I don't *believe* I've been here before, I *know* I have and there's a huge difference.

Even the Bible talks about past lives, in reincarnation. I say even, because most people don't realise that not only are past lives in most if not all Eastern religions, past lives and reincarnation are also in our Western religions. If you want to know more, please do your own web searches.

My story has not been written to convince or convert you.

It's been written in the hope it will help you. Help you to realise that there is far more to this life than perhaps you ever dreamed was possible.

I can assure you whether you want to believe me or not you have walked this life before, not once, not even twice, but many times. Yes of course I know this isn't fact, it's my belief, but it's the rock I've built my life on.

I just hope you will continue to read on with an open mind and if you are not sure then perhaps after reading my story you can have a really good think about everything I am writing down and then you can decide for yourself.

I am going to move forward now as if you are with me on this topic, but there is a little bit more that I would like to share with you, a little bit more information from this spiritual insight.

We do choose to come back into another life. We do choose to leave the Spirit world from time to time. We are not forced to. The choice to come back into an earthly life is entirely ours.

There comes a time in every Soul's existence when we

realise that we want to learn more. We want to progress and we also want to clear some of the karmic debts we have managed to accumulate over our many lifetimes.

I keep hearing people say to me, "I'm never coming back here. I don't want to," and I've even heard one or two people say to me, "I'm not coming back because I don't need to." And I just smile to myself.

I have often thought that our lives are a bit like a bank account. Now I know you think I've completely lost the plot but please read my next analogy and give yourself time to think about it.

If this was the very first life we had ever lived we would have been born into it with a beautifully clean slate, in other words a clean start. Or for the sake of my analogy, a nil bank balance. Then as we travel through our first life we will inevitably do a few things wrong, causing us to go into our overdraft. Then perhaps we might manage to do a couple of good deeds, helping to reduce our rising overdraft. When we left that first life and re-entered the Spirit world for the very first time we would have been slightly overdrawn.

Then back we come again.

But on re-entry onto this beautiful planet of ours and into our second life, this time we have come back into it with an overdraft.

And again we will do good deeds and again we will do bad deeds and our overdraft will go up and down like a yoyo. It might even almost get into credit if we have a few lifetimes being very kind and caring. (I'm not going to say lucky because luck doesn't come into it.)

But we have also done some horrible things to each other down through the eons of time. We've hurt each other in the most inhumane ways. We have committed some indescribable nasty acts, apart from all the simple everyday things we have done like lying and being deceitful, causing hurt and worry to our fellow human travellers along the way. We've poisoned each other and we've cut each other's heads off. We've stabbed and maimed and goodness knows what else. All the wars and conflicts, rape and pillaging, slavery and torture of the most horrid kind (and we have all been a part of this), man's inhumanity to man. I think you can begin to see that for the past few thousand years there has not been peace on earth or goodwill towards men like there should have been.

Are you beginning to get the picture?

We have all been horrid at some point during our many lifetimes which means we have all built up a mountain of karmic debt.

If we had learned all the lessons we needed to and had cleared all our karmic debts we would be in credit and it would not be necessary to come back into another life unless, of course, we wanted to.

All karma cleared. Wow, wouldn't that be great?

I'm going to leave all of this with you to think about. I will come back to the Universal laws as I understand them as we move through my stories.

If you've read this far, I hope I've helped you to realise just how amazingly connected we all are to everything and everyone around us. And when you have had time to think about all the above, you will also realise how very simple the law of karma actually is. So simple in fact some people find it hard to comprehend.

Go and get yourself a cup of tea or something a bit stronger and have a break, you deserve it.

CHAPTER SIX

"If you realised how powerful your thoughts are, you would never think a negative thought again."
Peace Pilgrim quotes 1908-1981

A little bit of knowledge is a dangerous thing, especially when it comes to things most people don't understand, like magic and I'm not talking about a magician on a stage. I'm talking about witches and things that go bump in the night. Many years ago a very dear friend said to me, "When people who don't understand anything about witchcraft talk about it you often hear them say there are white witches, they're the ones that use the good energy and there are black witches and they're the ones that use the dark energy. But there's no such thing as black magic, Isabella, and there's no such thing as white magic; there's just magic. Not black, not white."

Now I think I need to explain something to you here. This dear friend of mine knew exactly what he was talking about. You see, he was a male witch and if you didn't know, a male witch is called a warlock. In his role of warlock he worked with the Universal energy, using it to help him in his many spells and potions, but always for good. That was his choice. If he had wanted to, he could have used it for evil, but thank goodness he didn't.

Now in just the same way I want to say to you, "There's no such thing as bad energy and there's no such thing as good energy; there's just energy." Let me try and explain.

For me, there is a wonderful powerful energy surrounding this beautiful planet of ours. It actually fills the whole Universe and, of course, our minds can't really take that one in. But suffice to say, it's all around our beautiful planet and it's there for anyone and everyone to tap into and use in any way we choose, when we know how.

We can choose to use it for good or we can choose to use it for bad; the choice is ours. Choices again. We all have choices.

Just as my friend was talking about magic, the magic only becomes black or white depending upon how the user chooses to use it.

It's all in the user's choices.

Magic in the hands of someone with a loving kind nature can be a very powerful benevolent force. But in the hands of someone with vengeance in their heart, beware.

How the Universal energy is used is dependent on the choices the practitioner makes and I have always chosen to use it to heal people and I always will.

Not very longer after the death of a friend of mine's mother, I happened to go to her home to see her for a chat and, while we were talking over a cup of coffee, she told me that her daughter was having a really hard time.

Let's have a bit of background information here so we know who the family members are and we don't get confused. We have Mum whose name is Anne and her daughter Becky.

For the sake of my story I would like you all to know that Becky was the most clairvoyant child I had ever met. (A simple explanation of the word clairvoyant: 'clear-sighted' in French, 'having psychic gifts' or 'seeing beyond'). I had met her numerous times over the previous few years and we had chatted together about all sorts of things, so I did know her reasonably well.

Anne told me that her mother, Becky's deceased grandmother, was following Becky everywhere. She was even going into her bedroom at night when she was trying to get to sleep. She also said Becky was waking up in the middle of the night screaming with fear. She had twice run into Becky's bedroom in the middle of the night during two of her episodes to comfort her. But the most worrying thing that was happening was that Becky had told her she could see monsters chasing her in her sleep and as hard as she tried to run away from them they still caught up to her, and when she woke in the morning she had bite marks on her legs! Yes, actual bite marks!

"When did this all happen?"

"It just happened again last night, Isabella."

"Can I see her?"

"Yes, of course you can."

When Becky came into the room that day she looked exhausted. I said, "Hello sweetheart. You look very tired."

"I am. My grandma won't stop talking to me while I'm trying to get to sleep and then when I do fall asleep the monsters are chasing me. I wake up in the morning with marks on my legs where they have bitten me. I'm very fed up and a bit scared with everything that's going on. Mum says she thinks you might be able to help me. Do you think you can?"

"I think so, but I would like to sit and have a chat with you for a little while and try and find out exactly what's going on in your life at the moment, other than what you have just told me. How old are you now, Becky?"

"I'm thirteen."

"Do you have a boyfriend?"

"Well, kind of. There is a boy that I hang out with after school, but we don't go out anywhere together like the pictures or anything. I'm too young."

"Okay."

"But my Gran doesn't like him, and when we walk home from school together she follows us and she keeps shouting at me, telling me to tell him to go away. I just want her to go away and leave me alone. And there is this old man I keep seeing and I don't know who he is, but I don't like him (another Spirit person). He is often sitting on the grass at the side of the path when I walk home from school. But it's the monsters that I'm really scared of."

"Can I have a quick look at the bites on your legs, Becky?"

"Yeah."

She pulled the legs of her jeans up a bit so that I could see (not that I doubted her for a minute) and, sure enough, there were three what looked like scratch/bite marks on her left leg and two about the same size on her right leg. They all looked quite sore. Looking at her mum as I was speaking to Becky, I said,

"If Mum can bring you over to my home tomorrow afternoon after school, I will ask all my friends in the Spirit world to come and help us and I have a 'feeling' we will be able to sort this all out for you."

Anne said, "Thank God for that. I've been worried sick. It's just as if you were meant to come today to see us because I didn't know what to do. I didn't want to take Becky to the doctors. Can you imagine what he would say or do if I told him my daughter was both seeing and talking to her dead grandmother? He would have us both committed. And the thought of trying to explain a nightmare about monsters that gave her actual bites. We needed Mulder and Scully from the X-files but they are not real. But you are, Isabella. You are our very own X-file expert."

And we all started to laugh.

Before I left to go home that day I asked Becky to sit on one of their kitchen stools to enable me to work around her head in her aura, allowing the energy to calm and protect her to keep her safe until I saw her the next day.

Anne and Becky duly arrived at my home the next afternoon and thank goodness they were both smiling. Becky had had a peaceful night, no visitors.

Just before I began her treatment I explained to them both that, with the help of my unseen friends, we were going to close her third eye, and that would mean she would not be able to 'see' her Grandmother or anyone else for that matter ever again (unless someone in the future reopened it for her).

"How do you feel about that, Becky?"

"That will be great, but what about the monsters?"

"One step at a time, sweetheart."

"Okay."

Just in case any of you are wondering what on earth a 'third eye' is, here's a simple explanation.

Her third eye (and yours) is sometimes referred to as the sixth chakra centre. It's the chakra centre in the middle of your forehead, set right between each of your eyes. It's what I and other healers often refer to as your sixth sense. Quite simply it's our connection to our Spirituality. It's the eye we see Spirit people with. It's the eye that allows us to see things from other worlds.

I had already asked for all the help that Heaven and the Spirit world could give me and I also knew that as soon as I began to work in Becky's aura they would be there by my side helping me. Sometimes I can see my Spirit helpers and sometimes I can't. Sometimes I can see one or two of them and then there are other days I can see half a dozen Spirit people and more, all helping me in different ways. God bless them all.

I started by working around the whole of Becky so that she would feel very relaxed and sleepy and, within minutes, she fell fast asleep. Of course I can't make anyone fall into a peaceful sleep within minutes of me starting a healing treatment but, of course, it's not me that's doing anything, it's the wonderful healing energy.

I then sat on my stool at the top of my healing bed and held both of my hands out over her brow and third eye as I watched with my eyes wide open in sheer amazement as her third eye was closed. And the only way I can describe what I saw is to say it was like watching a film on an unseen movie screen no more than a few feet away from me. I'd never experienced anything like this before. I'm sure the powers that be were being kind to me that day, keeping things simple so that I could understand what I was seeing. Her third eye was presented to me as if it was a huge, very ornate wooden door, a bit like the front door of a fairy castle. But for the life of me I couldn't see what the door was attached to. As I was watching, the door began to close very slowly on its own. Then I watched as a very large golden key (already in the lock) began to turn very slowly all on its own, and with every turn the key made, I could hear a very loud clicking noise. For me, it felt as if each turn of the key sealed the door to Becky's third eye tighter and tighter. When the key stopped turning it disappeared before my eyes. The door was now locked tight shut, for as long as Becky wanted it to be.

Becky was fast asleep while this was happening and she

remained asleep for the next half an hour. After her third eye had been closed I then spent time working in her aura, taking away the shock wave that she had in her energy field caused by the frightening dreams she had experienced and also her anger at her grandmother and I must be honest and say at the time I was in a bit of a daze myself. I always knew nothing was impossible for God or the Universal energy. I always knew that anything could be done if I had help from hands from other worlds, and what I had just witnessed had left me in absolute awe and wonder.

After her treatment had finished and she had woken herself up, she got off my healing bed and joined her mum on the settee where Anne had been sitting quietly while I had given her daughter her treatment.

While Anne was giving Becky a hug I explained to them both what had happened and how I was sure that her third eye was now well and truly closed. Hopefully that was the problem of her grandmother solved for good. Now we needed to see what we could do about the nightmares and monsters. But before we did that I said to them both, "Let's all have something to drink. I'll go and make some tea and coffee and then we can have a chat to see what we can do to give you sweet dreams instead of your nightmares."

"Tell the negativity committee that meets inside your head to sit down and shut up."
Ann Bradford

Now I need to go on a little wander here and explain my understanding of what I think of as negative energy because, of course, I have kept saying to you there is just energy. The reason I'm doing this now is because the explanation that I'm going to give was in essence what I explained to Becky and her mum that afternoon all those years ago as we sat and had our tea and coffee.

First of all, there is the wonderful pure energy that God created.

And God filled the Heavens with it, pure energy. That is our Universe and all the other Universes that are yet to be discovered. We look up to the sky each and every day of our lives but I don't think very many of us stop and think that what we see goes on forever and ever, for infinity.

But that's what The Creator did. He filled forever with pure energy.

But we also create energy in every little thing we do ourselves, and I'll bet you hadn't thought about that either. When we wave our arms in the air that creates energy, when we swim in water we move the water, creating ripples and waves, but at the same time we are creating energy; everything we do creates energy. Our words create energy, our thoughts create energy and, just like the ripples on water, the energy that we create travels out and into the air around us and then into the heavens.

Actually, we are far more powerful than we will ever realise.

And we are all doing far more damage to the energy around us (the air or the ether) than any of us could ever imagine.

If I'm honest with you, I probably say something negative every day and negative words and negative thoughts create negative energy. I don't mean to and I certainly don't want to but there are so many negative words in our everyday language that we use without thinking and I'm as guilty as the next person for saying them. So I'm very aware that I need to take myself in hand and try and stop myself from saying negative words and thinking negative thoughts. I'm going to make myself a promise.

"I promise that from today I will try to stop myself when I hear a negative word coming out of my mouth, or a negative thought racing though my brain."

God did not create negative energy. He created pure energy.

And God did not create negative words and thoughts. We did. I know it sounds a bit strange but honestly, when we speak we do create energy and when we think, we again create energy. So our words and thoughts are creating all of the time.

So, in actual fact, what we are doing is changing the pure energy that is everywhere around us with our negative words and our negative thoughts each and every day of our lives. We are the guilty parties. Each and every member of the human race creates negative energy each and every day. So we are all the reason for all the negativity going around the planet.

Negative energy. We create this, God didn't make it.

God made pure energy.

Another way I could express this would be to say. Negative energy is pure energy used negatively by our thoughts, words and deeds. In our general everyday conversation people use the term negative energy so now you know where it comes from.

Us!

We, as human beings, take something wonderful and, with our words and thoughts, turn it into something nasty, without a thought as to what we are doing. And that was part of what I explained to Becky and Anne that afternoon and what follows is the rest of my explanation to them.

There is energy on this beautiful planet of ours being used very negatively, and anyone who thinks there isn't is being very naive. I personally try to have nothing to do with negative energy as best I can. Or better still I desperately try not to feed the negativity in any way.

Now you're going to ask me, "How can you possibly feed it?"

Well I hate to tell you, very easily.

Negative energy has a lot of different names and perhaps, as I go through some of the stories I have to share with you, we will come across a few of them. But to me, negative energy is evil and evil is the word nearly everyone uses to describe the most evil thing we can think of, the Devil.

Most people will say, "Well, of course, you wouldn't want anything to do with negativity, or evil in any form." But people don't realise just how easy it is to help 'the dark side of the force' and I make no apology for using those words, to help negative/evil energy without even realising it.

Let's say you are sitting watching the television and the news reader has just come on telling you that fighting has just broken out somewhere in the world and a lot of people have been killed. Your immediate thought might be, "Oh dear, that's terrible. It needs to stop."

Or, you might say, "That's terrible. I wish it would stop."

Or, "Thank God we don't live there."

I'm sure that would be the response of most people reading this or something very similar, and we would not think for one minute that we had said or thought anything that could help evil in any way or help the negative energy.

Maybe we all need to think again, because we have just given evil a huge boost, we have just fed it.

In effect we have just helped the Devil (and I'm sure that's not what we set out to do, was it?). We have just said or thought the worst thing that we could have. By saying or thinking what we did we unwittingly fed 'the dark side of the force.' Any prayer or thought asking something to stop is negative in itself and is actually feeding the fighting and making it worse.

When, in actual fact, our thoughts and prayers should be of peace.

Help them find peace, help them bring peace into the situation, help them live together in peace and so on. And that's a hard one.

Let me try and make this even more simple.

The word stop is negative. The words 'that's terrible', 'must stop', 'don't' - these words are all negative.

Negative words are evil at its most dangerous because none of us realise that they are dangerous. We can all see evil deeds but none of us ever realise that what to us seem very simple, inoffensive words are actually food for evil. Evil (The Dark Side of the Force) is so very clever it gets us nearly every time, and don't think I'm any different from you, it gets me too. Mother Teresa put it perfectly when she was asked to march against war. "I was once asked why I don't participate in anti-war demonstrations. I said that I will never do that, but as soon as you have a pro-peace rally, I'll be there."

In other words, she did not want to feed the negative of being against something, but she would march for the positive peace.

Negativity is evil in its simplest form and always at its most dangerous.

I'm sure all of you reading this know that to keep a fire burning you have to keep feeding it with fuel. And it doesn't matter what the fuel is. It could be coal or coke or paper or sticks and logs. Without the fuel the fire would simply go out. Well, evil is just like that fire; it needs fuel to keep it going, so with that thought in mind, I would love the whole world to stop watching the news on the television for just one day and night.

I would love the whole world to stop looking at newspapers during the same twenty-four hours.

And I would love the whole world to switch off every mobile phone and computer and disconnect from every social media hub so that the whole world would go quiet (for the same twenty-four hours) and nobody to look at any of the world's media links.

And I honestly personally believe that all the wars in the world would stop. I know that's just my thoughts and I have absolutely no way to prove it to you (unfortunately) but I am allowed my own opinion. I'm constantly telling other people to 'talk their talk' and this is me practising what I preach. Perhaps the wars would only stop for a few hours or, if we were very fortunate, for a few days but that in itself would be amazing. If no one in the world was giving the fighting any credence, if the wars were not on any of our minds on a global scale, then there would be no negative energy to feed them and, quite simply, the fire would go out of the fighting and the wars would stop.

No evil, no wars. Negativity is the food of evil. Food for the Dark Side of the Force!

The world's collective negative thoughts and words are causing more damage in the world than any one of us can ever begin to imagine and we all need to remember this!

So please, and I can't stress this enough - we all need to be watching our thoughts and words.

If we use that example and just expand on it, like massively expand it, what we all need to do to stop all the evil in the world is to send out good thoughts to, yes you've got it, the Devil!

Now this is a strange one, strange but true, and actually very reassuring for me. Within hours of me writing the above words down I happened to stumble on this quote by Mark Twain and when I read it I couldn't believe my eyes. I had been thinking to myself that perhaps you would think me absolutely wacky by saying we should pray for the very thing that represents the most evil we can all imagine. But how else are we going to stop evil?

So what did Mark Twain write?

He wrote, "But who prays for Satan? Who, in eighteen centuries, has had the common humanity to pray for the one sinner that needs it most…"

If I'm wacky then I'm in good company.

Now back to Anne and Becky.

I explained most of the above as best I could to Anne and Becky because I knew that all the negative (evil) energy that had been surrounding Becky had caused her own energy to become very imbalanced.

I then went on to explain to her that thirteen was a fantastic age to be, but very confusing. Periods not long started, emotions all over the place and her own personal energy rising, and then I explained that it's at this age that some families experience poltergeist activity in their homes because their teenage children can and do create very mixed up energy, causing things to literally go bump in the night.

This was the hardest thing I had to explain to her, the power of thought. No one realises just how powerful a thought can be. No one realises just how powerful we all are. Our thoughts can and do create, they can also hurt and harm, just like Becky created her very own monsters. How many times have you thought or wished for something and it has happened? This is actually one of the Laws of the Universe: *Action follows thought*. So watch your thoughts, because you're the one responsible for what you create in your life and no one else. I'm sure you have heard the expression 'Be careful what you wish for, because what you wish for is what you'll get'. And now you know the reason why.

"Becky, without realising what you have been doing you have created your very own monsters. There isn't any outside force wanting to harm you. Your own thoughts are so powerful you have created your own foul creatures out of your frustrations and anger at your grandmother. Your thoughts have been very angry and very negative. Negativity is evil and your evil thoughts have created your own fiends. You are a very clever young lady, Becky, with a very powerful mind. Of course you didn't mean to do this. You didn't realise what you were doing. No one ever realises just how powerful our thoughts are."

Much to my amazement (and relief), Becky and Anne completely accepted what I said to them that day and went home happy and calm because I told them both that the nightmares were gone for good.

I can tell you all that Becky never had another nightmare. The monsters never came back and she never heard from her grandmother or was troubled by any Spirit people again.

When I think back over the years I do still feel a touch of sadness. I don't have the right to say what Becky might have done with her life if I /*we* hadn't closed her third eye and stopped her clairvoyant vision. It was very necessary at the time and it was what she and her mother wanted (it was not my decision or choice) but she had such amazing clear vision. She could (in my opinion) if she had wanted to when she grew up, have gone on to be a wonderful medium. I can happily tell you that she has achieved much with her life to date, setting up and running her own very successful business. But I guess for me there will always be that touch of sadness. There are thousands of mediums and clairvoyants in the world today that would have given their back teeth to have been able to 'see' as clearly as Becky could all those years ago, including me.

This all happened well over twenty-five years ago now and Becky is still free from any nightmares and her grandmother. I know because I'm still in touch with the family.

I'm pleased this story was retrieved from my memory and I have written it down because it's given me a very good reminder to be more careful with my own thoughts.

CHAPTER SEVEN

"We are not put on this earth for ourselves, but are placed here for each other. If you are there always for others, then in time of need, someone will be there for you."
Jeff Warner

Many years ago my mother said to me, "Make sure you keep your girlfriends, Isabella."

"What do you mean, Mum?"

"As you get older you will come to realise just how important they are to you. They will be the ones that you can turn to when your husband doesn't understand how you are feeling or he doesn't understand the girly problems you may be having. When we get married and have families of our own, it's all too easy for us to forget to keep in touch. Then one day we turn around and realise they are gone and we have no one other than husbands to talk to and they haven't a clue what we are talking about, when what we really need is another woman to share our thoughts with, because they will understand what we are saying and how we are feeling. Keep your girlfriends, Isabella. Keep them close, keep in touch with them."

This was good advice then and it still holds true today.

Most of us have read the book 'Men are from Mars, Women are from Venus' so you will understand when I say her words have been proved right so many times over the years. My girlfriends are all very precious to me, as I hope yours are to you.

I've just realised that I'm being very sexist because I'm assuming that this book will only be read by women so, if you are a man reading this, please forgive me. But I'm sure the rest of what I'm going to say applies to everyone.

You can't make old friends; you can only grow them through time and love.

Those were the words that I put into my diary a few months ago when I lost a very close friend of mine. Her passing was very sudden and completely unexpected to her family and other friends. But I've got to be honest here and say, after I had thought about what had happened for just a few minutes, an initial shock for me yes but not so unexpected and I'll tell you why in just a minute. She had apparently been complaining about a headache for a couple of weeks prior to her passing. She mentioned it to me on the Saturday when we had a long chat on the telephone. We arranged to speak with each other on the following Monday teatime. She died of a brain aneurysm late on the Sunday night so we never got to have our Monday teatime chat. But I did hear from her loud and clear early on the Monday morning when she spoke to me for the first time from the great beyond, the Spirit world. And that was to tell me to make sure her family and friends wore bright colours for her funeral. Not quite the chat I would have liked to have had with her.

Apparently she was brain-dead when the ambulance arrived with her at the hospital. After they scanned her brain a doctor told her family it had been a time bomb waiting to go off and it could have happened at any time during her lifetime. When I sat on the Monday morning and thought about what had just happened I remembered that I had knowingly and purposely made sure I had given her lots of hugs and told her how much I loved her each and every time I saw her during the previous twelve months leading up to her passing (with her telling me to stop being daft). My instincts had been telling me to do this and I'd learnt a long time ago to make sure I followed them. So I think I must have subconsciously known that she was going to leave me sometime soon. Yes, I'm always cuddling the ones I love (but I do this without thinking). My actions had been different with her. It was done with thought and purpose on my part and I had known it.

If in this life we have one true friend we should consider ourselves very fortunate, because true friends are hard to come by. It takes years of caring, understanding, trust and love to turn a new friend into a dear old friend and that's exactly what she had been to me. A treasured friend and I'd lost her. I am going to miss her and that's an understatement. But I have lots of happy memories to recall in my mind and the knowledge that she knew how much I loved her, because I told her many times. Because of that I have no major regrets and that was and is very important to me, as it should be to you.

Having no regrets is probably almost impossible to achieve when we lose someone we care about, because the chances are there will be one or two small things we all wished we had done with them, or discussed with them. But above everything else we can make sure that we tell everyone we care about that we love them. Then if we should lose one of them unexpectedly at least we will have no regrets on that front, because we will know that they knew that we loved them. And that will help us all as we grieve the loss of our friends and loved ones.

I met her about sixteen years ago when I started teaching meditation classes in the area we had not long moved into. I had been teaching meditation classes for years where we used to live (and the 'old group' still travelled once a month to be with me for us all to meditate together), so after we got settled into our new home I decided I would like to start a new group. I thought it would be a good way for me to meet new people and make some new friends and my thinking was right. She was one of the first to join the class. I had taught her how to fly over the years, how to travel outside of herself during our meditations, and somewhere in my writings I will come back to this. Only this time, she had flown away and not come back to earth. She has been back to visit and talk with me since her passing but that's not going to stop me from missing her.

Somehow over the years I have been blessed to find more than one true friend. I love them all and I am very grateful to have each and every one of them in my life. Their love has and will help me through the coming months and years with the loss I am feeling. But I thank God because I know my friend is well and happy on the other side of life because she's been back to tell me.

During our lifetime friends come into our lives and then for lots of different reasons they aren't around anymore.

Sometimes they leave us because they have passed over, or they move away and we lose touch, or we may move away ourselves from the area. That's exactly what has happened with another close friend that I had some eighteen years ago now, Jean.

We moved away.

There are lots of different ways of healing and I can still remember my own healer, Nansi, saying to me when I first met her in 1981 that just by making someone a cup of tea and sitting listening to a person's problems, that in itself is an act of healing: listening.

So with this thought in mind, I'm going to go back to 1988 to tell you this story.

Do you remember me telling you about the close friend that I had when my father passed over from this life? Her name was Jean, she lived on our street and only about a five minute walk from our house. She gave me her permission to include her own healing testimonial in my first book and I was able to share it with you. Well, this is a story that involved Jean and myself some twenty-eight years ago now.

I was sitting doing my paperwork (I was an accountant at the time) late one evening and when I say late I mean very late. It was about two o'clock in the morning when I heard the tap on the windowpane. I was just about to pack in preparing a set of accounts ready to take into my office the following day and then go to bed when I heard the tap, tap, tap on the window. The light from our living room and the hall could be seen from the front street and that had indicated to Jean I was still up and working. She knew my routine so well. She knew all she had to do was see a light on in our home and I would still be doing paperwork and, of course, she was right. The tap on the window had given me a bit of a start but I had instinctively known who it was. I opened the door to Jean and let her in. She had just recently lost a very close friend of hers and she was still mourning her friend's loss so I understood why she had come in the middle of the night to find some company and someone to talk to. I told her to go straight into the lounge beside the fire where it was warm while I went into the kitchen to get us both a cup of tea.

It had only been a few days earlier, when I had been in Jean's home having a cup of coffee with her, that she had asked me if I could try and pick up something, anything from her friend that had just passed over into the Spirit world, to reassure her that her friend was alright and, to my amazement at the time, I had. I had been able to hear her friend's voice quite clearly as she described to me in detail the flowers that she had seen at her own funeral and quite a few other things as well. Jean had been a bit unnerved by my efforts. How the heck was I doing this? But she was pleased that I had managed to make contact.

When I went back into our lounge I found Jean sitting on the settee, crying. I sat down next to her and took hold of her hands to reassure her she was not alone. Tears are such a wonderful help when we are upset and I reminded her that having a good cry would release some of her built-up emotions.

Jean told me she couldn't stop thinking about her friend (Anne) as she was just beginning to realise how much she was going to miss her.

"Why can you hear her, Isabella, and I can't?"

The exact same words my mother had said to me a few months earlier when I first started hearing my father's voice so clearly after he had died. Only this time my answer was completely different. I explained to her that there was nothing stopping her hearing Anne's voice if she wanted to. I knew Jean had a very good awareness. It was just that she frightened herself sometimes as she would see things out of the corner of her eye and it made her feel very uneasy. One half of her desperately wanted to be able to see and hear from the Spirit world and the other half of her was a bit scared. It's not that she didn't believe, because she did. She just kept frightening herself.

I had been aware of Anne standing next to the settee beside Jean as she had been telling me how she felt. So I explained to her that her friend knew that she was upset at her passing and, because we had been talking about her, she had moved in close to be beside her. I asked Jean if she would like to be able to hear Anne's voice and Jean said, "Yes."

"Then if you just sit back on the settee and relax, close your eyes and take a few deep breaths you may be able to hear her voice. I'm here beside you and you're perfectly safe. Sit quietly for a little while and try and clear your mind and see if anything comes into your head without you thinking about anything in particular."

After a few minutes Jean suddenly opened her eyes and shouted, "The knob's come off."

"Pardon?"

"The knob's come off," she repeated.

We both looked at each other and burst out laughing. Jean said the words just seemed to 'pop' into her mind.

"Well let's face it, Jean, you're not going to forget those words in a hurry so you will just have to wait and see what happens in the next few days or weeks."

"But I can't have heard her."

I said to her, "I think you just have."

"What do the words mean, Isabella?"

I told her I had absolutely no idea but I had a feeling she would find out quite soon and not to worry about it. Jean eventually went home at about five o'clock in the morning. Needless to say I didn't get into my office until after lunch.

Jean had needed me to be there for her; she needed me to listen and I did.

About six weeks later Jean and her husband were invited to dinner by Anne's husband. Jean explained to me that she was a bit unsure about going as it would be the first time she had seen Anne's husband since her funeral and she didn't know how she would feel being in Anne's home when Anne wasn't there anymore. It might be very upsetting, but Jean did eventually decide to go. After Jean and her husband were given drinks on their arrival, Anne's husband invited her into the kitchen as she had offered to help dish up the meal and as Jean went over to the oven Anne's husband said to her.

"Be careful, the knob's come off."

Jean said she couldn't believe her ears and asked Anne's husband to repeat what he had just said.

"Oh, the knob's come off the front of the cooker. It fell off just after Anne died and I've not had a chance to put it back on."

So there was Jean's answer.

She had indeed heard her friend's voice that night in my home and when she relayed to me the next day what had happened she said she was pleased with herself but she also said she didn't think she wanted to do it again because it had frightened her a bit.

Hearing voices isn't for everyone and that's fine.

Not long after this event Jean hurt her back very badly and ended up having to crawl on all fours on the floor because she couldn't stand up for the pain. She rang me at my office and asked me to please call in to see her on my way home from work to see if I could try and help her. As Jean was sitting on her lounge floor when I arrived because she still couldn't stand up, I knelt down behind her and raised my hands above her head to start to allow the healing energy to flow. I then worked down her spine with my hands about six inches away from her. Jean was giving me a running commentary of all the different sensations she was experiencing as I was allowing the energy to flow. From tingling from head to foot, to heat on her back where her pain was, to a cool breeze that she said she could feel blowing around her feet.

"How are you doing this, Isabella?"

"Jean, I've told you before. It's not me doing it."

But Jean was having none of it.

I've got to be honest here and say Jean was one of my close friends at the time that began to look at me sideways. She became a bit uneasy with me, just like my friends had done at school, and I felt very sad about that because I didn't want to be different and I didn't want to lose her friendship. By the time I had finished, Jean got up off the floor and went to make us both a cup of coffee and all she could say was, "You must start helping other people, Isabella. You could help so many."

Her pain had gone.

As things turned out, it was only a few months after this that Nansi asked me to do some healing work with some of her long-term patients and I did.

My healing work had begun.

I would like to tell you another story that involved Jean and myself that happened a few years later in 1993.

Just as I was about to go upstairs to get ready for bed, late on a Saturday night, our front doorbell rang. Who the heck could that be at this time of night? That's roughly what my husband and I simultaneously said to each other as the front doorbell rang for the second time at eleven thirty on that particular Saturday night. As both our children were upstairs in their bedrooms safe and sound, we had absolutely no idea who would be ringing our bell so late in the evening. I hesitantly opened the front door to see who it was and there was Jean standing on our doorstep in a very agitated state.

"Can you please come with me, Isabella? John (her son) has had a bad accident and we need you to come and see if you can help him. He's in a bad way with himself. I think he's in shock. I'm in my car so I can drive you and bring you home again when you've seen him."

I said, "Of course I'll come with you. Just give me a minute to tell David where I'm going and I'll grab a jumper."

As Jean only lived about half a mile from us, we arrived at her home as she was still telling me what had just happened a couple of hours earlier. John apparently had gone to a friend's party that evening. They were having a barbecue and bonfire and, as boys will be boys, John had tried to light the bonfire more quickly by throwing some petrol or lighter fuel onto an already lit fire. The fuel caught fire immediately on contact and travelled back to its source, the can in John's hand. Fortunately, his friend's parents were in the house when the accident happened and they were able to rush John to the local hospital to get him seen to. They had also telephoned John's parents to tell them what had happened and ask them to meet them at the hospital. Once John had been seen by a doctor and after they visited the pharmacy in the hospital to pick up the pain killers he was prescribed, they were able to bring him home.

When Jean and I arrived at her home that night we went straight into their kitchen and there was poor John sitting on a chair next to the kitchen bench with his hand under the cold air blowing from a fan that Jean had positioned on the bench, in the hope it would help cool John's hand down. He was in a very distressed state. He told me his hand felt as if it was still burning and the pain was horrendous even though he had already taken two of the painkillers he had been prescribed. John was as white as a sheet.

I lifted my hands above his head and within seconds he shouted out that he was going to be sick, and by heck he was. Jean just managed to grab a bucket and put it into his one good hand before he started vomiting. The joke for weeks afterwards between John, our son and all their school pals was, "Don't go anywhere near Alexander's mum. She'll make you sick." After John stopped vomiting he looked a bit sheepish and admitted to us that he had drunk about half a bottle of whiskey before the event had happened. We didn't ask him where he had got it from because it was obvious he realised the mistake he'd made himself without anyone telling him off and, at fifteen years of age, it was no surprise he had been so sick; the contents of his stomach needed to come up. The thing Jean was now worried about was the fact John must have also sicked-up the pain killers he'd been given and she was in a quandary as to whether to give him some more, but she had been told to wait four hours between doses, so John would have to wait. John's hand was unrecognisable because of the bandaging around it. It was huge. It looked as if his hand had turned into a very large light bulb because of the shape of the bandage, just a massive bulge on the end of his arm instead of a hand.

Once the sickness passed, he felt a little bit better and I was able to continue working in his aura around his head and after about five minutes John said he wanted to go to bed to lie down, so Jean said she would take him upstairs. She asked me to give them both five minutes and then would I please come upstairs to his bedroom and sit with her and John and that's what I did. Jean was sitting on a small sofa on one side of his bed, while I sat on a chair at the other.

I began by putting both my hands above his head as I swept the healing energy down over him and after just a few minutes he became visibly calmer and sleepy. I then continued by keeping my left hand above his head and placing my right hand over his bandaged hand that was lying on top of his duvet cover, being very careful not to touch him. I kept my hands about six inches away from him and, to my amazement, I could feel what I can only describe as a freezing cold wind coming from the palm of my hand, a freezing cold, soothing wind. Then I moved my left hand to join my right hand and this doubled the cold healing energy flowing over his burnt bandaged lump. Jean asked me what was happening so I explained to her what I was feeling and suggested she place her own hand between my hands and John's bandage to enable her to be able to feel the freezing cold energy for herself. Jean's face lit up in amazement.

"That's like a wind from the Arctic, it's so cold."

Within minutes John had fallen fast asleep. I must have continued working like this for about fifteen minutes when I heard a voice say to me, "You can stop now."

I stayed in John's room with Jean for a little while longer to keep her company as she was very upset with what had happened but, as it was getting very late and I was very tired, it was time for me to leave and go home. There was nothing more I could do that night to help. Jean said she was going to sit by him all night as she wanted to be there beside him when he woke so that she could give him some more painkillers. The doctor had told her he could have three doses during the night if he needed them and then they were to take him back to the hospital at nine o'clock the following morning when they would redress the burns and give him some more medication.

I was driven back home by Jean's husband and I went straight upstairs to bed as it was about one o'clock in the morning. As I snuggled down (David was fast asleep) I lay there for a while thinking about what had just happened and I can still remember how amazed I was by the strength of the freezing cold healing energy that had flowed from my hands. I had never experienced such a difference in the temperature of the energy before and I was in complete awe. The healing energy had known exactly what was needed for John's burnt hand. That's why over the years I have often said to people, "If you were in my hands you would be in trouble but you're not in my hands, you're in the Universe's hands and the Universe knows exactly what you need."

Jean rang me at teatime the following day to let me know how John was. Apparently, Jean had stayed by his bed all through the night but John had slept soundly and had not woken. In fact he was still fast asleep the following morning. He was sleeping so peacefully she didn't want to wake him to take him to the hospital, so she waited until he woke himself at lunchtime. She took him back to the hospital later that afternoon and when they took his bandage off to re-dress his wound, she said they were amazed to see the burn was already healing. John only took two more of the painkillers that he had been given (on his mother's instructions when he first woke up that first day after the accident). The hospital apparently did give him some more painkillers to take home, but a week later he had not taken any of them because the pain had already left him by the time they got back home from the hospital and it didn't come back and his hand healed in record time.

I'm just very pleased Jean had come to get me that night all those years ago, because John could have suffered quite badly for hours, if not days, but he didn't.

Jean and I had met each other in 1983 when our family moved onto the same road where she lived. We met through our children as they all played on their bikes and skateboards on the street and we had remained close friends until 1998 when our family moved out of the area.

We did see Jean and her husband once more after we moved house. They came to stay with us one weekend. We all had some great times together over the years but, sadly, we drifted apart.

Some people pop into our lives and are close friends for a few years and then they pop out, and Jean was one of those.

CHAPTER EIGHT

"All that we are is the result of what we have thought. The mind is everything. What we think we become."
Buddha

I was about to meet a new patient. This gentleman had been recommended to come to see me by a colleague from his place of work and when he rang to make the appointment he asked me to give the directions to our home to his driver, as he would not be driving himself. He duly arrived in a chauffeur-driven car. He was in his late fifties, tall and, if I say so myself, a very attractive well-turned-out man. I invited him into the room in our home that I was working in, explaining to him as I did that I would like him to sit down on the settee so that we could have a chat to allow me to take some details down before his first treatment started. I sat down opposite him and asked him to tell me why he had sought me out and how could I help? It was obvious to me that he was having problems with his neck and shoulders, but I needed him to tell me himself. So he did.

He explained to me that it had all begun about three months earlier when his neck started to stiffen up. First on the right side of his neck, and then the left side which made it impossible for him to drive his car, because he couldn't turn to look in any direction (hence the chauffeur). Then both his shoulders started to be affected. His doctor had given him painkillers which he said helped a bit but they weren't taking the problem away, so he had come to me in the hope that I might be able to help him. He said that if he tried to move his neck just a little bit the pain was excruciating and he could hear it crunching, just as if a packet of crisps was being squashed. When he finished speaking I sat quietly for a few seconds looking directly at him and then, without any thought on my part whatsoever, I opened my mouth and out came, "Would it be fair to say you're a pain in the neck?"

The words were out of my mouth before I could stop myself.

Dear Lord what had I done?

I was sitting no more than three feet from him and the thought flashed through my mind that he was going to get very angry with me and storm out of the room and I would not have blamed him. I just wanted the earth to open up and swallow me whole.

I sat for what seemed like an eternity looking directly at him, expecting him to start yelling at me at any moment and then I saw the twinkle in his eyes and the smile that started to appear on his face as both sides of his mouth started curving upwards and then he burst out laughing.

"You couldn't be more right if you tried. I am a pain in the neck. My managers at work are constantly telling me the exact same thing. I was told you were good but I didn't know you would be this good. Can you help me?"

To say I was relieved by his response would be an understatement. I think I started breathing again when I realised he was not annoyed with me. As always, I explained to him that I couldn't make any promises but I had a feeling the healing energy would be able to help him. To what extent I didn't know. We would just have to wait and see. But it wasn't going to be an instant cure; it was going to take a few treatments.

He said to me, "You can't say fairer than that, so let's give it a go and see what happens."

'We are what we think' or 'we are what we feel' Remembering the tree on a windy day, if it didn't bend it broke (extract from my first book). In other words if we are stiff and unbending in our everyday lives we are going to have problems. Well, this story is a classic example of someone who was very stiff and un-giving. Spiritual healing actually goes for the whole of you. It doesn't just help the physical pain a person may be in, it also helps to rebalance the aura, the real you which, in turn, helps change your way of thinking. In other words, it can soften your thoughts, which in turn softens your approach to everything and everyone around you.

After a few treatments this gentleman was driving himself to his appointments, as his whole body had begun to relax. But the best was when, after about six treatments he met me with the words, "What the heck are you doing to me? I went into work this morning and smiled and said hello to everyone I met."

We were both laughing as he tried to relay to me all the funny reactions he had received from his very bewildered staff. I explained to him how the healing energy was beginning to have a very positive effect on his whole aura and if he could keep this up he would find everyone and everything around him reacting in a very positive way, making his job and workplace (he had hundreds of people working for him) a much happier place to be.

I can't remember how many treatments this gentleman had from me because this all happened so many years ago now. But there came a day when I said to him that I didn't think he needed to come to see me anymore. His neck and shoulders were healed and it was up to him now. He had listened to all the lessons I had taught him and he had taken everything on board that I had said and now he could get on with the rest of his life, pain-free with a smile on his face (for the first time in years).

Not long before my gentleman patient stopped coming for his treatments he asked me if I could help with something. I laughed so much when he told me this story. He explained to me that his father loved riding his bicycle even though he was eighty-two years of age. Wow. But over the last few months he said his father was finding that he was getting out of breath as he was peddling, especially when he was peddling uphill. Was there anything that I knew of that might help him? He then also explained to me that his father had three girlfriends. I think it was at this point in his storytelling that I was desperately trying not to laugh. You know the feeling when you start to splutter as you desperately try to keep your mouth tight shut. Apparently, one of his lady friends was in her fifties, another in her sixties and yet another one was in her late seventies. He then explained to me that his father rode his bicycle to two of his girlfriends' homes when he wanted to see them. But one of them lived up quite a steep hill and he was finding that ride quite a struggle to complete. Apparently, the third girlfriend lived in the same retirement flats where he lived so his bicycle was not needed to see her. That was the lady he took dancing every week. He then told me that his father was booked to go on holiday in a couple of weeks time with the lady in her sixties and he was hoping I might be able to help him. He didn't want to get out of breath! This time it was my turn to be quiet for a few seconds. I couldn't contain myself any longer. I burst out laughing and so did he. To be honest with you, I found it very hard to stop laughing, I had tears running down my face and I was in danger of having an accident I laughed so much.

He kept saying to me, "Honestly it's true."

"I believe you, I do," as we both laughed and laughed.

Could I help?

Yes, actually, I could. I'm not a homeopath and I would never suggest any remedies unless asked for. But in this case I was asked and I did know of a homeopathic remedy that could do his father no harm and might actually help to oxygenate his father's system. And yes it worked a treat. His father was able to ride his bike without getting out of breath and apparently a great holiday was had by the two youngsters.

Just before I close this chapter, the healing story that I have relayed to you is a great example of me saying something to a patient without any thought on my part. When I first met this gentleman patient, I asked him if he was a pain in the neck. The words were out of my mouth before I could stop myself. In other words, my knowing took me over and did its own thing, without getting my permission to speak in the first place. Over the years when this happens to me, time after time the words that I have just spoken have proved to be the exact words that were needed for the person I was speaking to at the time. This is just one of the ways that my knowing works.

CHAPTER NINE

> Truth is stranger than fiction, but it is because fiction is obliged to stick to possibilities; Truth isn't.
> Mark Twain

Have you ever had one of those days when nothing goes right and you wished you'd just stayed in bed? Well, this was one of those days for me.

The following events happened about twenty-three years ago but the day in question is still quite clear in my mind. This particular day got off to a bad start. Just after the children had left the house to go to school the post arrived and I opened a letter from one of our insurance companies. They were writing to inform me that, because the bank had not honoured the direct debits on the policy in question, for the previous four months they had cancelled the life and accident insurance policy on my husband and I hadn't noticed.

This was a time in our lives when my husband was driving through the night for a living and we both felt it was very necessary that we had his life insured to cover any unforeseen mishaps that might occur while he was driving. To cut a long story short, it was the bank's fault and the insurance company did reinstate the policy but I spent a very miserable morning on the telephone trying to sort the whole mess out.

Then just after lunch I slipped on the staircase in my stocking feet. You know how it goes. I had been upstairs to get changed when I heard the telephone ringing in the hall downstairs. I didn't have any slippers or shoes on my feet as I hurried down the staircase to get to the phone before it stopped ringing, when my foot slid on the stair carpet, sending me sliding down the stairs on my bottom at an alarming rate. When I reached the end of my journey I stubbed my toe on the post at the bottom of the staircase and I honestly thought I had broken it, it hurt so much. It was at that point that I burst into floods of tears. The telephone had stopped ringing so I had missed the call, my toe hurt like hell and I had a new patient due in half an hour, and all I wanted to do was run away and hide. I had to pull myself together, dry my eyes and wash my face so that my new patient wouldn't know that I had been crying. I needed to put a brave face on my bad day.

Do healers have bad days? Yes we do; we are human.

At the appointed time the doorbell rang and I answered it to, "Do you realise your gravel drive has just ruined my shoes?"

Not, "Hello," or "Have I got the right house?" or "Hello my name is..."

"You should warn people before they come to see you that you have gravel on your driveway."

I was so taken aback by her rudeness that I just stood there with my mouth open. It took me a few moments before I brought myself to say to her, "Would you like to come in?"

Let's be honest here, I was inviting her into my home but I didn't really want her in my house and the situation didn't improve very much, not for a while anyway. I directed her into the room I was working in and asked her to sit down so that we could have a chat, but she didn't give me a chance to ask her anything before I was met with, "My family insisted I come to see you. They told me I had to come because I have been taking too many tablets and they had heard you had helped a lot of people with back pain. I don't think for one moment that you can help me but I'm here anyway."

My mouth was open again (as I shouted out in my head to my guardian angels and anyone else that could hear me for help) because I had never had anyone come to me before that didn't want to be helped. Somehow I managed to ask her if perhaps she would like to go home now, or would she like to have a treatment from me?

"I'm here, so I might as well have a treatment."

Firstly, I asked her to sit on the stool I have in my room to allow me to work in her aura/energy around her head and then I asked her to lie down on my healing bed. She had no sooner lain down when she started to complain about everything and nothing. First she didn't like the colour of the sheet I had on the bed, then she complained that she didn't like the heat she could feel coming from my hands and then she was worried in case her skirt got creased and she went on and on.

I could feel my eyes starting to smart as I was about to burst into tears. Fortunately for me, I always start a healing session with my patients lying on their stomachs to allow me to work down their spine, down through their chakra centres. Also, if they have back pain I can work in the area that most needs help. Then half way through their treatment they turn over onto their backs and then I work in the aura around them and anywhere else that might need some help. So if I had started to cry she would not have seen my face. I had no idea what to say to this lady. I had no idea how to stop her constant complaining. I was pleading in my head for her to stop. Let me be honest with you here, I was shouting out to God to help me and that's when it started, breaking wind, or as my grandson would say she started 'pumping'. Every time she opened her mouth to complain about something else she broke wind and it was loud. So loud I thought the next-door neighbours would hear her and, as it kept happening, my tearfulness began to subside and I couldn't help but smile. There was no way on earth I could have stopped her complaining. Nothing I could have said or done would have worked but my cries for help were heard and God sorted her out for me. There's nothing like breaking wind to bring a person down off their high horse.

Please don't get me wrong, I wouldn't dream of wanting anyone to be embarrassed, but if God decrees that wind will break out then so be it. I can honestly tell you that in twenty-five years of helping people this was the only time that wind was the feature of my day.

This lady would never know I had been secretly smiling to myself because she never saw my face, so any embarrassment she might have felt that day would have been her own thoughts. She was very quiet for the second half of her treatment (thank you). She did, however, accuse me of hypnotising her just before her treatment was over because the pain she had been in had disappeared. She said I must have hypnotised her because there was no way her pain could have gone. The fact I had hardly spoken a word to her during her treatment had not registered with her. I did try and explain to her that if I had been capable of hypnotising anyone I would hypnotise myself to enable me to go to the dentist and get my front teeth seen to (large filling needed on my front tooth). That made her think, I think.

She got up from my healing bed with an amazed look on her face and said, "What have you done to me? My pain is completely gone."

I told her I'd done nothing. The healing energy had done its work and lifted her pain away for her. Then I tried to explain to her that I didn't know how long her pain would stay away for her. Her aura would only stay in balance for a short time after her treatment. She needed to learn to rebalance herself.

"What a load of rubbish," was her reply.

You're going to find this one hard to believe. She did come back to see me for two more treatments and, yes, she did complain again both times but not nearly as much as the first time. The outcome was she was able to go a few weeks without taking her cocktail of painkillers, nerve tablets, sleeping tablets and goodness knows what else but, unfortunately for her, she had no intentions of learning how to change her attitude towards everything in her life.

Her sister did ring me a few weeks later to thank me for trying to help her.

There was a lesson here for me. It had been her sister who had made the appointment for her in the first place and, at the time, I didn't question why she had not rung me herself. In the future I would only make an appointment for a person if the person spoke to me and arranged their appointment themselves, children apart obviously.

Every person that comes to me has a story to tell and I think I can honestly say I've learnt something different from each and every one of them. But this next story made me want to cry and if you've been thinking that perhaps I have made up some of the stories I have been telling you, then think again.

Even my wonderful imagination could not have come up with this one. Mark Twain said '…truth is stranger than fiction…' and I can assure you this story is the strangest I've ever heard. This is one story both you and I are not going to forget in a hurry!

I had been treating a husband and wife over the previous few months. They both worked together in their own successful interior design business. The husband came with a bad back and his wife had hurt her arm. Both problems were work related. Not only did they design things, they also made and upholstered furniture and fittings. After a few treatments they were both feeling much better, so much so that they had persuaded the lady's father to come to me for a treatment. They did explain to me he had so many problems they were not sure if I would be able to help him but they both felt it would be worth a try. They told me he was in such a bad way he couldn't even stand up long enough to cut himself a slice of bread or put the kettle on for himself, he was so breathless and in pain.

The day came and they helped him into the room I worked in. They all sat down so that I could ask him a few questions before the treatment began. I can still picture the three of them sitting in our lounge all those years ago (about twenty-two if my memory is correct). I will call the gentleman Colin. He explained to me that years earlier he had worked abroad and he had injured himself a few times while he had been away. I didn't know why I did this at that precise moment, but I asked him if he could stand up for me please so that I could go around his energy/aura to see if I could find where all his injuries were without him telling me.

"I'll try," he said. "I can stand for a minute or two."

"That's all it will take me."

By scanning him from top to toe, back and front, with my hands about six inches away from him, I knew I would be able to find where his energy was not flowing properly and that would show me where all his injuries were.

And I did.

Fortunately for me, he wasn't a very tall man and I

could just reach the top of his head with my hands, with my arms outstretched. So I started at the back of his head and slowly scanned him to his neck and then I scanned both his shoulders and then down both his back and his front. It didn't take me more than a couple of minutes and then he sat down again. I was able to give him a running commentary of all of his injuries as I was doing this and at the time I didn't think I missed one. I told him I felt I had been in the television game 'A Golden Shot' where the commentator used to say, 'Up a bit, down a bit, left a bit, right, now shoot.' He laughed and I could see him visibly relax. He said, "You were right every time. I'm amazed."

And so were his daughter and son-in-law.

Then he explained how he hadn't really wanted to come to see me because he didn't think I would be able to help him, but he said, "I've got to say I'm impressed."

I said, "Don't be impressed with me. It's the healing energy that does all the work." And it was then that the penny dropped with me and I understood why I had got him to stand up when I did. My little demonstration had given him the confidence that he had needed. He wasn't really interested in what I had just done or why; all he was interested in was could I help him? And he was beginning to realise that perhaps I could.

There is no need for me to give you a long-winded report on the next few times I saw Colin, other than to say he enjoyed his treatments and, as each week went by, he began to improve, so much so that instead of coming each week I was able to drop his appointments down to once a month. He could cook, he could go for walks. Colin was actually planning to go on holiday. The following month when Colin was due to come and see me I received a telephone call from him. He cancelled his appointment and I never saw him again. I was not due to see his daughter and son-in-law for another two months so I was going to have to wait to find out why Colin had cancelled.

When Colin's daughter and her husband came to see

me for their next appointments they both had very embarrassed looks on their faces. I was my usual happy smiling self (me most of the time) and I said to them, "Come on, it can't be that bad."

"It is," said Jane (Colin's daughter).

"My dad's not going to come for any more treatments and you're not going to believe the reasons why. If you could have seen him a few months ago you would have been so happy for him. He had bought a new greenhouse a couple of years ago but it had been left lying at the bottom of his garden, with weeds growing in and around it, because he wasn't well enough to do anything with it. But the other month he set to and built the whole thing himself. Then he went out into the field at the back of his house with his wheel-barrow and collected up all the soil from the mole hills to put into the greenhouse for his tomatoes. He was so pleased with himself and he didn't get out of breath."

I said, "That's fantastic, so why does he not want to come back for another treatment to help keep his energy/aura in balance?"

There was silence for what seemed like an age before Jane answered me and this is what she said. "My father said he doesn't want to see you again because you have made him too well!"

"Pardon!"

"I know, but that's exactly what he said. You have made him so well he will lose all his benefits. He's frightened in case someone from the benefits office finds out he built his greenhouse. He's even thinking about taking it down. He gets a lot of money, Isabella, because of all the problems he has had, so he is going to stop coming to you, knowing he will probably become ill again but he said at least he will have all his money."

"Dear God, that's so sad; I've heard it all now."

And that was out of my mouth before I could stop myself. I just sat and looked at her in disbelief and then I said, "I don't believe it. I really don't believe it. I could understand him not coming if I had not been able to help him after a few treatments, but to stop coming because I've made him well, that's got to be the strangest thing I'm ever going to hear."

And actually it was. In the twenty-five years I have been seeing people that's the one and only time I have heard those words.

"I don't want to come for any more treatments because you have made me too well!"

Twain was right, truth is stranger than fiction. You just couldn't make it up if you tried!

CHAPTER TEN

"You can't help those who won't help themselves."
Source unknown

"Is there anything that can't be healed, Isabella?" I've been asked this question at least twice a month over the past twenty-five years. It's obviously a question on many people's minds and my response is and always will be the same. For me there is nothing in this life that can't be healed, but there are people who can't be healed for a myriad of different reasons, and there are people who don't want to be healed (as hard as this is to understand) and I'm always asked what on earth I mean by this.

So this is my explanation for those people who don't want to be healed.

Do you know someone, perhaps an older lady, who has had a bad back for many years? Let's call this person Aunty Betty for the sake of my analogy. As Aunty Betty sits in her armchair beside her fire trying to rub her bad back, she will constantly tell you that no one can help her. Her doctor can't help her. The hospital can't help her. No one can. She will just have to grin and bear the pain. She will tell you that she needs help with her shopping and that she can't manage to do some of her housework. Aunty Betty doesn't actually want any help. Her bad back is her prop in this life and without it she would be lost. Without it she would have to take responsibility for herself and she doesn't want to do that. So she will spend the rest of her life in pain, relying on other people. If God himself came down from Heaven and offered to heal her, she would not accept His help. Please think about this. I'm sure you know, or have known, someone who fits this description. My example is sad, but very true.

I can't wave a magic wand (I often wish that I could) but we all need to learn to take responsibility for ourselves. We all have our own journeys to take on the road we call life and if someone, anyone, waved that magic wand we would not learn the lessons we came into this life to learn, and I hesitate to say this but if we don't learn our own lessons we will have to come back and do it all again.

None of us can tell someone else what to do and none of us can make someone take responsibility for themselves. They have to want to help themselves. We can try and help them understand that until they do take responsibility for themselves they are never going to be well.

If someone had told me thirty-five years ago that they were going to hang me upside down from a washing line with wooden clothes pegs on my toes, and that it would help me get well, I would have done it. I would have done anything to help myself, but not everyone is like me.

The title of this chapter is very similar to the title of chapter two but our subjects and their stories are very different and, as you read on, you will understand why I chose the quote I have used as the title for the following stories.

Like most people, I sometimes wonder why I bother to do what I do and I think the following examples will illustrate the point I'm trying to make quite well.

You are going to find that both our subjects in the following two stories were very feisty.

The first of my patients didn't want my help, and she actually told me she didn't want to come and see me, and the second one, well he was so frightened he threatened suicide if I didn't help him. It doesn't get much more bizarre than that!

It's always very important for me to remember that I'm not responsible for anyone that comes to see me, thank goodness and thank God. And I say this because sometimes I just want to stop what I'm doing and go home but, of course, I am home! Well, my home on earth anyway.

The first of these stories is about a lady with a very bad back problem, partly caused through the job she had when she was at work (she was retired due to her back problems) and partly caused by her very controlling nature (that was my personal opinion after meeting her). This is going to sound a bit strange because she was the second patient in a very short space of time that had been told by her family to come and see me and for almost exactly the same reasons, but I didn't know this until I met her for her first treatment. She had telephoned me herself to arrange the appointment. I will call her Helen for the sake of my story. Helen gave me some of her details; she had been a nursing sister on a men's ward for many years, and had a very abrupt and slightly sarcastic manner. But I was beginning to get used to dealing with awkward people and I was very patient with her, which actually made her even more sarcastic. I just can't win sometimes. Everything I tried to explain to her (just as Nansi had explained it to me) was met with, "That's ridiculous."

And everything I tried to say to her was met with, "That's not right."

And so our conversation went on. In fact she told me that nothing I said was right and my reasoning was stupid.

"Why did you come to see me please?" This seemed like a fair question to ask at the time.

"Because my family told me I had to."

That's when I found out that it was not her decision to come to see me; it was her family's.

"They are worried in case I overdose on the painkillers I have been given for my back pain."

She had spent about half an hour telling me how wrong I was and I was beginning to think I was wasting my time so I suggested to her that we either started her treatment, or perhaps she would rather just like to leave and go home.

"Oh, I want a treatment. If I don't have one my family will not be pleased with me."

I worked away as I always do, with Helen firstly lying on her stomach. I spent quite a while in the area on her spine that I felt needed special attention and then halfway through the treatment she turned over and I worked in the energy around her in her aura. All the while I was working she kept saying to me, "This can't possibly be doing me any good. You're not doing anything."

I said, "No I'm not, but the healing energy is."

"Hmm," she said numerous times.

When the treatment time was over I asked her to gently and slowly get off my healing bed. She did. The expression on her face was priceless. I wished I'd had a camera to take a photograph.

"But the pain's gone, it's gone."

I said, "Yes, that can happen after just one treatment."

"But that's impossible."

"Then the impossible has just happened."

Sorry but I was getting a bit fed up with her to say the least by this time and I am human, well most of the time. Then she tried to walk to the settee to get her coat but she could hardly put one foot in front of the other for wobbling all over the place.

"My God, you'd think I was drunk I feel so relaxed. I've never felt like this in my life."

"Perhaps this is to show you how nice the feeling is? Being relaxed is much nicer than being uptight all of the time."

"You're right. I've never felt like this before and it does feel quite nice, but very strange."

We did both laugh. I wasn't laughing at her, I was laughing with her.

"You would think I had just finished off two bottles of wine. I can't walk straight to save my life."

I suggested to her that she sat down for a few minutes until she found her legs again before she went home and she did. As she was leaving my home she said to me, "Well, that was strange."

And I never saw her again. Why? Her eldest daughter rang me a week later and told me that for years her mother refused to listen to her or anyone else for that matter. Nothing the family or her friends said to her was right and apparently she didn't have very many friends left. Her family were running out of ways to try and help her. She said her mother had told her she would not be coming back to see me for another treatment because she decided that she hated feeling relaxed!

She had not liked the fact she was not in control and never wanted that to happen to her again.

And that says it all.

And here's another story with a slightly different slant on the word control.

It was summer time 1993 when a man in his early forties came to see me for the first time and, without being rude or unkind, he was a little bit odd to say the least. He had no sooner sat himself down on my settee when he looked directly into my eyes and said, "If you don't heal me I'm going to commit suicide."

It was as if he was trying to hypnotise me or he was trying to frighten me with his staring glare.

I said, "Pardon?"

"I'm going to kill myself if you don't cure me!"

I sat for a few seconds holding his gaze and then I said in a very calm voice, "That's entirely up to you. If you want to kill yourself that's your choice."

"But you have to help me."

"I don't have to do anything. I may offer to help you but that will be my choice not yours. If you want to kill yourself, that's your choice."

Of course, this man didn't know me and he didn't know that a few years earlier I had been a Samaritan. I was trained to handle people who threatened suicide and I knew both how to react and roughly what to say. Obviously, every situation is different. That's why I said I knew roughly what to say. But the Spiritual side of me had known for many years that it's a person's own choice whether they take their own life or not. We all have choices. By the look on his face he realised I wasn't going to play his game, he wasn't going to be able to manipulate me in the way he obviously thought he could. Tough. I just sat looking at him, waiting for him to say something.

"Well can you help me?"

"I don't know. I never know. You can only give the

healing energy a chance and see what happens. But first it would be a good idea if you told me what your problems are."

"I am being haunted by very dark and frightening creatures and it's got so bad I don't want to close my eyes at night and go to sleep for fear they will grab me. It all started when a friend of mine gave me a book on kundalini energy (explanation of kundalini at the end of this chapter) and I taught myself to bring the energy up from the ground and up my spine and everything has gone wrong since then. I went to see a man who said he would rid me of the creatures I was seeing, by cutting cords from my past with his sword. He is very well known and supposed to be very Spiritual. His treatment cost me a lot of money, but it didn't work. I'm still very frightened and I think that guy was a fake. Can you help, please?"

I said, "Okay now I know why you are so frightened but you must accept that you have brought this on yourself by meddling in things that you don't understand. It's one thing to read a book about working with kundalini energy but it's altogether something quite different trying to use the energy on yourself when you are all by yourself and don't really know what you are doing. I think I want to say to you a little bit of knowledge is a dangerous thing."

"You're right. I think I've learnt my lesson but can you please stop me from seeing the nasty Spirit entities or monsters or whatever they are?"

This was not the sort of problem that I would normally deal with, but this poor chap was genuinely frightened and I knew that if the Spirit world helped me we would be able to close the door for him, so to speak.

'I can of mine own self do nothing....' John 5, Verse 30. Those words came into my mind (from my father's teachings), because I was being asked to help with a problem that was way out of my league, expertise and knowledge.

Boy, how right those words still are! But I knew at the time that, with the help of all my unseen friends, this man's problems would no longer be out of my league.

Firstly I explained to him that the only way I knew of stopping his manifestations was to close his third eye tight shut so that he never saw anything of the Spirit world ever again. There may have been another way to stop it for him but if there was, I didn't know what it was. I asked him if he was absolutely sure that that was what he wanted to do, because once I closed it tight shut it would remain closed until the day he asked someone to reopen it again for him. I explained to him that I was not happy doing this unless he was absolutely sure that that's what he wanted done and very clear in his choices.

"Yes, I'm sure."

"Okay, then we will close it for you."

I started his treatment just as I would anyone else's. The only difference I made was when he turned over and lay on his back. I worked in his aura for a little while to calm him down so that he was very relaxed (something he had not been for a long time) and then I sat down on my stool at the head of my healing bed just behind his head. I held my hands over his third eye while I asked for the Spirit world to help me close it down. I closed my eyes and watched as his third eye closed and this is what I saw. (Of course, I had been here before with Becky so I knew that my unseen friends would be able to help him, but I didn't tell him that.) When I say I watched as his third eye was closed, I watched from my third eye or my mind's eye metaphorically speaking. It's a bit like watching a movie in your mind. I saw very large wooden gates with huge metal bars going across them in three places (a bit like the gates out of 'Game of Thrones'). These gates were so big they could have held back an army and, as I was watching, they very slowly came together on their own and then the three huge bars of metal all slid into place, locking the door tight shut. Job done in a matter of minutes. I knew his problem had been solved. This might sound very surreal or even stupid to some of you reading this but trust me, the job was done. I finished his treatment by working around his whole body in his aura about two feet away from him as he lay peacefully resting on his back, oblivious as to what had just happened.

When he got up from my healing bed he said he felt lighter and much calmer. I explained to him what had happened and what I had seen and then he said, "Has it worked?"

I told him as far as I was aware it had but he would know himself in a very short space of time. He asked me if he could see me again in a couple of days time because he was concerned in case it hadn't worked and he was still very frightened. I did understand, so I agreed.

Back he came, but this time with a smile on his face.

"It worked, Isabella. It really worked. I've had the best two nights sleep in ages."

"Good. It's not for me to tell you what to do but might I suggest that you leave your kundalini books alone for a while? I think you need to promise yourself you won't let anything like this happen to you ever again."

"You're right, and if by any chance my nightmares start up again I'll be straight back to see you."

He had another treatment from me that day, thanked me and left my home with a smile on his face and I never saw or heard from him ever again.

Job done.

Thank you, my wonderful unseen friends.

One or two of you might be wondering or asking yourselves what on earth kundalini energy is?

It is said that kundalini energy is the life force that lies dormant within most people. In Hindu mythology, kundalini is a serpent goddess who lies asleep at the base of our spine, coiled three and a half times around our first chakra centre. It's seen as a coiled serpent lying at the base of everyone's spine. Let's face it, no one knows if it actually exists and I, for one, don't want to know. It's enough for me to know its representation is a serpent and that to me represents a negative image and remember negativity to me is evil, so for me kundalini is another word for evil (sorry folks if any of you like it, but I don't and this is my book). I read a bit about it many years ago and I can remember thinking to myself at the time that I didn't want to know any more and I didn't want anything to do with it. So if you want to know more, you do the research.

My patient was free and clear of it and happy and I can only hope he remains that way but the choice, of course, will always be his.

CHAPTER ELEVEN

"Whether it's a friendship or a relationship all bonds are built on trust.
Without it...you have nothing."
Source unknown

I have just realised that just about all of the stories I am going to be telling you in this book are from at least sixteen years ago.

About three years ago I sat down with a pad of paper and made a list of all the interesting cases I worked with in our last home, from the beginning of my healing practice in 1992 to the time we left the area in 1998 and, as I was travelling back in my mind recalling case file after case file, I realised that, in actual fact, I am still in touch with quite a few of the people involved. So when I have finished telling you some of the following stories I will be able to tell you honestly that whatever the problem was that they came to me with at the time, it was healed and they have remained healed to this day and that's nice for me (and you) to know.

Do you remember me telling you in my first book that I often know what people are thinking? In other words, I often find myself (for want of better words) reading someone's mind. I don't do it all the time and I don't do it on purpose. It somehow just seems to happen, mostly when I do actually need to know what a person is thinking.

I think you're going to love this.

Not long before I sold my business in 1990 (before I became a full-time healer) I had an appointment with a client to go over his year-end accounts. He duly arrived at the appointed time. He came into my office and sat himself down on the chair at the opposite side of my desk. As he sat down and faced me I couldn't help but notice a very large patch of angry raw skin on both his nose and forehead. It travelled the full length of the bridge of his nose and continued up and across both sides of his forehead. What a mess he was in and, by gosh, it did look sore and angry. You would have thought someone had used him as a punch bag or he had walked into a spiky rough wall. His face was in a right old mess. And before my brain gave me a chance to think about what I was going to say, I came out with, "By gum, that must have hurt."

"Not half," was his reply.

Now completely unknown to him, the minute I had seen the marks on his face I just knew how he'd done it and, in all honesty, I didn't even know at the time whether a voice from the Spirit world had quickly spoken to me telling me how he'd done it. Or, if the thought had just somehow popped into my head from out of the ether telling me exactly what had happened to cause it. But either way, I knew exactly what had happened.

I just couldn't stop myself. My mouth was open and out came, "I know what happened to you."

He looked at me as if I was stupid, shook his head and said to me, "There is no way on earth that you could possibly know. There is no way you will ever know."

He was right, of course. There was no way on earth I could have known. But the information hadn't come from earth, it had come from somewhere else entirely.

"But I do."

"Don't be stupid. No you don't. There is no way you will ever be able to guess how this happened."

"I'm not going to guess, but I do know how you did it."

"No, no. You will never know because I'm never going to tell you."

I just sat opposite him at my desk trying desperately not to laugh. Somehow I managed to go over his accounts with him without blurting out what I knew.

It would have been hilarious if someone could have videoed us. Me smiling at him every few seconds and him shaking his head at me each time he caught my smile. It was so funny. He was so sure there was no way I could know. And of course I was very sure that I did know what he'd done. An unspoken, "I know he thinks I don't know." And him thinking, "She thinks she knows but I know she doesn't." By the time I had gone over all his figures with him I was bursting to tell him what he'd done.

"Would you like me to tell you how you did it?"

"Go on then, give it your best shot."

And with a gleeful smiley voice I said, "You got up in the middle of the night a few nights ago to go to the loo. You sat down on the toilet seat and you promptly fell asleep. That's when you fell forward and the marks all the way up the bridge of your nose and the marks on your forehead were all caused as you skidded across the carpet on the bathroom floor, basically using your nose to skateboard across the carpet. Your weight pushed you along the carpet burning your skin. The open, very sore-looking wounds on your face are carpet burns. That's what happened; that's exactly what caused your injuries."

And without a doubt, this is one of the many times that I wished I had had a camera in my hand to take a photograph of the expression on his face.

It was priceless.

As I was explaining to him what he'd done he had been turning a very white shade of white. He ended up looking like a brand new bath towel, as his face gleamed, the purest shade of white imaginable.

"How the ***k did you know!?"

"I didn't. The minute I saw the marks on your face the thought just came into my head and I'm not even sure if the Spirit world told me."

He was silent for quite a few seconds and then he said, "I believe you. My God, there is no way you could have guessed; someone must have told you."

"I'm sure they did, or something did. Told you I knew how you'd done it."

"There's no keeping anything from you, is there?"

I just smiled at him and said, "I guess not."

And this brings me back very nicely to where I left off. Sometimes I get a thought into my head as to what someone else is thinking and I haven't got a clue where the thought came from. And at other times I clearly hear a voice speaking to me, telling me what a person is thinking. And sometimes this all happens so fast I don't actually know which was which, as was the case with the little story I have just told you.

So do I read people's minds? Yes I do, but I don't always know how.

And that is the end of that wander.

Now let's get back to the story I was about to tell you.

I can still picture the day this happened in my mind's eye as if it was yesterday, the picture is so clear. My memory file is in great shape.

This file is all about the day a teenage boy was brought to see me against his will. Now please don't be concerned, his father brought him to me because his mother felt sure I would be able to help him and, of course, the teenager (at the time) didn't. So to say the young man came up my drive kicking and screaming, metaphorically speaking, would not be wrong. But the kicking and screaming was all in his head. And I read his thoughts that day like an open book.

Let's have a little bit of background on the family.

We have mum who I will call Linda, father who I will call Geoff and the teenager who I will call Philip.

I met Linda some three years earlier when she came to me for healing after losing her beloved pet dog (and any one of us who has lost a treasured pet can understand how distressing this can be) and it was then that we discovered that we had both lived in the same area as children and young adults. But not only that, we had even attended the same school, although three years apart. Linda had left school to train as a hairdresser and she started her training in the very same salon where I, as a teenager, got my hair cut. I still have a memory of her in the salon as if it was yesterday (small world). So Linda and I have a connection.

Now back to my story.

I watched out of our lounge window as Geoff and Philip walked very tightly together up our drive. I'm sure Geoff did this to make sure Philip didn't try and turn and leave (he couldn't have turned to run because he was limping). And at every step Philip took I could hear him saying to himself in his head, "How the bloody hell do they think this woman can help me? They're crackers. No one can heal. Only God and the Pope can heal. What a waste of time." With each step he took he was berating his parents and me. The swearing that was going on in his head was actually far worse than I have recorded, but you get the idea. He just did not want to see me and, at fourteen years of age, well perhaps I can understand. I was smiling from ear to ear when they both came into our lounge, the room that I worked in.

"Hi, Geoff."

"Hello, Philip."

Geoff said to me, "You're going to have your work cut out with this one."

And absolutely no response from Philip.

"That's okay, Geoff. I've got quite a thick skin."

I turned to Philip and said, "I know you think that no one can heal except God and the Pope and your Catholic upbringing has been great for you, but if you ask Father Tom (their family priest) I'm sure he will tell you what Jesus said to his disciples regarding healing. And this is the exact quote taken from the King James Version of the Holy Bible. "Verily, verily, I say unto you, He that believeth on me, the works that I do shall he do also; and greater works than these shall he do; because I go unto my Father." John 14:12

What I actually said to him was, "These things you shall do and more." Well I almost got it right. "So come on, let's give this a chance and see if we can get you out of pain."

He did look at me with a very surprised look on his face when I had finished speaking.

I asked them both to sit down so I could find out exactly what had happened, and I realised straight away that Philip was not going to talk to me to save his life so I turned to his father to tell me the story.

"Philip plays football, Isabella, for the 'School of Excellence' in our local town."

"That's great. You must be really good."

"Two days ago he was kicked in the shins as he went to take the ball and he was carried off the pitch, shouting in agony. They took him straight to the team's physio practitioner and rang me to come and collect him, but the pain has only subsided a little bit and he's having difficulty walking up our stairs and he is hobbling around school, apparently, like a wounded soldier. But worst of all he can't play football. Can you help? Linda says she thinks you can."

"I can't promise anything but I'm fairly sure I/*we* should be able to do something to help."

I looked at Philip and said, "Come on, young man, as much as you don't want to, I need you to sit on my stool first so that I can go around your head in your energy (aura) and calm your energy down, because it's jumping all over the place."

I looked at his face and, without him saying a word out loud, I said, "The reason it's doing this is because your whole system has taken a shock. That's why your energy and your mind are all over the place and I'm sorry kid, but you don't have to speak, I can read your mind."

When I said that his eyes opened wide and, for the life of me, he looked just like I have always imagined the 'Lambton Worm' would look like from the Geordie song of the same name. The line reads, "An' great big googly eyes" and I knew at that instance it had dawned on him that I had been aware of him swearing at me in his mind. But I had got his attention and that's what I'd wanted to do. After a few minutes I asked him to climb onto my healing bed.

I worked down his spine as I always do, working both in his chakra centres and also the whole of the energy around him. I would do this even if someone came to me with a sore foot. Healing has to go for the whole of the person and not just the bit that hurts. That way the balance can be put back into the whole of the person and not just the area of damage. Then I asked him to turn over to allow me to go around his whole body in his energy field/aura, but more importantly so that I could work on the area of his leg that had been injured, and that is what I did for about half an hour. All the while I was working I was aware of Philip's thoughts (which made me smile numerous times) because, by heck, he knew some swear words and most of them are unprintable.

When he got up from my healing bed when his treatment was over, Geoff and I smiled at each other as Philip walked towards the door. He wasn't limping nearly as badly as when he had come into the room, but we both said nothing.

Linda rang me a few days later to let me know that Philip was running up and down the staircase at home with ease, so she could only guess that his leg was not hurting anymore. She told me she was guessing because Philip still wasn't speaking to her, although she said he had smiled at her a couple of times in the past two days and perhaps he would be speaking to her by the end of the week.

Boys!

About six months later I received a phone call from Geoff asking if I could please see Philip that afternoon because he was in agony. He had been injured yet again playing football, only this time he himself had asked his father if he could come and see me. Geoff told me that he had been at the football ground that afternoon to watch the boys practising when Philip had been tackled from behind, just as he had been in full flow as he jumped up into the air to kick the ball and, within a split second, he was screaming in agony as he fell to the ground doubled up in pain. Help had arrived immediately for him. He was stretchered off the pitch and told by the team manager that they were going to take him straight to the physiotherapist's room for an assessment and a treatment. But Philip himself had said, "No", as he shouted to his father, "Dad, please take me to Isabella. She will put me right."

What a turn around that was!

Geoff managed to get Philip into the car to bring him to me, but not before he rang me to make sure I could see him straight away which, fortunately for Philip, I could.

I don't think I had ever seen such a turn around in someone's attitude towards me. The look of relief on Philip's face as his father helped him onto my healing bed that afternoon was amazing for me to see. Philip actually smiled at me. He even spoke to me. And no swearing this time in his head, at anyone. He was just a very grateful young man with a smile on his face because I was able to see him at such short notice. And I'm very happy to report he was out of pain by the end of his treatment and his leg healed within days.

There is a little bit more to tell you about this story. Philip had wanted to use the experience he had had of healing in a talk he was due to give in morning assembly at his school. His year had been asked to come up with examples of how God worked through people to help other people. It was all part of their term projects at the time. I don't know whether this is relevant or not but he attended a private Catholic school. Philip wrote what would have been described at the time as a testimonial on Spiritual Healing and his form teacher had been all for him presenting it to the school, but the Headmaster vetoed it and Philip was stopped from giving his talk.

What a shame.

The Catholic faith does believe in healing but perhaps the Headmaster was trying to be politically correct at the time. Perhaps he was trying to stay on the right side of all the school governors.

You see, this all happened about the same time there was a lot of talk in the newspapers and on the television about Glenn Hoddle, the well-known footballer, and his faith healer. How sad is that? Sad because everything to me that Glenn Hoddle and his healer were trying to tell people is what I also believe to be true. Everything they were trying to say and explain was greatly misinterpreted by the media and because of this they were misunderstood by almost everyone around them.

I can hardly believe this, but this all happened over twenty years ago now.

I headed up this chapter by using a quote about trust and this last little bit of this chapter is the second reason why. The first, of course, was because Philip's mother trusted that I would be able to help her son, and the second part is because her son was later to trust me with one of the most precious things in his life, his very own son. Philip brought his wife, their young daughter and his eight-month-old son to my home just a few months ago to enable me to give his son some healing. He brought his baby boy to me for healing and yes, I/*we* were able to help him. His son was healed that afternoon and, of course, Philip was healed all those years ago and he never looked back.

But the most wonderful thing for me was that Philip had never forgotten what had happened to him all those years ago and he, in turn, now trusted me enough to bring one of the most precious things in his life to me and that for me was priceless.

CHAPTER TWELVE

"Our weakest points often become the place of God's greatest miracles."
Source unknown

God bless you, Father Tom, from the bottom of my heart.

In a very short while you are all going to know the reason why I have just used those words.

In Philip's story (the story you've just read) I mentioned to you that his mum, Linda, is a practising Catholic and proud of it. Her family priest at the time of Philip's story was Father Tom. And dear Father Tom is also in the story I am about to tell you.

Linda and I were both brought up in Christian households. Linda was brought up a Catholic and me, I was brought up a Methodist. I myself moved away from my conventional religious upbringing many years ago and Linda has remained a staunch Catholic to this day, not least because of the wonderful parish priest she had for many years, Father Tom. Linda told me many of the stories that Father Tom had shared with her as he tried to teach her by his simple story-telling. She relayed many of his stories to me when she came to me herself for healing treatments and, for all I never met Father Tom, I had always felt as if I knew him. I knew him to be a very kind, caring man from everything Linda had said.

So hopefully this helps to give you a little bit of background information for this, my next story.

For me, this is a very special story for many reasons, not least because our heroine in this tale was our daughter's best friend at the time and they remain friends to this day.

What I'm about to tell you all started to happen in 1993, but it didn't come to its conclusion until well into the twenty-first century.

On passing her GCSE's, our daughter then changed schools to complete her 6th form and A-levels but unfortunately she didn't pass biology and, because she needed it for the job she wanted to do, she decided to go to the local college of further education in our area for a year to re-take it (she did pass second time around) and this is where she met her new friend, Jane.

Marie used to tell me all about the things she and Jane got up to both at college and when they went out together on the town having fun. But, to be honest with you, I don't remember meeting Jane until her problems first began. Their friendship at the time encompassed both our daughter's and some of our son's numerous friends.

This was 1993 and I hadn't been healing outside of our family circle for very long when Marie came home from college one day very upset because she had just found out that her new best friend, Jane, had just been diagnosed with a tumour at the base of her spine. Essentially it was in the cheek of her bottom and the top of her leg and they were not sure if it had spread any further. Please remember I'm not medical in any way so if I've not used the correct terminology it's because I don't know it but even if I did, I wouldn't use it because it wouldn't be me.

"Can you help her, Mum?"

"Oh gosh, Marie, I don't know. Her parents must be frantic. I'm so sorry."

While I was giving my daughter a hug to try and comfort her, my thoughts went racing away and may everyone please forgive me for my honesty because my very first thought was, "Thank God it's not us."

And that I'm sure was a very normal instant response for any mother to have and then my mind went off on a roller-coaster ride of its own.

How would I cope with this situation if it happened to us? Could I cope? What would we do? Who would I ask to help us all? And a thousand other questions all tumbled around inside this mother's head as if someone had thrown a hundred different scenarios into a tumble drier and pressed the on button.

But I do clearly remember thinking, "Please Lord, help this family. Please help them through this."

All I really knew and could comprehend at the time was that my daughter's best friend needed help, her family needed help and I needed to try and do something to help everyone. And I needed to keep giving my precious girl lots of hugs.

"I never know, Marie. I never know if I/*we* can help but there's no harm in trying. There's no harm in me seeing her for a few treatments if she would like to see me (I think)."

Please allow me to go on another small wander here. I feel so ashamed of how I felt at the time. Ashamed because of my lack of trust in what I now know and have known for years was always there for me, God's wonderful healing energy. But I guess in 1993 this was all so new to me. My daughter was asking me for help for her best friend and she'd never done that before, so this was very important to me. I wanted to be able to help. But I was being asked to help with something that most people would have run a mile from. Even now the word cancer strikes fear into most people. Would the healing energy be there for me to use tomorrow? Would it be there when I needed it? Would it be there for my daughter's best friend? Could it help her with such a serious problem? I should have known better, but I was a very inexperienced healer at the time and I had such a lot to learn. I'm sure many of you will have learnt over the years (like me) that the best way to learn to do something is simply to do it.

More than twenty years have gone by since that day and yes, I have learnt a hell of a lot. So please forgive that woman (me) at the time for being a worried and unsure of herself healer.

Wander over.

"She knows what you do, Mum, because I've told her. I'll ask her and see if she would like to come and see you for a few treatments."

And that's how I left it with my daughter.

Jane did come to me for a few treatments within days of my conversation with Marie, before she went into hospital to have the tumour removed. This was all organised in a very short space of time after it was found. I think I was able to give her about four treatments before her major operation, which was to be followed by quite a few treatments of radiotherapy and then chemotherapy.

But what Jane and her family didn't know at the time, and probably still don't, was that I got Father Tom's phone number from Linda and rang him the week before Jane was due to go into hospital for her operation.

That phone call was so precious to me I'm never going to forget it.

I will never forget what Father Tom said to me.

When I rang him I introduced myself as a friend of Linda's and he knew immediately who I was talking about. I said to him I'm her 'non-Catholic friend' and he burst out laughing, saying he was sure God would forgive me (and I laughed).

I explained to him that I was a Spiritual healer and I told him all about Jane and her operation the following week and the reason why I was ringing him was to ask for his help. I explained to him that I truly believed that God could heal anything (or the healing energy, because to me they are one and the same thing). I also explained to him that I was going to tune in throughout the day of her operation. I was going to be asking for help for the surgeons to do an excellent job, the anaesthetist to keep her breathing safely and I was also going to ask that the healing angels would surround her with healing energy and fill the operating theatre with wonderful healing energy, and anything or anyone else I could think of to ask to help her.

I then explained to him that I personally felt I needed all the help I could get from Heaven, the Spirit world and anyone here on earth I felt I knew I could trust to help me. And he was the only person I could think of here on earth that I trusted to be there for me. If my father had been alive I would most certainly have asked for his help. I did anyway. He was on the top of my list of people in Heaven that I asked to help me. I think you must realise by now that I was gathering to me the most powerful prayers that I could muster.

His answer to me made me cry.

"What a wonderful faith you have. I wish my faith was as strong as yours."

And as our conversation went on he must have repeated those words to me at least three times.

Then he asked, "What would you like me to do? What can I do to help you?"

"Would you please join with me in praying for Jane? Please pray that her operation is a complete success and then I'll know that I'm not alone in my asking for help."

"I'll do more than that for you. I'll say a special mass for her. I'll have a day of prayers just for her. Is there anything else I can do to help you?"

"No, Father Tom. Knowing you are going to help me is a blessing beyond words to me."

And then Father Tom said, "Perhaps one day we'll meet. Your faith is like a ray of sunshine and by far the strongest I have ever known in anyone during all my years as a priest. God bless you."

And with that he put the phone down and I burst into floods of tears. And I was in floods for ages. As I have been writing this my eyes have been filling up with tears just remembering the wonderful Irish lilt in his smiley voice as he softly spoke his kind words to me.

Thank you, Father Tom, more than twenty years on, thank you.

I never did get the chance to meet him in this lifetime and he has now gone on to his home in Heaven. But one day when I travel back home myself I will most certainly seek him out and give him a great big hug and say thank you again for helping me all those years ago (and I wasn't even a Catholic, well not in this lifetime anyway).

The following week, the day before Jane was due to go into hospital for her operation, I gave her a treatment to help to keep her calm with a promise to her that I would be there by her side every step of the way.

And I was.

My way of praying I guess is very different from the conventional way that most people pray. When I'm asking for help for someone I can often see myself standing beside them (in my mind's eye) as if I am actually with them. And, as strange as this is going to sound, I have had people say to me, "I knew you were with me. I could feel you standing by my side," or "I could feel your presence in the room with me."

At the time I knew her operation was about to begin I sat myself down in a comfortable position and tuned in as I had often done before.

And that's when I stepped into the picture that started to appear in my mind's eye.

I found myself in an operating theatre where I stood and watched as beautiful blue (in Jane's case) healing energy filled the room. It was a bit like watching blue steam from a kettle billowing out everywhere, completely filling the operating theatre where Jane was lying. And I watched as what seemed like a crowd of people gathered around the table Jane was lying on, all ready to work. I had been told that the operation would last at least four hours so, once I knew she was in safe hands and I saw that there were angels by her side, I went to get myself a cup of tea and do a few little jobs around the house. All the while I was busy, I was asking that she be kept safe. Then sometime later in the afternoon I went to sit back down and I tuned back in again and I did this a couple of times.

Time is a very strange thing when you are tuned in to someone or something; it's almost as if you are beyond time and time does not exist. Sorry, but I don't know how else to describe it and all of that afternoon was beyond time for me.

But the wonderful thing for me now is that I can still see what happened next as if it was yesterday.

The operating room I found myself in that afternoon was a very noisy place. Lots of people talking and I could hear the sound of music playing in the background behind their voices, all mixed up with the sound of squeaky boots on the now wet floor. The floor around the table Jane was lying on was covered in blood (slight exaggeration but I'm trying to paint the picture I stepped into that day). There were splats and small puddles and watery, bloody foot-prints on the floor all over the place. I can remember thinking to myself that must be why we sometimes see surgeons on television programmes and in films with short green wellington boots on. The scene looked a bit gory to say the least, but Jane seemed fine. I was aware that all her vital signs were nice and stable and everyone working in the theatre seemed reasonably relaxed. But it was about to get very gory indeed as I watched in amazement as her operation reached its climax and I witnessed the whole thing as it happened. I could see a very large opening in Jane's buttock going down into the top of the back of her leg and it was being held open with what looked like shiny steel clips of some sort. Then I watched as the surgeon lifted out (with a struggle) a solid dark mass. It was both the size and shape of a rugby ball. It was huge and, without really looking at it, he threw it onto the floor and, fortunately for him, it landed in the bucket that had been placed on the floor to put it (or catch it) in. I can still see the content of the bucket in my mind's eye nearly twenty-one years on. The dark solid mass was just like a piece of very thick eel encased in its own see-through bag, or skin, the shape and size of a rugby ball. Yuck. I then watched as the surgeon cleaned the large area the lump had been taken from and then I watched as two other people started to prepare the open wound to be stitched up, and it was at that point that I knew the operation had been a success and I breathed a sigh of relief. Jane was going to be fine and, as I looked around the operating room, everyone was smiling. It was then that I stopped whatever it is that I do and said, "Thank you" out loud to the ether. I rang Father Tom and thanked him and again had a lovely chat with him and I also thanked and blew a kiss skyward to the Universal energy (God) and my dad and everyone else I had asked to help me. (Yes, I blow God kisses; so would you if you could see half the things I see.)

But like a lot of my stories this is not the end.

Jane did come for a few follow-up treatments.

I can remember her telling me at the time that the

doctors who were looking after her post-op were amazed at how quickly her wound was healing and, of course, she was still very close to our daughter so I was kept informed of her progress. Not only was she close to our daughter, she was now living with our daughter and a couple of their other friends. Things went well for her for a few years and then she started to have some more problems. She had been going for check-ups once a year and in 2001 her specialist told her that the cancer had come back and it had spread down her leg and it needed to be removed before it spread any further and she lost her leg!

Jane came back to me for more treatments before she had her second operation followed by radiotherapy.

I don't want to understate the worry this caused her family and all of her friends (including us) but on the other hand I don't want to spend ages repeating myself, so let me try and get a balance between all the emotions that were flying around and what happened next.

Operation day:

This time when I tuned in I didn't have Father Tom's help because he himself was now retired and not in the best of health, so I didn't ask him. But I knew I had Heaven's help and all the help of my Spirit friends including my father and, actually, that was now enough for me.

When I tuned in this time to watch the surgeon working I saw him cut a long incision into the back of her leg down to behind her knee. Then I watched him as he seemed to remove what looked like the tentacles of an octopus. O.K, I know that sounds a bit odd but that was exactly what it looked like to me. There was no tumour as such to remove, no massive lump to remove like the first time, just long, thin tentacles. Long, thin, cancerous tentacles that ended up in the bucket on the now bloody wet floor, just like the picture I saw during her first operation.

I watched in complete awe as the surgeon worked very slowly and methodically, removing one cancerous tentacle at a time as he followed the pathway of each of them as they wound their way down the back of her leg. That's the best way I can describe what I saw and when he thought he had them all (and I felt quite confident that he had, because I had watched him go over and over where he had been, clearly making sure nothing was left) he stepped back to allow different members of staff that were waiting in the background to step forward and start to stitch the back of her leg up. Her operation was followed with radiotherapy every day for five weeks to make sure all the cancer had been killed off. (And that was a lot of radiotherapy in anyone's book.)

I can still remember going into the hospital ward to see her with our daughter (Jane was in a side room on her own with a glass window looking out into the ward) as did many of our daughter's and our son's friends, trying to keep her spirits up during her stay with their high jinks and their antics, with hilarious results. When she eventually came out of hospital she again came for more treatments with me, mainly because part of her wound was in such an awkward place on the back of her leg behind her knee that it was proving very hard to heal. But heal it did with the help of the healing energy.

Now let me slightly change direction as I continue on with the story.

Jane had known for a long time that she would never be able to have a family of her own because of all the radiotherapy and chemotherapy she had gone through. There was no way she would be able to carry a baby. But just to make sure she went to a specialist centre to have some specialist tests. When the doctor met with her to give her the results, apparently (I am told) he was in tears. He confirmed to her that there was no chance she would ever be able to become pregnant because of the damage the radiotherapy had caused her. She tried to reassure him it was okay. She had known this for years, but now she knew for sure.

But this is not the end of my story.

A few years later Jane fell in love and got married.

We met her husband, John, for the first time when they came to our home to help us celebrate our silver wedding in the summer of 1999, a few years before they married.

I have often found myself saying to people over the past twenty-five years, "Please never say never because none of us can ever second guess what's going to happen next in our lives; we just don't know what life holds for us around the next corner."

We can all hope for miracles, we can all pray for miracles, often, but we can never be sure.

A year or two after their wedding, and not long after they returned from one of their holiday adventures, Jane wasn't feeling very well, so she took herself off to her doctor to have herself checked over. To her absolute shock, amazement and astonishment she was told that she was not ill, she was actually two and a half months pregnant! Now obviously her family doctor knew Jane's medical history and knew what the results from the specialists had been, so the wheels of the medical profession rolled into action in record time.

Jane was to have weekly scans.

There was great concern from very early on in her pregnancy because her baby was so very tiny and also because her baby never moved. Jane named her non-existent bump baby Peanut. Yes, Peanut. That's the name Jane gave to her tiny unborn child. Peanut never moved or changed position in the whole of the time Jane was pregnant.

Jane's consultant explained to her that they needed baby Peanut to get to 500gms in weight to give her baby a fighting chance of life, because any baby below that weight couldn't be helped. The medical profession didn't have equipment small enough to handle any baby below that weight so this was crucial. The tiny tubes they had to help premature babies were too big for any baby under 500gms. Every week Jane had her scan, checking to see how Peanut was growing. For all Peanut hadn't budged an inch from the very first scan Jane had had, there was a heartbeat. So from Jane's first ten week scan they watched and waited. Waited and prayed, hoping Peanut would be able to get to that magic weight. The weight at which there was a fighting chance she could survive.

Yes baby Peanut was a girl.

During the 29th week of her pregnancy Jane was being scanned three times a day, yes, a day. And, at some point during that week, Jane's consultant told her he wanted to get her baby out; he didn't want to leave her where she was any longer. He was fairly sure baby Peanut had reached the weight they would be able to help her at. He explained to the family that as soon as he could gather the correct team of specialists together within the next 24 hours they would perform a caesarean section and deliver baby Peanut. The team he wanted to perform this very tricky operation was to be seventeen strong.

Yes, I did say seventeen.

Every skill that he felt might be needed for both mother and child was to be represented in the operating theatre, all ready for any outcome. This was not going to be any ordinary caesarean section. Apparently Jane was to have what could be described as a double caesarean. Jane was to be cut in the shape of a cross across her tummy to enable them to get baby Peanut out from the very tiny space she had lodged herself into at the back of her mother's womb. And she had stayed there and not moved for the whole 29 weeks.

He gathered his team and they began.

Peanut was delivered weighing in at exactly 500grms. That equates to one pound two ounces. Her grandmother compared her weight and size to a tub of Lurpak butter but not as wide. She was so tiny she fitted into the palm of one of her father's or grandfather's hands with ease.

Now let's think about this.

Jane should not have been able to fall pregnant in the first place.

Jane should not have been able to carry a baby because of all the scar tissue inside her, due to her major surgery and the radiotherapy. The space for a normal-sized baby to grow in was not there. There was only a minute corner of her womb left untouched and that was where this little miracle had secured herself, stayed put and grown. And that was why baby Peanut was born so small.

When our family first heard the news that Jane was

expecting (not long before Peanut was born because Jane had not wanted people to know about her pregnancy in case she didn't get to term) obviously we were overjoyed for her. But within a very short space of time our joy turned to deep concern when we heard the news that the baby had been born but she was in serious trouble.

Baby Peanut's birth must have been a phenomenal mixture of jumbled-up emotions for Jane and John and both of their families. I can't begin to imagine the emotional roller-coaster ride they all must have been on at this time.

I was told that as soon as baby Peanut was safely delivered the hospital staff took her out of the delivery room on the pretext of giving her a thorough examination. But it was really because she was so incredibly tiny and apparently she looked so very strange the hospital staff thought she was very severely physically damaged and they didn't want either Jane or John to see her and get upset, so she was whipped away minutes after she was delivered.

Jane and John were apparently told by the staff not to go and see her so that they didn't form any attachment to her as she was surely going to die.

This little mite was left all alone to sleep away with no intervention from the medical profession whatsoever.

How this dear family got through the next three days is beyond me.

On day three, without any assistance from anyone, this 500gram mite was still alive and not only that, she had straightened herself out. To the hospital staff's amazement they found that she wasn't damaged in any way. She was, in fact, perfect and I do mean perfect. Baby Peanut had grown in such a small space that she was all scrunched up when she had been delivered, but she had grown perfectly. She had desperately needed to stretch and, of course, she was able to do that after she was born. A beautiful, perfect little girl and that's when the hospital staff started to assist her and feed her, on day three. And that was when Jane and John got to see their precious little girl for the very first time and they were able to touch and hold their very tiny miracle.

I don't think any of us can begin to imagine what those first few hours and days must have been like for Jane and John (and both sets of grandparents). It must have been horrendous. All of them desperately wanting to see their precious child, but being told by the staff that it would be far better if they didn't. And even though in their hearts they desperately wanted to see her and hold her, some part of them would have been frightened to see her. They were told she looked very strange and she was going to pass away, so better not to see her. What a nightmare those first hours and days must have been for them all.

When Marie rang me and told me the news that the baby had been born but that she was in desperate trouble, she was upset. So as soon as I put the phone down from her telephone call I went into prayer mode big time and I do mean big-style. I sat and asked (almost demanded) Heaven to help me. I asked Father Tom (who was now in Heaven), I asked my father, I asked for the baby's guardian angels, I asked for all the Spirit people that helped me in my healing work every day and I asked God. In other words I asked everybody I could think of to help me and join me in my prayers. I asked them all to help her to stay strong, to help her feed and grow strong. I sat and tuned into this tiny little girl with all my unseen friends morning, noon and night for days and weeks. And each and every time I did this I talked to her and, on some level unknown to us all, I know she was listening. And I also know you are all going to think that this is a crazy thing for me to be saying, but I know it to be true. She was aware of me, she was aware of the angels and all the Spirit people that were around her helping her to fight, and fight by God's good grace she did.

Now I'm sure, without a shadow of doubt, that all of her family and their friends were doing almost the same thing. So there is no way I am saying my prayers got this little girl through her first few weeks. But I do know my prayers, with the help of all my Spirit friends and loved ones, along with all her guardian angels and of course God's help, most definitely helped the situation.

Never doubt the power of your prayers.

I never do and I never will.

Yes, she survived and she is now a beautiful, very clever, and very aware little girl.

A family member told me that they were told by a stranger that she is an 'indigo child'. I will add to this and say I would like to call her my 'star child'. In other words she is very special. And I promise I will make a note to come back to this somewhere in my writings, sometime in the future to give you an explanation (or check it out yourself) as to what these terms mean.

I met our special girl for the second time (she is gorgeous) when she came for a visit last year. She was just a few months old when I met her for the first time and the recognition was there, even then, between us.

Before she left to go home with her grandparents she gave me the most amazing hug. She jumped up into my arms and put her legs around my waist, her arms around my neck, and she tucked her head in between my head and my neck and clung to me for what seemed like an age, without a word being spoken. I walked slowly around our garden with her clinging onto me. She didn't want to let go and, to be honest with you, I didn't want her to because her hug was so special. I knew it was her way of saying to me, I know you. I know who you are.

Everything about this child is special.

Everything about this child is a miracle.

It was a miracle that her mother ever became pregnant with her in the first place.

It was a miracle that Jane managed to carry her for 29 weeks.

It was a miracle that Peanut got to the magic weight of 500gms.

It was a miracle that she was able to breathe on her own from her very first breath and survive on her own with no help from the medical profession for 72 hours, weighing only 500grms, and then, of course, to be now growing into a wonderful, very inquisitive, very aware, gorgeous little girl.

I was told that her father spent an age looking for an appropriate name for their special girl and he found it.

Their special girl has been named Hannah.

And the meaning of her name, 'Gift from God'.

Perfect.

'Star-born, Indigo child'?

Definitely.

Looked after by angels?

Yes.

The title of this chapter was, "Our weakest points often become the place of God's greatest miracle." And now you know why.

I would like to take this opportunity once more to thank Father Tom, my father, and all my unseen friends and angels.

And last, but never least, the great 'I am' Himself for helping me to help our very special girl and allowing me to be involved in our star-born child's life.

Thank you.

CHAPTER THIRTEEN

"Remote viewing is the practice of seeking impressions about a distant or unseen target using subjective means, in particular extrasensory perception."
Wikipedia

The story in the previous chapter was actually a very good example of what I would describe as remote viewing. It might not be someone else's description but, what the heck, this is my story and quite simply, for me, the words mean viewing from a distance and that's exactly what I did when I tuned into Jane on the days she had her operations. I was able to be there in the room with her, watching everything that was happening as it happened, from the comfort of my armchair in our lounge at home. Quite remarkable when you think about it, but actually people have been remote viewing for as long as man first walked on our beautiful planet, so it's not that big a deal. It's just that, unless you have an interest in things beyond our normal senses, you probably have never heard the term remote viewing before.

I found some words on the internet the other day that I am going to quote from for you that will give you a very good description of remote viewing. The International Remote Viewing Association says on their web page, "Remote viewing is a mental faculty that allows a perceiver (a viewer) to describe or give details about a target that is inaccessible to normal senses due to distance, time or shielding. For example, a viewer might be asked to describe a location on the other side of the world, which he or she has never visited; or a viewer might describe an event that happened long ago; or describe an object sealed in a container or locked in a room; or perhaps even describe a person or activity; all without being told anything about the target - not even its name or designation."

The United States of America's Defence Intelligence Agency employed remote viewers in the 1970's and 1980's. Just look up 'Project Stargate' on the internet for more information if you are interested. You could also take a look at the hundreds of books that have been written on the subject, with some of them written by the people who did the remote viewing for the CIA. And it wasn't just the Americans that were using remote viewers. Other countries' agencies were also involved, including the British Government.

Now the honest truth is I have no idea how I do it.

I've never actually stopped to question myself because it's never been important to me. I've been doing it for as long as I can remember without me ever giving it a thought. I always just call it me tuning in to someone or something. It wasn't until I watched a programme on the television a few years ago that I realised that there was a name for what I do. I would love to go on a course and learn how to do it properly because I'm sure if someone were to teach me I could be better at it and, believe it or not, there are courses. Anyway, in the meantime, I do seem to manage reasonably well on my own.

A few years ago I received a telephone call from Rose, who was the daughter of a very good friend of mine, asking me for my help. Now that in itself was not unusual but what was a bit unusual was that Rose, her father Andy and their family lived in America and, up to this point in my life, I'd never been there.

Well, not in this lifetime anyway.

Rose had rung me because her father had asked her to. Andy had asked her to ask me to please tune into him and the reason for this was because he had been rushed into hospital about two weeks earlier and they still hadn't managed to find out what the cause of his problem was. The doctors, apparently, were still doing loads of different tests on him, with little or no success, and Andy was getting very frustrated and a bit angry by their lack of progress.

Rose explained to me that her father had asked her to ask me to come and visit him as he lay in his hospital bed and would I please scan his body in the hope I could somehow find out what his problem was and could I then please email Rose with my findings? He said he would then tell his doctors what my findings were because they were getting nowhere!

Rose said to me, "I've got to be honest with you, Isabella, my father seems to have a lot of faith in your abilities and, if I'm being honest, I don't know how the hell he expects you to do this, but he seems to think that you can. Can you? Can you come across the ocean in your meditation and visit him? Can you scan his body and find out what the heck's the matter with him and then report back to us, because no one here has a clue what's wrong? Can you?"

"The honest answer, Rose, is I'm not sure but I'll give it my best shot and see what I can see."

"Well you can't say fairer than that."

"I'll tune in tonight after my family have all gone to bed, when the house is quiet so I won't be disturbed, and see if I can get to him and I'll see what I pick up. Whatever happens, I'll email you when I have finished to let you know what I find or don't find so that you can pass the information on to your father."

"That would be great. I'll tell Dad what you are going to do. I'm going to see him later this evening."

And with that we said our goodbyes.

After my family had all gone to bed I made myself a cup of tea and, as I was drinking it, I can still remember thinking to myself, "How on earth am I going to get to the other side of the world, let alone find my friend in a strange country? Oh well, all I can do is try.' After I had finished my cuppa I went into my treatment room and I sat myself down on a cushion on the floor. I reasoned with myself that if I sat on a chair I might fall off it, but if I sat on the floor then if I did manage to travel outside myself if I was sitting on the floor on a cushion with my back to the settee I would be safe (nothing for me to fall off).

Honest, I'm not crazy, well at least I don't think I am.

I had been told Andy was in a hospital somewhere in the Bay area of San Francisco. But I had no idea where or what the Bay area was. The only pictures I had seen of San Francisco were from television programmes or films that I had watched so, as far as I was concerned, he could have been on the moon. I would be lost within seconds of setting foot on American soil (or the moon's).

I closed my eyes and took a few deep breaths as I tried to still my mind and, of course, as I did this I asked for help. "Get me to him please, Lord," was my first plea. "Please take me to him," and within seconds of these thoughts I found myself flying at great speed high above the earth.

The best and only way I can describe what I saw is to relate my adventure exactly as it happened.

I didn't feel myself lift up out of my body as I had done on previous occasions when I had gone travelling. My first realisation of what was going on was when I looked down at the earth far below me as I flew at great speed through the dark night sky, which I found a bit disconcerting because one minute I had been sitting on the floor in my home, safe and sound, and the next minute I was a mile above the earth.

This was me doing my version of Superman.

Some part of my brain must have been working because I can remember thinking to myself that the sky would start getting lighter the closer I got to the West Coast of America because I knew I had set off from England at about one o'clock in the morning in the dark, so I should be landing in what I hoped was San Francisco in daylight. But I misjudged the timing slightly because it was early evening on a winter's night when I felt myself starting to slow down and descend to the ground as the golden rays of the sun were disappearing fast in the sky to the west of me, where the sun had obviously just set.

I landed with a bit of a thump onto a concrete path in front of a low modern two-storey building. I stood for what seemed like an age, trying to get my bearings.

As I had started to descend, ready for me to land, I saw the shape of the building I was approaching from the air and it was shaped like the letter T. As I stood now at the front of the building it stretched to both my right and left for about fifty yards in each direction. I had landed right in the middle of the building, right in front of the double glass sliding front doors. I was aware (and I had seen from the air) that behind the front doors was a long corridor going straight back with shorter corridors branching off in each direction. (Hope you get the picture.) This was most definitely a very new building; I could almost smell the paint as it was drying. Apparently it was a very new hospital for veteran soldiers, what they in America call a VA Hospital, but I had no idea whereabouts I was. And as strange again as this is also going to sound, I didn't for one minute stop to think I might have landed in the wrong country or I was standing outside the wrong hospital. Something in me just seemed to know that I was exactly where I was meant to be.

    I stood where I had just landed, taking in what I could see of the building around me as my eyes adjusted to the low light as the sky was turning dark, but my eyes were very quickly drawn away from the building in front of me to a very bright light in the sky to the left of where I was standing. I was now looking at the lights on the top of what I thought was a lighthouse, a very tall white round structure that looked for all the world like a white upside-down ice cream cone. It had a very bright yellow and orange light shining from the top of it. It really stood out because it was the only tall building I could see clearly within about a mile of where I was standing, other than the hospital, with all its lights glaring out into the now darkness. I can remember thinking to myself I must be very close to the sea and I was a bit surprised that I couldn't hear the waves breaking on the shore or rocks, as the shoreline must have been very close by.

    Having stood on the pavement looking around me for what seemed like an age, I instinctively knew it was time for me to go inside the building, so I did. I floated in through the closed doors and straight down the long corridor almost to the end, when I found myself floating into a side room on my left (if you've seen the film 'Cocoon' you'll know exactly what I mean when I say I floated down the corridor) and as I entered the room there was a lady sitting on a chair next to the bed

Andy was lying on. The lady had very long jet-black hair as it hung down her back in long, glossy waves. I couldn't see her face because she had her back to me and at almost the exact same moment that I saw the lady I found myself shrinking, yes shrinking, to the size of a small matchstick and not much fatter, at which point I felt as if I had almost disappeared, and then I landed quite gracefully and very lightly onto the end of Andy's nose.

Okay, so you are all going to have me committed and you are all reading this thinking what a load of, but as God is my witness, that's exactly what happened to me and believe it or not, I wasn't in the least bit bothered or fazed by any of this at the time; it all seemed quite normal to me.

'Normal'? Who the hell am I kidding?

It's nights like this that fill me with wonder.

It's nights like this that allow me to say to you, "I just love the world I live in."

My world, my life, my bubble.

Dear Lord, my life can be very strange at times but I love it, I love my adventures.

And my story is about to get even more weird.

I can clearly remember asking Andy in my mind for his permission to enter his body and he said, "Yes," and this is where the real fun began.

I found myself as a very little person entering the front door, so to speak, of his house (his body) and the front door was his left nostril and this was where I started my journey into the wilderness of the inside of the human frame. I travelled quite slowly down his throat. I guess I was acting a bit like the camera on the end of a probe as the camera investigates and takes pictures of everything it can see as it passes along on its way. I can still clearly remember feeling as if I was in a warm tunnel of soft pink as a very soft light shone all around me, showing me the way, as I travelled down through his throat and into what I can only describe as passageways or tubes. And all the while I was looking at what looked like soft pink walls of flesh gently pulsating to the beat of my friend's heart and me thinking this was all very normal.

As strange and weird and unbelievable as all of this sounds, it did happen, and it happened exactly as I'm telling you.

I kept on travelling down through his tubes very slowly, and I'm going to use the word down as I seemed to twist my way along, and all the while I felt as if I was going downhill. I could both feel the pulsating of his heart as it was beating and I could also feel a gentle, and I want to say a gentle, wave, as the rhythm of his heart gently carried me along as I passed either through or around his heart. To be honest, I have no idea if they were valves or the arteries, but as I travelled along them his heart occasionally seemed to miss a beat and I felt myself jump. It was as if his heart was hiccupping and, just like me when I get the hiccups, it happened three times in a row and then it stopped for a little while and then it did it again, and each time it did this I felt myself slightly jump and be pushed forward ever so slightly on my journey and then the steady rhythm would return and I would slow back down again.

As I continued I passed through and along what I thought at the time must be the miles and miles of his intestines and they, or the tubes, did seem to go on forever and, at some point in my journey, I found what I could only describe at the time as a small hole in the wall of his tube as I passed by it. The only reason I spotted it was because I felt a slight breeze coming out of the wall and when I went back to have another look I spotted a sort of spurt of what looked like smoke come out through the small opening. If you can imagine squeezing a small spray bottle filled with a smoky-coloured liquid, then that's the sort of light spray that came through the opening in his wall. There was a fluid-like liquid in the form of a spray leaking out from one side of the passage I was travelling along, through the wall or lining of his intestine, and that's the only way I can describe what I saw. A hole in the wall of his tubes, or the wall of his gut and there was rubbish getting into his blood stream and the whole of his system was being poisoned.

He was poisoning himself without even knowing it.

The next thing I knew I was at the foot of his bed and I was back to my normal size again.

Wow, what an amazing journey.

When I looked at my friend lying on his bed he was fast asleep, completely oblivious to what had just gone on and the chair beside his bed was empty. His visitor had left.

I blew him a kiss and I left the building the exact same way as I had entered.

As soon as I arrived back, which only seemed to take a matter of seconds, I felt myself land onto my cushion on the floor and I sat for a few minutes trying to comprehend what I had just seen and experienced and then I got myself up and I went straight to my computer. I sent Rose a very detailed explanation as to what I had just witnessed and, in a way, I think that's what has helped me to remember in such detail what happened to me that night all those years ago. By me writing down my journey just after it happened, I think I must have reinforced my memory files by going over my adventure, so in a way I imprinted it twice onto my memory banks while it was fresh and clear in my mind.

Three days later I received an amazing response from America.

Rose told me that she had printed out and taken a copy of my email to her father in the hospital and he had read it at least half a dozen times and that afternoon he told his doctor that he felt as if he might have a tear or rupture in the wall of his intestine, causing faecal matter to get into his blood stream. And after two days of tests that's exactly what was found to be one of his problems and yes, his heart was apparently misbeating just as if it kept getting hiccups. Rose apologised to me for doubting me. She apologised for not believing what her father never doubted, that it was possible for me to do what I had done. She had not believed it was humanly possible, but her father had. She then went on to say that she hoped that perhaps one day we would meet. I didn't think so, but I never say never and as for the lady who I had seen sitting at his bedside that night, it turned out that his name was Chris. He was a young man in his mid-thirties, a great friend of Andy's and a Native American with very long, black, wavy hair, just like a woman's and apparently he had sat at Andy's bedside that night for about two hours. The night I travelled to visit Andy.

And that's what I call remote viewing, viewing from a distance.

But this story doesn't quite end here. There is more to tell.

About nine months later Andy was unwell again and he desperately wanted to see me. He had visited us here in England a couple of times and he had desperately wanted to come back for one more visit but his health was failing and he wasn't well enough to travel. Well, I'm sure you have heard the phrase, "If the mountain will not come to Mohammad, then Mohammad must go to the mountain."

I had been receiving both emails and telephone calls from my friend's wife on almost a daily basis keeping me informed as to how Andy was doing and he wasn't doing well. His family were very worried. They didn't think he had long to live and was there any possibility of me coming to America? Me, America? As Andy desperately wanted to see me one last time.

Just to let you know, I had met Andy and his wife a few years earlier when they had travelled to England with some other people for a conference, a conference I had attended and that's how we met. The recognition between us was instant. It had been like meeting a long-lost friend and Andy and his wife had come back to England to stay with me and all my family a couple of times since for holidays. Andy was a lot older and like a second father to me and all my family thought the world of him, so when I was asked to go to America my daughter volunteered to go with me as my guardian angel. I don't like flying at the best of times and the thought of doing a long-haul flight on my own was unthinkable.

It just so happened that my daughter and I travelled to America six weeks after September the eleventh.

Now this was a strange one. As the day of our departure drew closer I had an uneasy feeling that there was going to be a plane crash and, completely unknown to me, my daughter had a similar premonition. She, however, didn't tell me until after we had landed on American soil and, needless to say, I didn't say a word to her before we flew either. If I had thought for one minute it was going to be the plane we were flying on I wouldn't have got on it. And she didn't tell me, bless her, because she said she felt that I was on a special mission and God would keep us safe.

Once we were through passport control we were met by Rose (along with her friend Beth) who, after lots of hugs for us both, took us straight to her car in the airport car park to drive us to Andy's home. It was then, as she was putting the suitcases into the boot of her car, that she told us about the plane crash that had just happened a few hours earlier (while we were in the air).

"Did you know that while you were in the air a plane went down at Kennedy Airport, killing everyone on board?"

"Dear Lord, no, we didn't know."

Now I feel I ought to tell you that I said all of the above just after I picked myself up off the floor of the car park after I had kissed the ground several times. I was so grateful that my daughter and I had been kept safe and that we were both now on solid ground.

Rose then went on to explain to us what had happened. It was thought at the time that the plane that crashed had been sabotaged and, sadly, everyone on board had been killed. And the other bit of information that Rose told us was that all planes flying over US airspace at the time of the crash were sent back to where they had come from. They'd started clearing the skies in case of another attack. Because we were very close to our destination, flying down the west coast of America, Rose thought that was why our flight had been allowed to finish its journey.

It was later found that the flight crashed because one of its engines had fallen off.

Rose loaded up the car with our cases and we set off from the airport on our journey to my friend's home where we were going to be staying for the coming week.

Rose explained to us that Andy had been in bed for the previous three weeks but, apparently, he was very excited about our arrival.

I sat in the front of the car with Rose, like the big kid that I often am, allowing me a fantastic view of all the sights as we drove along and Marie sat in the back with Rose's friend Beth. We left the airport and drove through part of the city and then we went over one of the bridges that crossed the bay, but not the Golden Gate Bridge. I was a bit unnerved by the sight of the armed police standing at each side of the bridge as we approached it. When we crossed there were more armed police at the other end. They were armed with machine guns, not exactly what we are used to here in England. Apparently the whole country was on high alert.

As we were driving along I got my first close-up of all the skyscrapers which I didn't like, then we seemed to leave the city behind as we entered the suburbs. Rose had said the journey would take us about an hour to get to her parents' home, allowing for traffic but, fortunately for us, the roads were fairly quiet.

We must have been driving for about forty minutes when I let out an almighty shriek and I mean shriek. I didn't mean to make anyone jump but I had just got such a shock myself. Rose and Beth both shouted out at the same time, "What's the matter?"

And I said, "That's the lighthouse. Dear Lord, that's the lighthouse."

And as my words tumbled out of my mouth in excitement I said, "Rose, was the hospital your father was in just behind that lighthouse?"

And Rose answered me and said, "Yes, it's about half a mile away."

But it wasn't a lighthouse at all.

It looked like a lighthouse.

You would have looked at it and said it has to be a lighthouse.

It was the shape of a lighthouse.

It was the colour of a lighthouse.

But there on the top of it, in a half-moon shape in huge letters that were shining out in bright yellow and orange light, was the word 'Casino' for all the world to see. No sea or beach or shore for miles around. And then Rose said, "I never gave it any thought at the time when you sent your email describing what you saw that night. Of course, that's the lighthouse you told me you'd seen; your description was spot on. But, of course, I knew it was an advertising sign so it never crossed my mind to correct you, because you were actually right in what you described. And now you've seen it for yourself."

Wow.

I couldn't believe my eyes. Who would have thought?

I've got to be honest with you, I did keep repeating the words over and over, "That's my lighthouse," while the contents of the car laughed at me.

It fooled me on that dark night a few months earlier and I think it would have fooled anyone if you could not see the words. It turned out I was standing about half a mile away behind it on the night I visited Andy in the hospital, so I could only see the lights shining on the top and not the words the lights actually spelt out. And that was one of my remote viewing adventures.

Just to let you know, by the end of our stay Andy was up and out of his sick bed and he remained up for the next few years until again I was asked to go back and be with him for his final days here on earth.

CHAPTER FOURTEEN

"Past lives and all that jazz"
Me

Past lives. What a multitude of pictures those two words conjure up if you think, hope, believe or, better still, know that you have been here before. I mentioned in chapter one and chapter four that I would continue as if you were with me on this subject. There is a chance that if you are still not sure, then perhaps some of the following stories might actually help you make up your mind.

But, of course, the choice, as always, is yours.

One day I would like to write a book about past lives. Am I qualified to do this? I'm not sure if I am but, then again, who is?

So from the many past-life stories that I would love to share with you sometime in the future, let me give you one or two of them now to whet your appetite.

I love it when I suddenly find myself in a past life belonging to someone else. I can often see where a person has been and what that person was doing in the particular life I have homed in on. Now I realise that must sound a bit strange to all of you reading this but, quite often, when I am giving a patient a healing treatment, pictures start to appear in my mind's eye. It's as if someone turned a television screen on in my mind and I'm sitting watching it. I have often wished that I could put an extension cable into my mind, just like the lead that you would use to charge your mobile phone. If I had a plug in my head then what I see could then appear on a large screen and we could all sit and watch, just like watching a film. Anyway, I mentioned at the very beginning of my book that I would give you some examples of past-life healings so I'll make a start now (we can always have some more another time) and I know you're going to love this first one.

One day in late summer 1989, while I was still an accountant, I went to visit a client at his home in the early evening. The appointment had been arranged so that I could spend some time with his wife going over his business paperwork and then I could spend some time chatting to my client.

After we had concluded all the work-related business Sophie made us all a cup of tea. I moved away from the desk and chair where I had been sitting and sat myself down on their comfy settee to drink it. But just after I had sat down I felt the most awful pain in my left shoulder and for the life of me I had no idea where it had come from. I started rubbing my shoulder with my right hand and Sophie said to me, "What's the matter?"

I explained to her that I had a terrible pain in my shoulder that had suddenly come on from nowhere.

"That's funny. Mark (their young son) injured his left shoulder two days ago. He fell off his bicycle and he's upstairs right now in his bedroom feeling very sorry for himself because his shoulder is still hurting him."

Sophie had no sooner told me about Mark's injury when the pain in my shoulder left me, as if by magic.

Thinking back, that's the only time in twenty-five years of my healing work that I have taken on someone else's pain, thank goodness.

"Can I see him?"

"Yes, of course you can."

Sophie came back into the room a few minutes later, followed by a very sheepish-looking young Mark. I think he would have probably been about seven years old at the time. I asked him if he would like me to see if I could ease the pain in his shoulder for him and he said, "Yes please."

So I did.

Now I've just told you about his shoulder because that's what brought Mark down the stairs into the lounge to meet me. Mark was now looking much happier. He actually had a smile on his face. It was then that his mum said to me, "Mark has another problem, Isabella, but I'm not sure if you can help with this one because it's not a physical problem, it's an emotional one."

I looked at her with a puzzled expression on my face and said, "Well, if you tell me what the problem is I might be able to help."

Mark at this point looked decidedly embarrassed but his mum gave him a reassuring smile and started to tell me his story.

"Mark is due to go away next week on his very first cub camp and in some ways he is very excited about the whole thing. The idea of going away from home for the first time with a lot of his friends sounds like a big adventure, but he is also very worried because he doesn't know how he is going to go to sleep at night."

"O.K, now you've lost me."

"Well, Mark has gone to bed every night since he was a little boy with his teddy bear as his companion and one of my nightgowns as a comfort blanket. He realises he can't take them with him to camp because he will be laughed at and made fun of by all of his friends. That's why he is getting worried because he doesn't know how he will manage to go to sleep without them and I don't know what to suggest for him."

As Sophie was talking to me the strangest thing began to happen to me. It was as if I was being transported to a different time and place. I could still hear her voice in the background as she was telling me the story. Half of me was very aware of what she was saying, but the other half of me was transfixed by the pictures I was looking at and the sounds that I was hearing.

I found myself high up in the mountains somewhere in the Himalayas on a very large, rocky outcrop that seemed to be a mile above the nearest clouds that I could see floating far below me. And before me was a temple with its doors flung wide open. I could both see and hear what was going on inside and I could also smell the sweet fragrance coming from the incense that was burning both in and around the outside of the temple. The sound of tinkling bells was all around me; they were so clear. The sound they made was so crisp and pure.

Every note seemed to penetrate the whole of my being, filling me with joy.

As I looked inside the temple at the colours of the wall hangings and the wall coverings, the colours of the clothes the monks had on and the coverings on the seats that surrounded all the walls, they all completely overwhelmed me. From rich peacock greens and blues to the deep reds and rich golds, to the bright yellows and greens of the satin cushions that were scattered on the seats and on the floor, it was the most amazing sight to behold.

I could hear chanting in the distance. It sounded as if children were singing because the chanting was so sweet and gentle to my ears. Many voices raised in joyful union. I could feel myself becoming very tearful, with tears of pure joy.

Trust me, that may all sound very fanciful but twenty-five years on and I can still see that picture in my mind's eye as clear as if it was yesterday and I can almost feel the feelings of happiness and joy that I felt at the time.

"Isabella, Isabella, where are you?"

That was Sophie trying to pull me back into the room.

"I wish you could all have seen what I have just seen. I turned to Mark and said, "I think I know now why you are so fond of your comfort blanket. I'm not sure about teddy at the moment, but I will try and relay everything I have just seen to you."

So I did.

After describing exactly what I had seen to Mark and his mum and dad Sophie then said, "Mark's teddy has two little bells, one in each of his ears that tinkle away when he hugs him."

I smiled at them and said, "Well, now we know where teddy comes into the story."

I was then able to explain to Mark that because his life in the temple had been so happy the memory was still very strong with him. So strong that I was able to pick up on it very easily and see his memory so vividly for myself.

Little teddy bear with his two tinkling bells just like the

bells in the temple and his mother's deep green satin nightdress, the same material as the monks' robes and also the same colour and material as some of the cushions I saw scattered all around the inside of the temple.

I explained to him that this particular memory was such a powerful one he didn't actually need to have his teddy or his mum's nightdress with him to be able to access the memory. It was there in his memory file very strongly. So when he went on his cub camp there was no need for him to take them with him, and no need for his friends to know anything about them and ridicule him. All he needed to do was go to bed and picture the scene I had just relayed to him. I promised him the memory would come flooding back to him and he would go to sleep with a smile on his face.

And that's exactly what happened.

He went to his cub camp and came home after the weekend, smiling. And actually, not very long after, he apparently stopped taking teddy and his comforter to bed with him, he didn't need them anymore. Once he understood why he had needed them, needing them left him. He now knew that he had all he needed to comfort him for the rest of his life; it was all in there in his own memory files, and now he understood.

That story always makes me smile when I read it and I hope it made you smile too.

The next story I would like to share with you is about a lady who came to see me with what, at the time, I thought was a very minor problem. Now that probably sounds a bit mean of me and that's not my intention. I was used to dealing with people with quite serious issues, so when this lady told me that she was stressed because she couldn't swim, well let's be honest, that did seem like a rather minor problem, especially in comparison to some of the stories I have already shared with you. Anyway, she had come to ask me if I could help her because her problem was a very serious problem for her.

Let me describe this lady to you. She was beautifully and expensively dressed from head to toe. She was very exact in both her speech and her movements. She was very neat and precise in every way. In other words she tried to achieve perfection in everything she said and did. And I've got to be honest and say she was one of the smartest, best-dressed ladies I've ever had the pleasure of meeting. I thought this was going to give me a bit of a problem (me, I look a mess most of the time and I'm not bothered). I was worried in case she wouldn't want to lie face down on my healing bed for fear of spoiling or creasing her beautiful skirt and blouse (now that was me a bit bothered for her, not her being bothered). But when I asked her to lie face down she did without hesitating. I explained to her that the only thing I thought I/*we* might be able to help with was to rebalance her aura around her. It was way out of balance because she was so stressed because she couldn't swim. Then she explained to me that she had just come back from a two week course. Two weeks in the sun learning to swim through a specialist company that guaranteed that at the end of the two weeks she would be swimming. She told me that everyone else on the course had learnt to swim, everyone that is except her. The company had been as good as their word. If you didn't pass the course they guaranteed to give you your money back in full and with this lady they had, including the cost of her flights. Then she explained to me that over the previous thirty years she had tried and tried to learn to swim and it was now becoming an obsession with her.

    She enjoyed her first treatment with me very much and asked if she could come back for a few more. So I booked three more appointments for her. It was after she left that first time that I realised that I had hardly said a word to her during that first session, which was unusual for me.

    I learned very early on in my healing practice that I needed to chatter merrily away when my patients are lying on their stomachs and I do this because if I didn't, nine times out of ten they would fall asleep and I don't want them to, not yet anyway. I need to keep them awake to be able to ask them to turn over about half way through their treatment, enabling me to work in their aura from the other side, allowing the healing energy to rebalance the whole of them. So it's important to me to keep my patients awake until I have asked them to turn over. And I still chatter away to this day. Once a patient does turn over, I can then work away and perhaps also spend some time on other areas that might need some extra help, such as a leg, or arm, or shoulder or even a big toe. Once they are comfortable lying on their back I am always quiet. I sometimes stay very quiet for the whole of the second half of their treatment and yes, nearly everyone falls asleep or drifts away into a very relaxed space. But there are a few patients who chatter away for the whole of their session and that's fine by me; the choice, as always, is theirs.

Now back to our lady.

The second time she came to see me she was still upset because her learning to swim holiday had not worked. She was blaming herself for being a wimp. She said she was feeling that she had now tried everything so she was going to have to face the fact that she was never going to be able to swim and that was very upsetting for her.

I worked as I always do with all my patients, on her front first and then, about half way through her treatment I asked her to turn onto her back. It was then, just after she had turned over, that the pictures began to appear in my head, just as I explained to you at the beginning of this chapter. I was sitting by her side watching my television screen in my head.

My hands at this point were on this lady's shoulder, her left shoulder to be precise. I had one hand under her shoulder and my other hand on top and I was sort of sitting there in a dream-like state, not really thinking about anything in particular, and that's when I (without any thought on my part) jumped back in time into one of this lady's past lives.

You might ask me why I had my hands on her shoulder when the problem she had had nothing to do with her shoulder. Because my hands take on a life of their own during a healing session. I don't stop to think, "Oh I need to be here or there." I just work away with no thought on my part. So my hands just go wherever they like. They do their own thing and, without exception, they always go to the right place because my hands are being guided by an outside force and not by me (thank goodness). But in this case I think I can say, metaphysically speaking, she was carrying a lot on her shoulders, so that was why my hands were there.

I don't ask for the pictures. I'm not thinking about anything in particular. The pictures just start appearing in my head as if by magic, and I never know what I'm going to see or sometimes hear next and I love it!

I found myself looking at a very cold, dark blue almost black sea with peaks of white crests breaking on the top of very troubled water. I'm actually shivering as I'm writing this, just as I did all those years ago when I first saw this picture in my head. That's how cold this scene looked to me on that day many years ago. I can remember thinking to myself, "Okay I'm at sea on a very cold dark night. So what's this all about?"

And that's when I saw the ship, and lots of icebergs.

And yes, you might have guessed it.

The ship was the Titanic.

I saw the name on the side of the boat as I seemed to fly past it in my dream-like state. I can remember taking an intake of breath when I saw the name and my patient asked me if I was alright. Up until that moment I hadn't said a word to her. I had been so transfixed by the film I was watching in my head.

Now how was I going to approach her with what I had just seen?

I didn't want to upset or frighten her in any way but I needed to say something, so I said, "Have you ever at any time had dreams about being shipwrecked, or perhaps you have dreamt of being in a ship as it sank?"

"No, but ever since I can remember I have had a fascination with the Titanic. I even bought a book about it about six months ago."

Followed immediately by another intake of breath from me!

"Have you ever given any thought to the possibility that

you may have lived before, that perhaps you may have had other lives?"

"I'm not sure. What do you mean?"

There was nothing for it. I was going to have to tell her what I had just seen, so I did. She was quiet for a few minutes and then she said.

"Do you think I knew someone on the ship?"

"No, I think you were on the ship. In fact, the feeling is so strong with me I not only think you were on the ship, I'm sure you went down with the ship. I'm sure you lost your life on the Titanic when you were a child (I had a very strong feeling that she had been a child when she drowned) and that's the reason you are finding it so hard to learn to swim in this life. You now have an overwhelming fear of drowning and, let's be honest, it's not surprising when you know and understand what happened to you many years ago, in another lifetime.

I honestly thought she would get upset by what I had just said but no, she held her composure and after what seemed like ages she said, "I think what you have just said makes a lot of sense to me, but is that really possible?"

"You can never know for sure, not in this lifetime anyway. But does it sit right with you? Does it feel right to you?"

"Yes, it does."

"Then perhaps we are right."

I did see this lady for one more treatment and, as I worked with the healing energy, I explained to her that I felt she had most definitely drowned in her previous life and there was no need for her to drown again in this one. So perhaps if she could think about this and accept what had happened to her, she might just be able to let go of the fear from that life and move forward, let go and perhaps even learn to swim, knowing her fear was not related to this life.

Did she learn to swim?

The honest answer is I don't know, because I never saw or heard from her again. I would like to think that she did so that's the thought I will always hold for her.

Now if I had told you that you lost your life on the Titanic the above story would mean absolutely nothing to you. If I said to you that you had gone down with the ship you might shrug your shoulders and possibly say to me, "Okay, if you say so, but it means nothing to me."

And you would be right. It's all very well me or anyone else picking up on your past-lives but they have to mean something to you for you to be able to benefit from the knowing.

The great thing for me is that every past life I have found myself in or have somehow homed in on for other people, up to now, each and every person has been able to relate to the things I have seen and heard for them. So, to date, the information I have been able to pass on has both meant something to the person and has helped them to understand why they feel the way they do now.

Even if you don't believe in past lives it really doesn't matter, they are still there in your memory files regardless of how you feel, or what you believe. And I can almost guarantee that at least one of your past lives will be having some sort of an effect on this life of yours now. You may not be aware that what you see sometimes in your mind's eye, that fleeting glimpse that you catch of something - that means something to you - but you're just not quite sure what it is. Or perhaps the feeling that you get when you visit a place for the first time and it feels very familiar to you, yet you had never been there before. Or perhaps even someone you have just met that seemed uncannily familiar. These are the type of things that are probably coming from a previous lifetime of yours.

Let me give you some more examples to help me explain it to you.

Some people have a terrible fear of heights and others of snakes. Some people have a fear of spiders and yet others of rats and mice. Yet there is nothing in this life to have prompted the fear. I, for one, had a fear of vertical drops. When my daughter and I visited America to allow me to spend time with Andy his family very kindly took us to the Napa Valley to see the vineyards and sample some of the wonderful wine and also to allow us to swim in the hot springs in the village of Calistoga. We went on a cable car ride up and over one of the vineyards and there was me with my head and shoulders hanging out of the cable car window saying, "Yippee, my fear has gone."

As my daughter was frantically trying to pull me back onto my seat to stop me falling to the ground way beneath us, I was so pleased with myself. I would have expected me to be hanging on to the sides of the cable car being too frightened to look out of the window, let alone be hanging out of it but no, there was me hanging out, enjoying the wonderful view and my daughter having a heart attack in case her mother went head first to the ground (slight exaggeration but you know what I mean).

But, and it's quite a big but, I still don't like walking along a cliff edge. I will come close and I may, if you hang onto my arm, be very brave and try and see over the cliff, but only if you hang onto me. Just looking at photos of roads with sheer drops on one or both sides still gives me the shivers yet, as I have said, there is nothing in this life to have prompted this fear in me. But I now know where this fear came from, so it doesn't bother me nearly as much as it used to.

Okay, so you want to know why?

This is one of my past lives that I myself have not been able to access but a dear friend of mine called Keith was able to home in on it for me. When he told me the pictures he could see it made perfect sense to me, because without a shadow of doubt it was one of my past lives.

Many lifetimes ago, apparently I was out walking with my family along a cliff face when the rocks beneath my feet gave way, tumbling both the rocks and me almost to the bottom of the cliff, injuring me very badly. I didn't die, but I was paralysed from below the waist for the rest of my life. The lesson for me in that lifetime was to learn to allow other people to help me, a thing I still have a little bit of difficulty with even now. I love helping other people, but I find it a bit difficult to ask for help for myself. (I promise I am trying to learn to ask for help when I need it.)

We also bring back with us some of our nice memories, which often include what I will call gifts from our previous lives. The gift of singing for example, the gift of dancing, painting, playing a musical instrument and the list goes on. The love of animals, especially horses, that's always a strong one. The gift of caring for other people is also strong; if you were a caring person in a previous life the chances are you will be again in this one. I personally know one or two people who have worked in the clothing industry in this life and I have seen that they also worked with textiles in previous lives. Without ever realising it we all bring back memories with us from our previous lives (those memory files of ours). They might be beneficial memories, or memories that can cause us problems until we can overcome them. But that's what they are there for, for us to learn from and then let them go.

This next story is a very simple example to help clarify what I have just been saying.

This particular lady patient came to me because she had broken her leg rather badly in a riding accident only weeks earlier and she was worried in case it was going to leave her with a long-term problem. Her leg healed very quickly and she continues riding to this day with no ill or after-effects whatsoever.

So let me tell you what happened during one of her treatments with me.

After I had spent quite a while working on and around her injured leg, I then started to work in her aura, just as I do with everyone, and that's when the pictures started to appear in front of me. I want to say to you that the pictures appeared in my head, but it's also as if they are in front of my eyes just like a film being shown on a screen on the wall for me to watch. A bit strange and a bit difficult for me to describe exactly how I see what I see, but the pictures are always very clear.

I felt as if I had just walked onto the set of 'Dances with Wolves'.

I was definitely somewhere in North America and I am going to say to you The Midwest on the plains. But actually I have no idea where that is. The truth is I have no idea where I was. But the impression I was given, the awareness that I had, the feeling I was picking up from the picture I was looking at were all telling me I was on the plains, in The Midwest of America wherever and whatever that meant. Those were the words and those were the impressions that came into my mind at the time that this all happened.

It seemed as if I was riding in the air just above and behind the back of the horse, as the horse and the rider rode across the vast open landscape that seemed to go on forever. I knew the man that I was following was a US Cavalry Officer by the clothes he was wearing. Just like Kevin Costner in 'Dances with Wolves.'

Now you might say to me, "Well, this lady obviously likes horses," and that would be a fair comment. Actually, she loves horses and she has two of her own and I knew that.

Without telling her what I had just seen I asked her if she had ever felt a pull to visit North America, perhaps the Midwest?

"No," she said. "What have you seen, Isabella?"

She knew by the tone of my voice that I was quizzing her for a reason and she was immediately intrigued.

"I've just seen you riding a horse at full gallop across the plains somewhere in North America and you were in a Cavalry Officer's uniform, complete with your sword at your side."

"Never in the world."

"Yes."

"Isabella, you're not going to believe this because I've never told you. I am a member of the 17th Century English Civil War Battle Re-enactments Society and once a month I dress up in my full Cavalry Officers uniform, complete with my sword. I am a full Colonel and proud of it. I come alive when I'm riding at full gallop on my trusted steed towards the enemy, with my sword at the ready."

"I'm lost for words."

And that's exactly what I said to her.

Don't judge a book by its cover came to mind.

This lady is in her early sixties, very petite, and the last person in the world I would have expected to be involved with what to me is a very strange and definitely not your everyday pastime.

This past-life memory was so strong with her that I could see it very clearly. Also it had never been a problem for this lady but at least now she would always know where the love of all things to do with riding her horse in her full uniform, complete with her sword at her side, had come from.

Without a shadow of doubt in my mind and hers, she was a Cavalry Officer sometime in the eighteen hundreds, somewhere in North America.

Simple but true.

Let's have one more.

This next story is about the connections we have with other people over our many lifetimes, rather than a specific event. It's amazing how our feelings can come along with us for a ride over many lifetimes and affect us more than once. Our feelings for other people sometimes travel through time and come back to us in this lifetime and this next story is a very good example of exactly that.

Over the past twenty-five years many of my friends and patients have sent their friends to me for healing and this was how I met this lady. She was a friend of a patient of mine and I will call this lady Harriet.

The first thing Harriet said to me after she had sat herself down on one of our settees was, "I'm really not sure if you are going to be able to help me with my problem because there is actually nothing physically wrong with me."

I said, "That's okay. If you can explain to me what the problem is then I might be able to tell you if I/*we* will be able to help and you can then decide for yourself if you would like me/*us* to try."

So she began.

"I'm married, Isabella, with three children, I'm very happily married and I love my husband very much but, and this is a huge but, there is a young man I have come into contact with at work recently and I can't begin to tell you how attracted I am to him and him to me. It's crazy. He's about thirty years younger than me. But when I see him it's as if a surge of electricity is passing between us. It's so strong it makes me feel woozy. I'm in a crazy situation. I am a happily married woman with a grown-up family and I feel like a stupid teenage girl. This has got to stop, but there doesn't seem to be anything I can do myself to stop it. I love my job and don't want to leave. I've been with the company for nearly ten years and he's not long joined the company but he also loves his job. Our offices are on different floors in the building we work in, so I have tried to avoid the floor he works on. But I end up spending every minute of my working day thinking about him and then, of course, every day he comes downstairs to my office to see me. Every time I see him I want to run to him and throw my arms around him and he feels exactly the same, the pull between us is so strong, but we don't, we hold back. But it's hard, so hard. This is driving me spare. He would have me run away with him so that we can start a new life together and, as tempting as this seems to my very irrational mind at the moment, I know that's not what I'm meant to do. Please can you help me? I'm desperate! This needs to stop."

Frantic might have been a better word for her to use. She really was frantic, bless her.

"Harriet, have you ever given any thought to the possibility that you have been here before, that this life might not be the only life that you have had?" (And that was out of my mouth before I could stop myself).

"Yes, I have and I did wonder if this attraction towards Ken (the young man) had something to do with that but I didn't think I would still have an attraction towards someone I knew before. I didn't think feelings for someone could transfer into another life. I didn't think that could happen."

"I have such a strong feeling, Harriet, that you have

both been together before in a previous life. You could have been married to each other, you could have been lovers, or perhaps you were attracted to each other in a previous life but were never allowed to be together. Unrequited love can be a very powerful memory. Whatever your relationship was, I think it's safe to say you did know each other before, and you were attracted to each other then."

"Yes, I'm sure you're right."

"Would you like me to see if *we* can clear this for you?"

"Do you think you can?"

"I'm not sure, because I've never been asked to do anything like this before. But it's got to be worth seeing what the healing energy can do. It may be able to clear the feelings from your aura and I'm more than happy to try for you. Would you like me to?"

"Yes please."

So I started as I always do with Harriet on my stool as I worked in the aura around her head. I don't know if I have mentioned this to you before but, by me doing this first, it allows me to tune into my patients' energy allowing me to sometimes see pictures, scenes from my patients' lives and also my voice might give me some information, as well as me being able to gauge the strength and balance of the patients' aura. This is all so helpful for me. So the few minutes that my patients spend on my stool it is almost more for me than it is for them.

I then asked Harriet to get onto my healing bed so that the healing energy could start doing its work. After what seemed like an unusually short space of time I found myself asking Harriet to turn over onto her back and as she did I placed a pillow on the bed for her to rest her head, and this is when things started to turn really strange. So strange that when I did eventually realise what I was doing I burst out laughing at myself.

I have mentioned before to you how my hands just go where they want to (in a nice safe way) without any thought on my part and always to where a patient needs some help, sometimes because of pain and sometimes just to allow me/*us* to move the energy around in a more balanced way. Well, this day the whole of me and not just my hands did its own thing, with hilarious results.

Without thinking, I went across the room and somehow I managed to manoeuvre my very large duet piano stool to beside my healing bed. Next I climbed up onto it so that I was what seemed like a mile above Harriet who was lying on the bed way below me laughing. Okay, so that's an exaggeration but that's what it felt like at the time and that's when I realised that Harriet was laughing her head off at me and that's when I joined her and burst into fits of laughter myself as I wobbled, what seemed like miles above the ground.

What a picture I must have made. I must have looked an idiot. Me standing on top of my piano stool laughing, but almost too scared to move in case I fell off. I could have almost touched the ceiling, I felt so high. But I had absolutely no idea why I had done this.

While I had been tuning into Harriet when she had been sitting on my stool my voice had told me that the past life I was going to be looking for had been a very long time ago and I just knew (and I can't explain my knowing) that the further back in time the life was that I needed to find, the further out into her aura I would need to go to find it. In other words, if the past life was very recent where the memory was coming from it will be found in the aura or the energy quite close to the human body. But if the memory (the past life) was from a lifetime hundreds of years ago, the longer ago the past life the further out into the aura I would have to go to find it.

So there was me on my piano stool with my arms outstretched at least nine feet above Harriet's head, searching through the layers of her aura looking for the life they were both together in, and I found it!

And this was how I found it.

First and foremost I asked for help because I knew (and know) there is no way I could find it on my own. I asked my unseen friends and helpers to help me find the exact life that this very strong connection/attraction between Harriet and Ken was coming from. Having asked for help, I then began.

Firstly, I moved the piano stool into position. Then I stood on the floor beside it, with my hands outstretched about one foot away from Harriet's body. I then very slowly raised my outstretched arms up as far as I could stretch, but I didn't sense or feel anything different. So I then climbed onto my piano stool and, from a kneeling position, I continued to scan her aura, with my outstretched arms slowly moving up through the layers as I stood up slowly and carefully until I felt a coolness and sensed a very thin ripple in my hands, and that's where I stopped. I was about seven to eight feet above her body with my hands outstretched above her. And that's when I realised what I had just done, and where I was, and that Harriet was laughing at me. I can still see the picture in my mind as if it was yesterday because the scene I began to witness was so beautiful and completely unexpected. That is after I got over my giggles at what I had done without thinking, and I had steadied myself on my wobbly legs.

I found myself looking into a rainbow of very beautiful pale shades of pinks, blues and mauves, almost like a painting of a very pretty, serene sunset and there in the middle of my picture was a very thin wispy layer of silvery pale grey. The grey thin line seemed to be pulsating ever so gently just like a ripple on water and I instinctively knew that this ripple was the memory that needed to be cleared for Harriet. I held my hands as steady as I could (on my wobbly legs) and asked the powers that be to clear this memory away from her to free her. And as I watched it was as if a bolt of lightning shot across the scene in front of me, a bolt of golden colours that went whoosh across my vision and then the scene settled back down again. And when it did there was no silvery grey band to be seen in my picture anymore and no ripple.

I climbed back down off my piano stool and breathed a sigh of relief. I was back on solid ground once more. I looked at Harriet lying on my bed and she said, "I feel so light, Isabella. I'm floating on air."

I wished Harriet could have seen what I saw that day. In actuality, I wish you all could have witnessed what I saw that day, because it was so beautiful.

What an amazing experience for me and I was very sure the job was done.

But was it?

Had it worked, you are going to ask?

About a week later Harriet rang me to tell me that she felt a miracle had happened for her during her treatment and she apologised for not ringing me sooner to tell me. She said all the feelings she had had for Ken had left her. She also said she had felt wonderful all week, as if a load had been lifted from her. And Ken had also spoken to her and he also felt as if the attraction between them had gone away and could they please remain friends, which apparently they did.

It's probably at least twenty years ago since this all happened and I do know that Harriet is still a very happily married wife and mother.

I love a happy ending.

Do our past lives look like ripples in our aura? I have no idea. I don't pretend to have the answers. I can only tell you what I see and hear and feel. I'm sure the powers that be are often very kind to me and show me things in a very simple way so that I can understand what's going on and that's fine by me.

There is one more thing that I need to say before I move on to something else. Sometimes it's very worthwhile knowing what has happened to us in a previous life because it can help us in this life and that has to be good. We need to be able to learn and move forward. But it's also very important for us to know that this life is the most important. This life is the most precious. It's this life that will lead us on to greater things if we can get it right.

So please if you have a serious problem and you have absolutely no idea where your problem has come from then yes, ask the question, "Could this be from a previous life?" But I've got to be honest with you, serious past-life problems are rare. They are not the norm, if that's the right word to use?

This life is so precious.

Live it.

Enjoy it and do the very best you can with it.

That's all you can ask of yourself.

Don't have any regrets when you go back into the Spirit world.

Be able to sit with your guardian angels and say to them, I think I did okay, I think I got it right, didn't I?

CHAPTER FIFTEEN

Instinct: "A natural or intuitive way of acting or thinking"
Dictionary definition

Now it's not unusual for me to get a phone call asking to make an appointment for the caller's partner and, on this particular Monday afternoon in August 1993, that's exactly what happened.

I will call the lady who rang me Michelle. She rang to make an appointment for her husband. Michelle was very chatty with me that afternoon on the telephone as she told me about her husband, Andy. He apparently had been feeling very down over the previous six months and Michelle said she was worried about him. She had asked around amongst her friends to see if anyone knew someone, anyone, that they thought might be able to help him and one of her friends had come up with my name and phone number. She told me that once she had my contact details she then told Andy about me and he had agreed to come and see me. In fact, Michelle told me he had actually said he was pleased she had found someone he could see to talk to. She explained to me that he was at work during the day and that was why she was ringing me to make the appointment for him, but he was going to have next Friday off work, so could she please make an appointment for him for sometime on that Friday afternoon? So that's what we did. His appointment was for two o'clock in the afternoon.

When Friday came around and I looked in my diary to see who was coming that day, I had two patients booked in for morning appointments and I had two more booked in for the afternoon. My afternoon appointments were for one o'clock and then Andy at two o'clock so I knew I would be finished working by about three and then I could go out and do a bit of shopping on our local high street. My day was planned, or so I thought.

After my one o'clock left I had about fifteen minutes to get myself a quick cup of tea before Andy arrived. As I sat in our kitchen drinking my cuppa I started to watch the clock on the wall. I wanted to make sure I had time to finish my drink and go to the loo before the doorbell rang. But the minutes kept ticking by as I sat looking at the clock, and the doorbell didn't ring. When it got to twenty past two I picked up the telephone and rang Michelle. She was very surprised to hear my voice when she answered the phone and when I told her that Andy had not arrived yet she was a bit dismayed. She explained that he had left the house in plenty of time to make sure he wasn't late in getting to me. He did have a little bit of shopping to do but he should not have been late. Michelle said perhaps his car had broken down. I told her not to worry, he may still arrive, so why don't we give him a bit longer? She asked me to ring her as soon as he arrived as she felt sure he would be with me soon and, of course, I promised her I would. You must all remember this was 1993 and very few people had a mobile phone. They were very expensive at the time, very large and very heavy. So there was no way that Michelle could get in touch with Andy while he was driving his car.

It was now three-thirty and Andy had still not appeared.

It was at about this time in the afternoon that I began to feel very uneasy and I hadn't a clue as to why. My stomach was churning. When four o'clock came I rang Michelle again. She said she had been ringing around all of their friends and colleagues trying to see if anyone had seen or heard from him, but no one had and, of course, he hadn't come to me. And that's when, and I took myself by surprise by the words that came out of my mouth, I found myself saying to her, "I don't quite know what you might have to face later today, Michelle, but whatever it is, please remember that I am here for you, should you want to speak to me. I'm here for you if you need me. Try and be strong and remember that I'm only a phone call away."

And with that we said goodbye to each other, with her promising me she would ring me as soon as he got home. But as I put the phone down from her that afternoon I had such a strong feeling that he wouldn't be going home and I didn't know why. The uneasiness I was feeling was getting stronger by the minute. Something was very wrong but I didn't have a clue as to what it was.

I didn't go to the shops that afternoon, even though there were a few things I needed to buy, because my stomach was in such a knot. I was a bit worried in case I might need the loo in a hurry so I stayed where I was. I reasoned with myself that it would be best to stay at home just in case Andy had had a problem with his car and ended up arriving late.

Tea time, I was in our kitchen preparing our evening meal with the radio on, tuned into our local radio station as I always did, with me singing along to the music when the six o'clock news came on and, within a few seconds of the newsreader speaking, I shouted out "Dear God, no!"

"What's the matter, Mum?"

That was our son, Alexander, as he walked into the kitchen just as I was shouting the words out loud.

I said to him, "That's the man who was supposed to see me this afternoon at two o'clock."

My husband then piped up.

"Don't be daft. It won't be him."

"It is him. I know it is."

"What's going on, Mum?"

"The newsreader has just said a man has driven his car off the cliff at the coast and killed himself and I just know it's Andy, the man who was supposed to come this afternoon for a treatment from me. But instead of coming to see me, he's killed himself."

The words were no sooner out of my mouth when I burst into tears.

David kept saying to me, "You will be wrong."

And I kept saying, "No. I know I'm not."

It was 1993 and if this happened today David would (I hope) not be saying, "You will be wrong." I've been right far too many times over the past twenty-odd years for him to start doubting me now.

All I kept thinking was, "If only Andy had come to see

me I might have been able to stop him from ending his life." I was still crying when I distinctly heard a man's voice say to me, "I'm sorry. I'm so sorry."

And then he was gone. And again I instinctively knew that I had just heard Andy speaking to me. I told our son what I had just heard and he said, "What are you going to do, Mum?"

"I'm going to ring Michelle and let her know I'm thinking about her because I know, without a shadow of doubt, that Andy is gone and she needs to know I know," so I did.

A close friend of Michelle's answered the telephone that evening but when I told her who I was she said Michelle wanted to speak to me. Michelle came on the telephone and said, "Have you heard, Isabella?"

"Yes sweetheart, I've just heard it on the radio and I instinctively knew that it was Andy the newsreader was talking about. I'm so sorry."

She said to me, "You knew something was wrong didn't you, this afternoon when you spoke to me on the telephone, you knew?"

I explained to her that I had a feeling something wasn't right, but I didn't know what it was. I then explained to her that I thought he might have been in a car accident and he was seriously injured. And then I said to her, "In my wildest dreams I couldn't have guessed what he had done, but as soon as I heard the news on the radio I had instinctively known it was your husband. I'm so sorry, Michelle. If you ever need me, you know where I am."

She said she would be in touch with me when she was ready to be able to face people. I gave her my love and put the phone down and I burst into tears again.

David came back into the kitchen after a few minutes and I told him I had been right; it was Andy. Our son said, "I knew you were right, Mum. I never doubted you."

Why is it that our children know us better than our partners?

For weeks afterwards I kept thinking about Andy and I

kept asking the air around me, "Why? Why did you do it? If you had only come to see me that day perhaps I could have helped you to stay." I was really sad about what had happened. I never met him, I had never met Michelle, yet they were in my thoughts and prayers constantly during the months of late summer and autumn. I found it hard to get what had happened out of my head.

It was probably about six months later when Michelle rang me and made an appointment to come and see me. She said she was still in a muddle with herself and she desperately needed to talk to me as well as have a treatment.

I, of course, had never met Michelle before that day (well, not in this lifetime anyway) but we had an immediate connection between us. You will know what I mean when I say it was as if we had known each other for years and we were old friends. There was an instant rapport between us.

When I opened our front door to her she stepped inside our home and gave me a big hug as if she was greeting a long-lost friend (and I guess in many ways she was). I invited her into the room I was working in and asked her to sit down so we could have a chat. She told me that she had brought the letter Andy had left for her before he took his own life and she said she wanted me to read it. As she handed it to me I said to her, "I realise you must have talked many times to your friends and family over the past few months about Andy taking his life, but I don't actually know what happened Michelle, so perhaps you could tell me."

She said she was sorry she forgot I didn't know the story. And this is the very sad story, as she told it to me.

"Instead of Andy coming to see you, Isabella, that Friday afternoon, he drove to the coast and parked his car in the car park next to the cliffs right on the seafront. He apparently got out of his car and stopped a young couple as they were walking their dog, handed them a letter with my name and address on it and asked them to give it to me. Then he turned and ran back to his car, started the engine and within seconds he drove his car straight through the fence at the edge of the car park and over the cliff edge. The reason I know all this, Isabella, is because the young couple stayed at the scene and gave the letter to the police when they arrived, along with their story of what happened. The police apparently arrived on the scene very quickly after receiving numerous phone calls from people telling them a man had driven his car off the cliff. The young couple were able to tell the police exactly what he had done. They had stayed at the scene because they had not known what to do. Let's face it, who would? They apparently were both in shock (the police told me that) as were quite a few other people who had witnessed what had happened."

    I just sat there that afternoon, listening to her telling me her story as if I was in a dream. Then she said, "I would like you to read the letter, Isabella."

    I sat and read the letter that Andy had left for Michelle. And even now all these years on I can still remember how much love came from his words on the page in front of me, for both Michelle and his family. And how terribly sad the letter made me feel as I read it. I can remember that he told her he felt she would be much better off without him and that, because he loved her so much, he felt she would have a far better life if he wasn't around her!

    Michelle explained to me that Andy had been recently diagnosed with manic depression. He apparently had watched his mother suffer very badly from it over the years, before he himself started showing signs of the same symptoms. She told me that he had been such a proud man, he hadn't wanted her or his family to see him like that (how his mother had been) and that's why he felt he wanted to end it all. He had wanted to save Michelle from seeing him the way he had seen his mother. He hadn't wanted her to have to cope with him the way he had had to cope with his mother.

    How sad.

    I obviously can't remember everything that the letter said because it's so many years ago now since this all happened. But I can and do remember some of the treatments I was able to give to Michelle over the coming months and the few times that Andy came to call, and some of the things he was able to tell her. So let me relate some of them to you.

Michelle always came for her appointments with me on a Friday afternoon at two o'clock (the same day and time that Andy should have come to see me) and if I did have another patient to see that afternoon it wasn't until three-thirty. But nine times out of ten I was free for the afternoon, or my next appointment wasn't until four-thirty. Now I'm telling you all of this for a reason. Each and every time Michelle had a treatment from me, without fail, she would fall asleep after she had turned onto her back. After I finished giving her her treatment I would always cover her with a blanket so that she would be warm and cosy and I would leave the room. (Watching someone sleeping is a bit like watching paint dry!) I would leave her to sleep for at least an hour and sometimes even longer. To be honest with you I sometimes left her as she slept and I went to the shops on our local high street and did my shopping and when I got home she would still be fast asleep. Did she know I left the house and went shopping? Yes she did, because I told her.

Michelle called these sleeps her 'sleeps of peace'.

She told me that she would often feel herself starting to turn over on the bed but someone would tap her on her shoulder and she would turn back away from the edge. No one in twenty-five years has ever fallen off my healing bed, and please God, no one ever will. But Michelle is the only person I have left all alone in the house, no that's not true, there was one other lady many years later, but that's for another book.

Michelle told me that she would never be able to fully understand why Andy did what he did (manic depression apart) because there had been so much love between them and their family and it was when she told me this for the first time that I heard a voice say to me, "He did have something wrong within his brain."

The words I was given were, "It was wired wrong."

So the fact he took his own life had been what could be described as a bit out of his hands. There had been extenuating circumstances, manic depression and his brain being wired wrong (or perhaps that is why he had manic depression because his brain was wired wrong?). I explained to Michelle what I'd heard and she told me that there had been an inquest and it had been found that there was something not quite right medically, so she could accept what I had just heard.

During one of her treatments Andy told me that she had recently ordered a new bathroom suite and he didn't like it! In fact he told me that he thought it looked awful. He said to me, "Go on, tell her I don't like it."

So there I was giving Michelle her treatment and me not being sure what to say to her when Andy explained to me that he didn't like it because he thought the colour of the new bathroom suite was, well actually the word he said was a swear word so you get the gist. So I asked him what colour it was. He said, "It's the same yucky colour as the jumper Michelle is wearing today."

And, I've got to be honest, he had me giggling so there was nothing for it, I had to tell her.

"Michelle, Andy tells me you have just bought a new bathroom suite."

"Yes, I have. I got it cheap in the sales and it's being fitted next week."

"Well, Andy doesn't like the colour of it. He's told me to tell you it's the same wishy-washy ivory colour of your jumper!"

And at that I put my hand to my mouth to stop the giggles (because I could hear the laughter in Andy's voice).

"He's right, it is."

And, bless her, she started to laugh too. Her jumper was a wish-washy pale colour and I've got to be honest and say it wasn't a very flattering colour on Michelle; it did nothing for her. But it did give us all a giggle. Anyway, Andy obviously knew exactly what Michelle had been doing over the past few months right down to the colour of the new bathroom suite she had just bought (and her jumper) even if he didn't like it. Michelle seemed pleased to know he was still around her, but obviously very sad that he was not here with her.

I'm not going to go into all the treatments Michelle had because that's not necessary for this story, but there was one more thing Andy told me to tell her so that she would be in no doubt whatsoever that he had been talking to me.

Now this is a bit personal, but I can guarantee that most married women over a certain age will smile to themselves and recognise exactly what Andy was meaning.

Andy said to me,

"Tell her I'm telling you about her special dress, 'our special dress'. Go on, tell her."

So I did and she became a little bit embarrassed when she tried to explain to me what it was. Now I can't remember but I'm fairly sure Andy also told me what the colour of the dress was so there could be no doubt in her mind that he had been talking to me. And you're not going to believe this, but as I have been writing this a man's voice has just told me that the colour of her dress was blue. And guess who the voice belonged to. Thanks Andy, after all these years. Thank you.

Andy did pop in from time to time over the next few weeks and months as Michelle slowly started to put her life back together.

The healing energy was able to take away the horrible knotted feeling that Michelle had said she had in the pit of her tummy. It was able to help her to get back onto her feet but, as she said to me at the time and she would probably say to you now if she had the chance, nothing will ever be able to mend her broken heart.

I lost touch with Michelle many years ago now and I'm really sad about that. So the only thing I can do now is send her my love and blessings over the airwaves and say it was a privilege to have known her (and Andy).

I could just walk away and close the book on the above story, but I don't want to. I feel the need very strongly to reflect for a few minutes on Michelle and Andy's story and that's what I'm going to do.

It saddens me every time I think about them both and writing it all down has brought it all back for me again and that's okay. I was involved and yes, I'm going to question the 'if only' of it for the rest of my life. If only Andy had come to me that afternoon, if only he had told Michelle how he was actually feeling, if only he had sought help sooner.

I need to give myself time to ponder on the sadness Andy's suicide has left behind.

There is so much more I could write on this subject. In all honesty, it's such a very complex and emotional subject it deserves a whole book to be written. I think if I started to delve the floodgates would open and I would lose the rhythm of this book so please forgive me for now. Another book, another time, I promise.

But just before I do end this chapter I would like to say to you all, if you or any of your friends are feeling overwhelmed by this life, please seek help.

If, by chance, you are reading this and you have lost a loved one because they committed suicide, my heart goes out to you and, if I could, I would give you a hug. So if you need one I'm sending one to you through the ether with my love.

If you are the one that's struggling, please try and talk to your friends and loved ones. Life is far too precious to end it.

Or, please try and help your friends and loved ones if you feel they are struggling. It's amazing what a kind word, deed or a cuddle can do. There are lots of professional people out there that would be glad to be of help if they were asked.

If Michelle could talk to you all I'm sure she would tell you that even now, after all these years, she has moved on with her life but she is still heartbroken and will be for the rest of her life here on earth.

In my experience as a healer over the past thirty-six years, and as a Samaritan for a few years many years ago, I can say with some authority that most people who have lost a loved one from a suicide will tell you they were devastated by what happened and most of them will spend the rest of their lives blaming themselves. And again most of them will also tell you that they wished that the person who passed into the Spirit world had told them there was a problem because they didn't actually realise they were feeling so desperate.

If only they had known, if only someone had known.

Please seek help if you need it.

Please just ask.

CHAPTER SIXTEEN

"Ask a power that when its source is tapped will flood you full of warmth and drive away all fears of yesterday's bad thoughts"
Me from my Dad

About nineteen years ago we were looking for a house to buy in an area we didn't know very well, but the area we wanted to live in. It took lots of trips out and many miles of driving to try and find a suitable home and, of course, at the other end of things we had to sell our house to enable us to move on.

Now I'm quite sure a lot of you will have gone through exactly the same thing. They (whoever 'they' are) say moving house is one of the top stress events in a person's life and I was beginning to remember what they meant.

We found a new home in the area we wanted to live in and we found a buyer for our home without even trying and you know what they say, 'if it seems too good to be true, it probably is'. Well, that was certainly the case with this buyer. We didn't even have our 'for sale' board up outside our home when we got a letter pushed through our letter box, asking us if we would get in touch with the letter writer should we be interested in selling our house. Wow. We were just about to put our house onto the market when this happened. So we passed the letter on to our estate agents who got in touch with the gentleman in question and, lo and behold, he came within days to view our home with his wife. He consequently offered us our asking price and asked our estate agents to put a 'sold' sign on our 'for sale' board. Fortunately for us, our agent refused. Our agents told him that until contracts had been exchanged there was no way a 'sold' sign would be put up. Thank goodness.

It turned out, at the end of the day, he couldn't afford our home. Was it too good to be true? Yes it was and he managed to waste about six weeks of everyone's time. Now, while this had all been going on we had found ourselves our new home and, thinking we had sold our house, we put in an offer and, to cut a long story short, our offer was accepted but then, of course, we lost our buyer through no fault of our own. That's when I began to feel a bit stressed, to say the least.

It was a beautiful late summer's afternoon about a week after we heard our house sale had fallen through, and just at the point in time that our estate agent was arranging for an advertisement to be put into our local paper for the following weekend. I had been gardening all that afternoon in the warm sunshine, lost in my own thoughts, when I realised I needed to walk to our local shops to buy some fresh food to make something for our evening meal. So I cleaned myself up and changed from my gardening clothes into a cotton skirt and lightweight jumper. But before I set off I made myself a cup of tea. And I can still picture myself standing at the bench in what was our kitchen all those years ago, having just poured my cuppa, when I said out loud to the air around me, "Please Lord send me a smile. Please send me a smile. I need one."

I had no sooner got the words out of my mouth when the thought struck me, "What a funny thing for me to ask for."

I had been feeling a bit tearful for a couple of days because I was worrying in case we wouldn't find a buyer (silly me) for our home and I was worried in case we lost the house we wanted to buy because I loved it so much. So I suppose that had something to do with me asking for a smile. But then I thought to myself, "How on earth can God send me a smile? You silly girl," and with that thought in my head I left our house and headed for the shops.

It was a beautiful warm sunny afternoon so that made me feel a little bit lighter as I crossed over the road outside of our home and started to walk down one of the side streets that would lead me onto the High Street. And as I was walking I noticed a lady as she turned off the main road a few hundred yards away from me, as she started walking up the road towards me. The closer she got to me I could see her staring at me. Actually it freaked me out a bit because she hadn't taken her eyes off me from the moment I caught sight of her looking at me and I had no idea who she was. Then as she got nearer to me I could see that she was smiling at me, and the nearer she got to me the bigger her smile grew. Just as she was a few steps away from me she said, "You look so beautiful. Do you realise how beautiful you look? You look a picture in your pale blue skirt and your pale blue jumper. You look lovely."

I somehow managed to mumble the words, "Thank you," by which point she had stopped walking and so had I as she continued, "You look so lovely dressed all in blue. You are a ray of sunshine. You have brightened up my day. Thank you so much." And with that she continued walking past and away from me.

I was dumbfounded.

And all I had managed to get out was a mumbled, "Thank you."

I had smiled at her as she was telling me how lovely I looked, but I couldn't speak, I was so taken aback by her words.

As she turned and walked away from me I had the biggest smile on my face that I think I've ever had in my life.

I continued walking down the street and along the main road, beaming like the Cheshire Cat from the Mad Hatter's tea party, and I kept on smiling all the way along the High Street, into the shops and back home again.

I can still picture the scene in my head as if it was yesterday. I can see and remember that everyone I was walking past was looking at me and as they did they started smiling. It was as if my smile was infectious and everyone I passed caught it. People were turning their heads in my direction and looking at me, not only on the side of the road I was walking along but I also caught sight of people looking at me from the other side of the road. It was all a bit surreal, but amazing at the same time, and somehow that seemed to make my smile even bigger, if that was at all possible. And me, my smile never left my face all the way to the shops, back home again and for the rest of that day. In fact for a few days afterwards, whenever I thought about what happened I can remember thinking at the time that I had the strangest feeling that I had floated my way to the shops and back home that day as if my feet never touched the ground.

Was I sent a smile from Heaven that day? You bet I was, within minutes of me asking. I was sent the best smile I've ever had.

Have you ever heard the expression 'Angels come in strange disguises'.

Well, I have often thought about what happened to me on that summer's afternoon, and I have often wondered if perhaps the lady that spoke to me and gave me my smile was in fact an angel sent from Heaven.

I wonder? What a lovely thought.

But angel or not, thank you Universe for answering my prayer.

Now this next story is a little bit different but just as amazing. Many years ago our precious daughter decided she would like to travel the world for a few weeks before she started her very first job. She wanted to have a really special holiday, enjoy herself and have fun before her working life began, because as she said, "Mum, I may never get the chance again."

She had worked very hard over the previous two years, along with her newly made friends, to qualify in their chosen profession. And another one of her newfound friends decided she would also like to travel with her. Just the two of them, but safety in numbers even though the number was just two. The funding for this came from savings. Well done to them both for having some savings in the first place. And this was their itinerary.

England to New York
New York to Seattle
Seattle to Sydney via a stopover in LA
Sydney to Fiji
Fiji to LA for a twenty-four hour stopover
LA back home to England

Now for our twenty-three-year-old young lady and her

very nervous travelling companion this was all very adventurous and very exciting. Six weeks away from home would be a new experience for them both and something they would both remember for the rest of their lives.

Marie had travelled to America twice on her own before this holiday so she considered herself an experienced traveller. She had been to numerous countries, and I had explained to her over the previous years how to keep all of her transportation safe. I had taught her how to put golden light around every car, plane and train she might travel on at any time. By using the golden light she would keep them both safe on all their transportation, with her companion at the time (apparently) making fun of her for the first couple of times Marie did this even though her companion stood shaking every time they had to get on an aeroplane because she was so nervous.

I'll sidetrack here for a couple of minutes for me to explain to you what the golden light is all about.

Each and every time I go out to my car to drive somewhere, before I start the engine, I put golden light around it. Every aeroplane, train or vehicle I drive in or go on all get the golden light treatment, including my bicycle. I wouldn't dream of going anywhere or on anything without me asking and seeing the golden light of protection going around my transportation. Can you picture the 'Ready Brek' instant porridge advert, the one that appears on the telly in the wintertime, you know the one? The little boy comes out of the house on a cold frosty winter's morning and he looks as if he is completely surrounded in a golden orb of light, his own warm 'Ready Brek' glow-coat of protection. Well, that's what a halo of golden light around our cars, bikes, transport looks like. So the next time you get on an aeroplane, picture a beautiful golden light of energy going all around it, covering everything from the wing tips to the end of the aeroplane and back again, or your car surrounded in a lovely golden glow and it will keep you safe; that's what I mean by the golden light.

But then Marie said, "Mum, by the time we were due to

get on the aeroplane to fly to Australia, Pam (her travelling companion) was pestering me to make sure I'd put the golden light around the plane, much to the amusement of a gentleman who was standing right next to us in Seattle airport. He turned to me, Mum, and said, "I do it every time I travel and it's good to know you do it too."

"And with that the man smiled at me and turned and walked away from us, leaving Pam standing with her mouth open. She never thought in a million years, Mum, that other people might actually do it too."

Now it was towards the end of their trip that things went a little awry for our daughter.

And before I go any further we all need to remember our children didn't have mobile phones. This was 1998.

Marie was due to start her first job about eight days before Pam, so Marie had planned the trip to allow herself time to get back (but only just) to England the day before she was due to start her new job and, of course, Pam would have plenty of time when she go home before she had to start hers.

Fiji. From what Marie has told me Fiji sounds like a magical island. Marie learned to snorkel there for the very first time and when I tell you she is terrified of fish there must have been something very special about the sea-water, her teacher, and the fish for her to have been able to learn to do this. I've told her many times over the years that I think she must have been Jonah, swallowed by the whale and then spat out again. So for Marie to say she absolutely loved swimming in the sea surrounding the island it must be a very special place indeed. Perhaps one day I might get to go and swim there myself.

The day before they were due to leave Fiji to fly back to LA for their twenty-four hour stopover, before their return flight home, Pam informed Marie that she wasn't going to be going home with her. She told Marie that she was going to stay on the island for another week because she didn't need to be home just yet.

Marie (apparently) was dumbfounded and very hurt.

This had been a trip of a lifetime for them both. It had

been 'we will always take care of each other and not leave the other one alone' trip. So for Pam to be leaving Marie to travel back home alone was not what Marie had expected to happen, or wanted to happen.

There was nothing for it. Marie had to head for home on her own, feeling very hurt and very let down.

When she arrived in LA she found herself a taxi and headed for the hotel she had booked them both into on her own. And this is when she went into meltdown.

You can picture the scene, can't you? She would have been feeling very sorry for herself because Pam was still back on Fiji in the sunshine having a fabulous time and there was Marie on her own in a strange city. Not a good place for anyone to be in. And that's when she left the safety of her hotel and took herself for a walk to find a telephone booth so that she could phone home. And that's when I got the call, and thank God I was able to answer it for her. I could have been out of the house, I could have been sound asleep in bed because of the time difference and then there would have been no one at the other end of the phone for her to speak to, but thank God I was there!

"Hello Mum, it's me."

"Marie, what's the matter?" (The minute I heard her voice I knew something was wrong.)

"I'm all alone, Mum!"

"I don't understand."

"Mum, I'm all alone."

"But why Marie? Where are you?"

"I'm in LA, Mum."

"But why are you there alone? Where's Pam?"

"Pam is still on Fiji."

"What?"

"She's still on Fiji, Mum. She wouldn't come home with me."

"Good grief, Marie. Why on earth not?"

"She met someone, Mum, and she wanted to stay longer to be with him."

I was that mad at this point, and I didn't want to get into Pam staying on Fiji. I just wanted my girl to be safe.

"Where exactly are you, Marie?"

"I'm in a phone booth a few hundred yards from my hotel, Mum. I left the hotel to find a phone so that I could call you."

And, of course, Marie had started crying the minute she heard my voice and I was fighting back the tears because I didn't know what to do or what to say to her. My precious girl was on the other side of the world all alone, upset and a bit frightened because she was feeling vulnerable (which was not like her) and I couldn't get to her to help her and keep her safe. I was very angry with Pam at this point.

Marie had been the strong one when they started out but the roles seemed to have been reversed. Pam staying on in Fiji because she had found a guy and deserting Marie who was left feeling very hurt, vulnerable and very alone.

"Are you all right, treasure?" Stupid question really but I didn't know what else to say to her.

"No Mum, I'm not. That's why I've rung you."

I needed to think on my feet. Marie needed me to be strong for her and I needed to turn the conversation around somehow.

"How is Pam going to get home, Marie? She was booked on the same flight as you. Will she be able to change and organise new flights for herself?"

"I don't know, Mum, but will you please ring her parents and tell them what's happened? Please let them know that Pam won't be on the flight back home with me because she's still on Fiji. They don't know what's she's done, Mum. They will be expecting to pick her up at the airport when our flight gets in but she won't be on it. Will you please ring them?"

"Yes of course I will."

I then said to her, "Marie, when we have finished talking I want you to promise me that you will go straight back to your hotel and stay there until the taxi picks you up in the morning to take you to the airport. I need to know that you are going to be safe. Promise me?"

"Yes, Mum, I promise I'll go straight back."

"And promise me you won't talk to anyone unnecessarily?"

"I promise."

"I'm going to ask for help for you, Marie."

"Will you, Mum?"

"Yes sweetheart, of course I will as soon as you put the phone down."

We talked for a few more minutes until she stopped crying and I knew she would be alright walking back to her hotel.

"Okay, Mum, I'll go straight back to the hotel now."

We said a very tearful goodbye to each other with me promising I would try and get help for her. The minute I put the phone down from her I shouted out into the middle of our empty kitchen, "Dad, I need your help and I need it now. Please Daddy, help me. Marie needs help, Dad. I need you to send someone to her, Daddy, to watch over her. I need you to send someone she can feel safe with. She needs a friend to be with her. Now Dad. Please!"

And if my memory is correct I also asked him to go to be with her, knowing she would not be able to see her grandfather, but at least I would know she had a guardian walking beside her. What a worried state I was in!

Don't ask me why I asked my father and not God because I don't know. It could have been because I knew how much he loved her. I really don't know. Now trust me on this, I didn't stop to think about how he could help her. I had no idea whatsoever what my father could or could not do. I just simply trusted that he could do something. Or that God would somehow help him to help Marie. That must sound so stupid to some of you reading this.

I have said to you before that I just trust like a child and, believe me when I say, I wouldn't have asked if I hadn't thought that something could be done.

After I had asked my father for his help I then turned

my attention to the fact I needed to inform Pam's parents that she wouldn't be on the flight home with Marie in twenty-four hours. I needed to take a few deep breaths, blow my runny nose and pull myself together a little bit before I rang them.

I had their phone number in a file with all the paperwork to do with our girls' trip. All the hotels they were going to stay in, their passport numbers, all the information that might be needed in the event they lost anything or needed help. So I didn't have to hunt for Pam's parents' number, it was to hand. Pam's mum answered the telephone and I said, "Hi, it's Marie's mum here. I'm not sure how to tell you this but I've just had Marie on the telephone from LA and she's there on her own because Pam is not travelling home with her; she's still on Fiji. Marie thought you should know she will not be on the flight home tomorrow so there is no point in you going to the airport to meet her because she won't be on the aeroplane."

Now I think you can guess the reaction I got. I really felt sorry for Pam's mum. She had absolutely no idea what her daughter had done (or in this case had not done). She was furious with her. She was also very concerned because she didn't know how her daughter was going to rearrange her flights from Fiji and her accommodation for her stopover in LA, let alone her flight home to England. No mobile phones remember.

We had a rather odd conversation.

Obviously I told her I was very cross with her daughter because my daughter was in LA on her own in a distressed state, all because Pam had not followed their promises to stay by each other's side through thick and thin no matter what. Even if they fell out they had promised us as parents that they would stay together.

Pam's mother was very apologetic and, of course, it wasn't her fault. She asked me what I thought Pam was going to do. Had she given Marie any idea how she would get home? And, of course, I had absolutely no idea because that's not what Marie and I had talked about during our telephone conversation. I did say that obviously Marie would be home in the next twenty-four hours on the flight they had both been booked on so she might be able to tell her something when she landed. I would get her to ring her as soon as she got home.

What a to-do. All because a young lady had met a guy and not kept a promise to her girlfriend!

Apparently Pam's mother and father spent the next few days absolutely frantic because they hadn't a clue what their daughter was up to. They had rung the hotel on Fiji that Pam was staying in and left more than one message for their daughter to ring home, but Pam had not rung them back, so there was no way they could speak to her and they didn't know what she was doing or how she was going to get back home. Bless them.

We, on the other hand, had only twenty-four hours before Marie landed and I couldn't wait to get to the airport to meet her.

She did look well with her golden suntan (but very tired) when we picked her up from the airport. I ran to her to give her a big hug followed by lots of cuddles and then home for a cup of tea. And that's when she told me what had happened.

"Mum, you're not going to believe what happened to me after I put the phone down from you the other day. I headed straight back to the hotel like I promised you I would and as I got about fifty yards from the front entrance I saw someone sitting on the hotel steps and I recognised him. Pam and I had met him in Seattle five weeks earlier and he knew we were coming to LA for a stopover and Pam had told him where we were going to be staying. So he had travelled down from Seattle especially to meet us. Actually, Mum, he had travelled down to meet Pam and, of course, Pam wasn't with me. He was a bit disappointed she wasn't with me, but he said he would stay with me for the rest of the day and evening and make sure I was okay until bedtime, ready for my flight the following day. We went out for a burger and then he brought me back to my hotel. I was safe, Mum, and I had a friend. I wasn't alone any more.

Now come on all of you, was my prayer answered?

Did my father and the Universe answer my call for help?

Did my daughter get the help she needed and did she get it 'Now'?

Let's face it she couldn't have got it any quicker.

Within minutes of her leaving the phone booth, within minutes of me asking for help for her, the words were no sooner out of my mouth here in England than the help was there for her in America, and that's what I call amazing.

The Universal energy, or God, or whatever name you give to 'your God' has an amazing or, better still, miraculous way of working things out for us. A truly miraculous way of knowing what we need before we even need it, or before we ask for help. Was it my father that got the help there so fast for her that day or was it God? It doesn't matter a jot. The fact is the help arrived for her immediately and that's all that matters to me.

Thank you ten thousand times over. Thank you.

CHAPTER SEVENTEEN

"Sometimes the most important life lessons are the ones we end up learning the hard way."
Author unknown

It was funny how the summer of 1993 brought a lot of people to me with similar back problems. I must have had about six patients all come to me within a very short space of time and all with problems with their backs caused by lots of different reasons. I have chosen two of these stories to tell you at this time, both of which taught me a thing or two, and you might also find them interesting.

Just a note for you to remember, the summer of 1993 was at the beginning of me treating people outside of my family and friends, outside of my comfort zone.

The first lady I'm going to tell you about was in her mid-sixties when she came to see me and I will call her Alice.

Alice was a small, very well dressed lady with silvery-grey hair and as she entered the room I worked in she said to me, "I've come to see you because I had a fall about three years ago. I fell backwards and hurt myself quite badly and I'm still in pain. I've been told by some of my friends that you might be able to help me."

I explained to her that I couldn't promise her anything but if she was willing to give the healing energy a chance she would soon know if it was going to help. I tried to explain to her that her problem wouldn't go away overnight and she would need to allow the healing energy time to heal her and to allow herself a few treatments to be able to clear the problem, if indeed it could be helped.

"Well, I'm not sure about that. If you can't guarantee to cure me, if you can't say for sure it will help me, I don't want to pay you. I don't think I should."

Where my next words came from I didn't know. Put it this way they weren't mine.

"Alice, I'll not charge you for any healing you receive

but I will charge you for my time. My time is valuable to me as I'm sure yours is to you. So if it's alright with you I'll only charge you for my time."

"Well how much will that be?"

"Fifteen pounds a treatment."

"I can't afford that. That's too much."

"Then what can you afford?"

"I can afford ten pounds."

I thought about it for a few moments and said to her, "Okay then, I will only charge you ten pound a session." I didn't have the confidence at the time to say no to her.

So we began.

Alice came for six treatments and if my memory file is correct, after only two treatments Alice began to notice a difference. The pain she had been experiencing was beginning to leave her and by her sixth and final treatment with me/*us* she said she felt wonderful. So wonderful in fact that she told me she had planned a holiday.

"A holiday, Alice?"

"Yes. Because I was in so much pain I haven't been on holiday since the year before I fell down and that's four years ago now."

"Are you going to go somewhere nice?"

And as proud as punch she announced to me, "Oh yes, I've booked it already. I'm going to go on the QE2 to New York, stay for a few days to see the sights and then I'm coming back home again on the boat."

I was speechless.

With that said she paid me her ten pounds, thanked me for healing her and she left my home never to be seen by me again. I watched her as she walked away down our drive with a definite skip in her step.

Alice was healed. Do you know what I did next? I sat down and cried. I was feeling so stupid and cross with myself. She had told me six weeks earlier that she couldn't afford to pay me my going rate so, me being me, I had tried to help her (or so I had thought) by giving her a reduced rate to enable her to have a few treatments. I found out later she was very wealthy and could have afforded to pay ten times my rate! I decided on that day that I must have the word mug written across my forehead. As you can imagine I've never forgotten Alice.

After a bit of thought as to what happened I realised that I had agreed to treat Alice for ten pound a session so there was actually nothing for me to be cross about or complain about. So the lesson for me at the time was to make sure I was happy with what I decided to charge (or not charge) someone regardless of their circumstances.

It dawned on me that Alice had been unfair in her dealings with me. So the wonderful law of karma would come into effect and I didn't need to think or do a thing about what had happened, because the Universe would balance the scales for me.

Have I done the same thing again? Have I reduced my rate for someone else and got walked on yet again? The honest answer is yes I have, but in twenty-five years it's only happened to me about three times. Three times out of the hundreds of people I have seen and helped. That's actually not bad going and the few times I have been aware that someone has just walked all over me I have always left the person to the wonderful universal law of karma.

So there is no need for me to feel annoyed.

I'm not going to change just because a few have got one over on me. Alice's back was healed and that's what mattered. I will always help where I can and if I can because I know that when I ask for help, the help has been and always will be there for me every time and that to me is priceless.

Now this next story is a little bit different, but lessons for me nonetheless.

I can remember this lady telling me she had a bad back but then she immediately changed the subject and spent ages telling me all about her mother, who was apparently driving her crackers with her never-ending complaining. Now for the sake of my story I will call this lady Brenda. Brenda was not an easy lady to communicate with because she was so set in her ways (which I found out within a very short space of time) and, like a few patients I had already seen with similar problems, she was very stubborn and from the outset I found it difficult to find common ground. Brenda's overriding problem was her mother, not her back. Brenda's bad back was secondary to her complaints about her mother. But, of course, Brenda's bad back was primarily caused because she would not bend when it came to anything to do with her mother. Apparently, for the previous two years her mother had kept telling her there was something wrong, that she didn't feel well. But every time Brenda took her to the doctors the doctor could find nothing the matter, so Brenda was getting angrier by the day with her mother's seemingly unnecessary complaints.

The second time Brenda came for a treatment she asked me to book an appointment for her mother so that I could give her a treatment and would I also please tell her mother to stop complaining, because she wasn't ill. (I, of course, had no intentions of doing that.) Brenda told me she was sick of telling her mother she needed to pull herself together and get on with her life. So we arranged for Brenda to bring her mother for a treatment the following week. They would both have their appointments back to back as they lived quite a distance from me and this meant that Brenda only had one journey to make instead of two.

Brenda duly arrived at her next appointment accompanied by her mum who was a lovely lady, very quiet and very timid, the complete opposite to her daughter.

As soon as mum sat on my stool for me to go around her energy in her aura around her head I knew straight away that there was something very wrong and when she lay down on my healing bed I can clearly remember that all I wanted to do was cry.

This lady was very ill and no one knew.

I can also clearly remember as I was going around the bed, allowing the healing energy to flow both over this lady and through her, the words, 'Be very gentle with her, be very gentle' were going over and over in my mind. And as I looked across the room at her daughter sitting watching me with a cross look on her face, what on earth could I say to her? She thought her mother had been complaining for the past two years for no reason because her doctor kept telling her that there was nothing the matter with her. And who on earth was I to tell them any different!

It wasn't my place to tell Brenda that her mother was seriously ill and only had a very short time left here on earth. And it wasn't my place to tell her mother either. Although I had a very strong feeling that mum knew.

After I had given her mum her treatment all I wanted to do was put my arms around her and give her a big hug. I did, much to the annoyance of her daughter. Brenda then had her treatment almost in silence, while her mum sat restfully waiting.

The following week when Brenda came for her fourth treatment with me she was furious because I hadn't told her mother to stop complaining. I knew I couldn't tell her about her mum (it wasn't my place) but I needed to say something without actually coming out and saying the words, "Your mother is dying."

I'm not medically qualified so I have no right to be diagnosing anyone and rightly so, but sometimes I wish I could be allowed to say something to allow people the time to put things right in their lives. To give people the time to make amends, to be able to clear bad feelings, to help save them years of grief but I can't. But I can try in a roundabout way to say what's needed. And on that day in 1993 I tried my hardest to make Brenda realise that her mother was actually very ill.

"Brenda, I really feel your mum's not very well. I honestly think it would be really good if you and your mum could clear the air between you. It would be even better if you could tell her you loved her, because you can never know for sure how long the door will be open for you to be able to make peace with her."

"I'm not doing that. She's driving me crackers."

All through that final treatment I was to give Brenda I

tried my best to tell her in a roundabout way that her mother was not long for this world. But everything I said fell on deaf ears.

Now Brenda was very cross with me for not telling her mother to stop complaining and because of that she didn't come back to me for any more treatments.

I can remember thinking at the time that that was going to be a blessing for me. She was so stubborn and stuck in her ways and, of course, her bad back was all due to her stubborn nature and her very controlling attitude towards her mum. I had found her very trying and very tiring for me to deal with.

Because I knew someone who knew both her and her mother I found out not more than two months later that her mother had been rushed into hospital about four weeks after I had seen her and she had died the following day. Her autopsy had shown that she had died of heart complications and that she must have had a heart problem for many years. God bless her.

Now, about six months later I was out shopping in our local town. I was in a very well-known department store looking at scarves when something made me turn and look to my right and there standing staring at me was Brenda, not more than a few feet away. I stood for a few seconds looking at her and I couldn't help myself as my head turned slowly from side to side. My head was saying to her, "I tried to tell you, I tried to warn you but you wouldn't listen." I watched as she slowly dropped her head down and she stood looking at the ground for what seemed like an age and then, without speaking, she turned and walked slowly away. I could tell by the look on her face before her eyes dropped to the floor that she knew I had tried to warn her, but she had chosen not to listen.

There is a very strong chance she will go through the rest of her life knowing she should have been more giving towards her mother, more forgiving. She had been given the chance to make peace with her mother, but she had chosen not to.

I took away from this never to assume that the doctors

are right, but I guess I knew that anyway from my own experience, but this confirmed it yet again for me.

Never forget to follow my instincts. I had given Brenda's mother a cuddle that day just as she was leaving our home, much to Brenda's annoyance when I knew she was mad at me. I was so glad that I had when I heard that she had passed over about four weeks later. And last but not least, no regrets.

Please God I'm never in the same position as Brenda when I lose a loved one.

CHAPTER EIGHTEEN

"Anything is possible in this world. I really believe that."
Liza Minnelli

When I opened our front door on this particular afternoon to greet my new patient, I got quite a shock when I first saw her. I'd never seen anyone's head look quite so lopsided in my life. It was bowed forward so that her chin touched her chest, but at an angle. It was as if her neck had broken and her head was resting on her raised left shoulder to support it, but then both her shoulder and her head had then fallen forward which made the top half of her body look all hunched up. I don't mean to be unkind in any way but, in all honesty, she reminded me at the time of Quasimodo from 'The Hunchback of Notre-Dame' and I hope I have painted a clear picture by me using those words. And even now, all these years on, when I try and put my own head into the same position that hers was in on that first day it's actually almost impossible for me to replicate and painful to even try, and Penny had been like that for about two years.

Now this story is both sad and very strange but I think you will find it very interesting.

Penny had not rung me herself to make the appointment, her mother had. She told me that she had heard about me through a friend of the family and both she and her husband wanted to know if I could perhaps help their daughter Penny who had only recently come out of a mental health facility after receiving treatment due to a very bad breakdown. Her mother then went on to tell me that she felt I might be their last hope because she and Penny's father felt they couldn't cope with her anymore and they were thinking of having her sectioned again. It was at this point in the conversation that I was beginning to wonder what on earth I might be getting myself into if I said yes. But I had no sooner thought this as her mother was speaking to me when I had an overwhelming feeling that I needed to see Penny regardless of what her mother was saying to me, and what Penny's problems might actually be.

It was then that I asked her mother, "How old is Penny please?"

Because of the way her mother had been talking about her I was quite sure she must be a teenager.

"Oh, she's forty-three."

Now that took me by surprise.

By the way her mother had been talking I had been sure she was quite young, not a grown woman. She then told me that she and her husband would pay for as many treatments as I thought Penny needed. She said she would make sure Penny had the money each time she came to see me. I've got to be honest I didn't like the tone I was hearing in Penny's mother's voice as she was talking to me. She was referring to her daughter as if she was a child and she was coming across as being very controlling and very severe. Not the sort of lady anyone would want as a mum at the best of times, but especially if you were not well.

The picture I was looking at in my head as this lady was speaking to me was of my own mother putting my dinner money into my purse and telling me to be very careful in case I lost it (the money and the purse). I would have been about six years old at the time and this lady had the same controlling tone in her voice as my mother had when I was six, as she described her forty-three-year-old daughter to me.

There and then over the telephone an appointment was made for Penny to come and see me and that was how Penny ended up at my door that afternoon with her very lopsided head, looking very sad.

It only took me a couple of seconds to get over my initial shock at Penny's appearance as I invited her into our home and into the room I was working in. I asked her to take her coat off and I invited her to sit down so that we could have a chat. I always take down a few details from new patients, just simple things such as their address and telephone number and date of birth and I always ask why they have come to me, what brought them to my door? And that's when Penny spoke to me for the first time.

Everything about Penny was timid. It was as if she wanted to hide herself away so that no one could see or hear her, but at the same time she desperately wanted to let someone know how she felt. Her voice was so quiet I had trouble in being able to hear her speak and there's nothing wrong with my hearing. It was as if she was too frightened to speak in case she was in trouble for saying the wrong thing. She reminded me of a timid little mouse, frightened in case a cat was hiding ready to pounce on her. After Penny had given me the details I needed, she said very slowly and very quietly, "I know my mother made the appointment for me but I desperately need help, Isabella. I need someone to listen to me and not shout me down all the time. I don't expect you can help me with my neck because my doctor tells me that there's nothing that can be done. Whenever I ask her for help because my neck is hurting she just gives me more painkillers to take and tells me to pull myself together or I will have to go back into hospital. She's not very nice to me, but no one is. I just need someone to listen to me."

"Who's your doctor, Penny?" I asked.

"Doctor Angus," she replied.

"I don't believe it. That's my doctor and she's been horrible to me too."

So, without thinking, I sat and told Penny the story of what our doctor had said to me the day I asked her for help when she told me I didn't have MS and never had and then the day I went to see her with terrible earache. That was the day she refused to give me anything for the pain I was in (full story in my first book). It had only been a few months earlier that one of those things had happened to me. Penny and I had something in common and when I had finished telling her I could see that she had visibly relaxed. She realised that our doctor had treated us both badly, so she had not been alone in the way her doctor had both treated and spoken to her. My story helped her to realise it wasn't just her that our doctor had been horrid to and I expect we were not the only ones.

Why oh why do some people do jobs they just shouldn't?

I explained to Penny that I couldn't promise her anything but I felt sure that the healing energy would be able to rebalance the energy around her and I promised her that I would explain everything that I was doing to her as we went along. She seemed to like the sound of that so we began.

As she sat on my stool so that I could go around the energy around her head I was picking up all sorts of things. Firstly, an overwhelming sense of sadness and grief and a feeling as if she was trying to hide away. Then I was aware that the energy down the left hand side of her head and down the left side of her neck was non-existent. There was nothing supporting her head and neck, no aura. It was just as if someone had stolen her energy from that side of her and run away with it, very strange. It was no wonder her neck had flopped onto her shoulder; there was nothing in her energy field to support it. So as soon as she got up onto my healing bed that was my starting point. I/*we* needed to put her aura back, we needed to replace a non-existent energy field down the top left hand side of her and I needed to try and find out why this had happened, because I had never seen anything like this before or since. This was a new one on me.

It had been obvious to me when we first met that she was worried in case she was meeting yet another woman who was not going to care about how she felt and I could now tell she was very relieved she had met someone that would actually listen to her and try and help her, the way she wanted to be helped.

As promised, I explained everything that I was doing as I worked down through her energy centres, down her spine and then when I got her to turn over I explained to her how there was no energy on the left hand side of her head and that was why I felt her neck and head had collapsed and if I/*we* could put the energy back there was no reason why her head shouldn't straighten back up. It just made sense to me. No big deal. No energy supporting her neck, neck collapsed. Energy put back around her neck and head, her head would be helped back up again. Common sense when you think about it, so I felt there was hope for Penny, the first hope she had been given in a very long time. I explained all of this to Penny during that first healing session and for the first time I saw a glimmer of a smile on her face.

"Do you really think this might help me?"

"Yes Penny, I do. Now that I can see what the problem is with your head I'm feeling very hopeful that the healing energy is going to be able to help you in a very positive way. Perhaps the next time you come for a treatment you can tell me a little bit about yourself to help me understand how this has all come about."

"I will."

She left me after her first treatment feeling much more relaxed and with hope for the first time in years.

The following week I was looking forward to seeing Penny because I was hoping that I might find out what on earth had happened to have caused such a terrible shift in her aura. I'd never seen part of an aura disappear before, or run away. I wasn't quite sure which it had done.

Back Penny came but this time, when I opened our front door to greet her, I knew what to expect and, to my joy, Penny smiled when she saw me, albeit a wonky smile. I invited her in and asked her to sit down so that we could have a chat before I began her second treatment, in the hope she would tell me what started all of her problems.

Now the story I'm about to tell you was told to me over a period of about four weeks. It all came out very slowly in bits and pieces. So rather than me trying to break Penny's story down into the bits as they were told to me at each healing session I'm going to give it to you in one helping, so here goes.

"In my early thirties, Isabella, I went to live and work in London. I was desperate to get away from home because my parents were so controlling with me and had been all my life. I'm an only child. Mum was thirty-seven when she had me. My mother is eighty now and dad's a year older. They have always been old-fashioned but it was getting so that they were not allowing me to go out at night and if I did I had to be back in by nine o'clock otherwise I was in trouble and trouble meant they locked me in my bedroom! I was a prisoner in our home. I was thirty-two years old and being told to be in bed by ten o'clock. So I decided to get as far away from them as possible. I had managed to keep in touch with a few of my old school friends who lived and worked in London. I kept in touch by telephone although that was difficult because mum didn't like me talking to them and she would listen in on my conversations whenever she could. Anyway, I managed to pack a bag and get on a bus to London. I stayed with one of my girl friends until I got myself a room in a house with a few other girls. I found a really good job in a hotel and I loved it. I was free for the first time in my life."

"What do you mean they locked you in your room?"

"They locked me in my bedroom overnight a couple of times and they locked me in during the day. My bedroom has an en-suite bathroom so I could go to the toilet but they once locked me in for twenty-four hours. It was just lucky I had a bottle of water to drink and I could refill it in my bathroom sink. But I was starving hungry by the time they opened my bedroom door."

"You're joking!"

"No, I'm not."

"London was great. I could go out whenever I wanted to and I made friends with a lot of my work colleagues from the hotel. That's where I met my husband."

"You were married?"

"Yes, Isabella, I was married. My husband was a chef in the hotel when we started going out together. We were married when I was thirty-four.

I did keep in touch with my mother and father. I rang them about every three to four weeks but when I told them I was getting married they got very angry over the telephone and told me in no uncertain terms not to. They didn't want me to get married so I didn't invite them to our wedding. About a year later an uncle of my husband's invited us to go and work for him in the South of France. He had a restaurant and was looking to employ another chef as he was expanding his business and he said he could also give me a job. So we packed up our flat, hired a van and moved all our belongings to France. It was lovely. We lived above the restaurant for the first few months until we found ourselves a house to rent within walking distance of the restaurant and we both started to learn the language. I was so happy. We also got ourselves a rescue dog so that when John (my husband) was working late I had company and I could take him for walks. The countryside around where we lived and worked was lovely. We had been there about two and a half years when the accident happened. John had bought himself a motorbike a few months earlier so that we could go and explore on our days off.

John was killed, Isabella.

He died when a truck knocked him off his bike about a mile from where we lived and when the police came to tell me what had happened, I fell apart."

"I'm so sorry."

"I was thirty-seven when this happened. I was in such a state I didn't know what to do or how to organise the funeral. My husband's uncle tried his best to help me but I was in such a bad way he said he had no choice. He rang my parents and told them what had happened. They immediately drove to France to take control of the situation. They took control of everything and I mean everything. I've got to be honest, Isabella, I'm not exactly sure what happened and in what order because my doctor at the time had me sedated. My parents apparently arranged the funeral but I didn't go because they didn't tell me when it was happening. I don't know who went. They apparently didn't go! They took complete control because they said I was in no fit state to do anything. They got rid of all of our possessions within days of arriving at our home and they got rid of our dog. Within a couple of weeks everything that John and I had owned was gone. I still wonder what happened to my dog. I loved her and I wish I knew where she was. Everything that my husband and I had owned was either thrown away or given away. I was brought back to England with only one suitcase full of clothes. It was as if my life in London, my marriage and my life in France had never happened."

"Dear Lord."

"I was brought back to England under sedation and they kept me sedated for weeks and then my parents and the family doctor managed to get me into our local mental hospital. My parents told me I was being sectioned because I wouldn't stop asking where John's ashes were and what happened to our dog. Because the more they wouldn't tell me, the more distressed I became. That's when I ended up in a mental institution and I was there for months and months. My parents did eventually tell me where and when John was cremated. They didn't know where his ashes were and they hadn't gone to John's funeral. I asked them if John's uncle had gone and had our friends from the restaurant gone? They said they had no idea as it wasn't any concern of theirs and I wasn't to ask them about it ever again, so I didn't. I gave up."

"Penny, I don't think I've ever heard such a sad tale. I can't begin to know how you must have felt at the time this was happening to you or how you are feeling now. I'm so sorry this happened to you." I didn't know what else to say, I was so upset for her.

"Penny, can you remember when your head and neck started to be affected?"

"Yes, it started going down when my parents arrived in France before the funeral. I remember that by the time we got back to England, about three weeks later, my head was right down where it is now. Mum took me to the doctors and she tried to get me to lift it up and then she actually tried to force it up herself, but I yelled out in pain so she stopped."

"If I said to you that I have a very strong feeling that you were desperately trying to hideaway at the time, hide yourself away from everything that was going on around you and your parents, does that make sense to you?"

"Yes, it does."

"Well, that's what I think has happened. By putting your head down it's as if you were turning away from the world around you so that you couldn't see what was going on. I think it's now time for you, Penny, to lift your head up again and find yourself. It's time for you to heal and move forward. What do you think? Would you like to do that?"

"Yes, I would."

"Then that's going to be our mission over the next few weeks."

And that's exactly what Penny and I did.

With the help of the healing energy Penny started to put her life back together and, as each week went by, she became stronger and stronger and her neck became straighter and straighter until eventually her head and neck looked normal again. It was truly amazing to see the transformation.

But there was a problem.

As Penny began to get better the problems at home got worse for her again. It was obvious to me that as Penny became stronger her parents started to lose control and they obviously didn't like that. They had brought their little girl back home from France, but their little girl was becoming a woman again and she had started to stand up to them. It wasn't long before Penny began to look for somewhere else to live, much to the dismay of her parents. They even tried to have her sectioned at some point while I was seeing her (desperately trying to control her, which would have been funny if it hadn't been so mean and horrid of them). Needless to say they didn't have a leg to stand on. Penny was getting better in every way and she was now well able to speak very sensibly for herself.

Her parents apparently had stopped giving her the money for her treatments about six weeks into our sessions because they had wanted her to stop seeing me. They had not liked the fact Penny was getting better. (They must have thought that I would not be able to help her when they sent her to me in the first place). What they didn't know was that Penny actually had some money of her own in a bank account that they knew nothing about. It had been a savings account that she and her husband had had. Penny didn't tell me about the money situation until her last healing session with me. She said she hadn't wanted me to worry (bless her) so Penny had paid for her final few treatments herself and she was very pleased that she had.

Penny, of course, had still been visiting our doctor as her parents were insisting that she keep an eye on her, even though it was obvious to everyone concerned that something good was happening for Penny. And, bless Penny, she told our doctor exactly why she was getting better. She told her that she was coming to see me and that the healing energy was not only helping her get better emotionally it was also healing her neck and head. Apparently our doctor was lost for words. The last time Penny saw her before I moved away she apparently had had the decency to tell Penny that she had been amazed at how well Penny looked as she walked into her surgery, because two years earlier she had remembered telling Penny that her neck and head would never heal. But there was Penny standing in her surgery with her head held high, looking great.

Completely healed.

The last and final time I was to see Penny was actually quite tearful for both of us. She was healed and there was no need for me to see her again. We hugged and as she walked away down our drive, I've got to be honest, I cried. Cried for joy for her and a tinge of sadness for me because I knew I would never see her again and I haven't. But that's okay because my job was done.

The next time I had cause to see our doctor she spent the whole time I was with her looking at me sideways. You know what I mean. She really wasn't sure what to say to me so she didn't say anything. But often actions speak louder than words and her responses or actions towards me that day spoke volumes. If my memory is correct I only saw our doctor that once more before we moved out of the area and I'm really glad I didn't have anything more to do with her because to me she was most definitely in the wrong job.

Penny, perhaps one day you will find this story and read it and remember.

But in the meantime I am sending my love to a very remarkable, very brave lady.

CHAPTER NINETEEN

"It's amazing how easy the truth is to accept, no matter how strange."
K.C. Ranadll

I had a lady who come to me with what I thought at the time to be a minor ailment (silly me and when will I learn?). That was until she explained to me how she could hardly bear to put one foot down in front of the other because of the pain it caused her.

Why? Because she had a host of verruca's on both of her feet! Now I realise that this is not an earth-shattering problem but actually it is was very debilitating for this lady as it would be for anyone.

She explained to me that she had had them for a long time and she was sure she had picked them up from the swimming baths while she had been staying with friends a few years earlier. She then went on to explain to me that over the past few years she had used various creams to try and get rid of them and her doctor had tried to burn them off for her on more than one occasion, and also freeze them off. But everything that had been tried had failed and that was why she had come to see me. Was there anything I could do to help her?

Let's face it this was not the sort of thing I was used to helping. This was going to be the first, and so far the only, time I was ever asked to help with verruca's.

But here's the strange and interesting thing.

When I started to work down and around this lady's aura I found it stopped just below both of her knees, there was no aura around each of her feet. Her body didn't know her feet existed. Her aura and subsequently her body didn't know they existed so it was no wonder her feet wouldn't heal because as far as her aura and body were concerned they weren't there.

Only this lady's aura hadn't disappeared from around her head, it had gone from the bottom half of this lady's legs completely. How very strange.

Obviously her verruca's were not caused because of an accident of any kind or mixed-up emotions. They were caused because her immune system was a bit low at the time. She told me she could remember being very tired during that particular short holiday. It was just after she finished university and that was some fifteen years ago now. This, she felt, had left her immune system in a weakened state and susceptible to a virus, and the virus she happened to pick up was the wart virus. She had had the verruca's ever since.

Actually the thought of being in pain every time you put your foot down is no joke. Now we knew the reason she had picked up the virus, but why on earth had her aura run away?

I explained to her that her feet would never heal until her aura had been put back around them and, of course, this must have sounded a bit strange to her and even stranger to try and grasp and understand. It would sound strange to anyone who doesn't understand about the human aura, or energy field.

I did ask her at the time if there was anything she felt she had wanted to run away from about twelve years earlier, but she couldn't remember. The reason I asked was because it was as if the bottom part of her legs had run away, as if there may have been something in her life that she had wanted to run away from but, if there was, it was lost to her now.

We never did find out.

It only took about four sessions to put her aura back around her properly and then all of her conventional ointments began to work. It did take a few months for her verruca's to completely heal, but heal they did.

Many years have now passed since that lady's feet were healed but she still comes to see me occasionally when she needs an extra boost or she is feeling a bit down. She comes because she knows that the healing energy will leave her feeling very relaxed, completely chilled and, within hours of her treatment, raring to go again. And you will be pleased to know her verruca's have never come back, thank goodness.

I've lost count over the past twenty-odd years of the number of times I have opened our front door to be met with the words, "I'm ready for my fix."

And I keep saying, "One day you'll get me arrested," and we all have a good laugh. The healing energy does fix people in the most wonderful way and I'm so grateful.

Now what should we have next? One more healing story and then I think we will have a change of scenery. My next story is about a mother and daughter and as I'm sitting writing this I can still picture them both very clearly as they sat on the settee in our lounge about twenty-three years ago now.

I will call the mother Emma and her fourteen-year-old daughter Lilly.

It's almost as if this next story just happened yesterday because the picture I have of them both sitting in my lounge is so clear. And the reason for this is because this was one of the very few times over the past twenty-five years that I have met a woman who understood why a 'dis-ease' (I know this is the wrong spelling but I'm trying to make the point of being 'out of ease' with yourself) had occurred in her daughter when everyone around her told her she was wrong, without me having to try to explain it to her. She just knew.

Emma brought Lilly to see me because she was suffering very badly from asthma and had been for three years. Emma told me it had been so bad that she had had to dial 999 on numerous occasions over the past three years to have Lilly rushed into hospital to relieve her symptoms, which was very frightening for all the family and she was getting desperate to try and find a way to help her daughter. She also explained to me that Lilly was getting upset because of all the schooling she was missing. She was now trying to study for her GCSE's in two years time and she was falling behind because of her illness.

"Can you help, Isabella?"

"I honestly don't know but I do know the healing energy will do Lilly no harm and it might just help."

Emma then turned to Lilly and asked if she would like to give the healing a try and Lilly said, "Yes please, Mum."

"Then yes, Isabella, we will give it a go."

My response was instant.

I didn't stop to say "Yes" or "Good", I just opened my mouth and blurted out, "What happened to Lilly about four years ago, please?"

And that's when Emma got very excited and almost screamed at me, her voice became so loud.

"I knew it, I just knew, I knew I was right but the doctors wouldn't listen to me."

"You knew what, Emma?"

"I knew that Lilly's accident four years ago had sparked her asthma but no one would listen to me. Every time I mentioned this to all of the doctors treating Lilly they told me I was wrong, but I knew I was right, I just knew. It was the accident that started Lilly's asthma wasn't it?"

And I said, "Yes."

Without me knowing the reason why, I think I just heard the words 'accident' and I responded.

"I knew it."

And even now, after twenty-three years, I can still see Emma sitting on the edge of my settee, shouting at me in a very excited state as she said, "I was right."

"Yes Emma, you were."

This is how Emma told it to me:

Apparently when Lilly was ten years old she had fallen off her bicycle and broken her ankle. Now that in itself could have been the trigger, because it would have created a shock wave in Lilly's aura. She had been taken straight to casualty after the accident happened where her ankle was X-rayed and then it was plastered but, apparently, after three days Lilly was still complaining of being in pain. So Emma took her back to the hospital. They X-rayed her ankle again and found that it had been set wrongly. Lilly was then admitted into hospital so she could be operated on. They had to re-break her ankle and then reset it all over again. The trauma of having to stay in hospital overnight and everything else that followed had sent Lilly and her aura into shock and, within months of this happening, she developed a very serious case of asthma.

 I never got the chance to explain to them both how an accident or a fright can trigger an imbalance in the aura and if left can then trigger a dis-ease to develop (cause and effect) Emma had figured that out all by herself. She may not have understood exactly how or why her daughter's broken ankle caused the asthma to develop, she had just instinctively known that it had. But she did understand that for every cause there would be an effect and, of course, she was right.

 As I said at the beginning of this story, this was the first time a new patient (albeit the mother of the patient) had understood the implications of a trauma and the effect it could have on the human body and that made my job ten times easier.

 Without hesitating and without me having to explain, I was able to say to her, "I'm not going to try to heal Lilly's asthma, Emma, I'm going to concentrate on mending and rebalancing Lilly's aura by taking the huge shock wave out of it. And then I'm going to heal metaphysically speaking her broken ankle because that's where her problem came from in the first place. And, as strange as that might sound to you, that's exactly what I and the healing energy did. We healed the break and we took the shock wave out of her aura.

 Within a matter of a few weeks Lilly was feeling so much better and mum hadn't had to ring for an ambulance since Lilly's healing sessions began.

 After a few weeks Lilly's asthma was almost completely gone and the very few minor bouts of shortness of breath she experienced on an odd occasion were of no consequence to her compared to the horrendous bouts she had suffered a few weeks earlier. Emma decided to stop bringing Lilly to see me at this point because she was a bit tight for money. But also because she felt there was a good enough improvement in her daughter's condition and Lilly did speak up at this point and say to me that she was feeling great. So, on that note, we all said our goodbyes.

I did get a message passed onto me from them both about three years later. The message was sending me love and to let me know that Lilly had passed twelve GCSE's and she passed ten of them with 'A stars'.

Then about two years after that another message from them to say she had achieved four A levels, three A's and one B. This was a very clever young lady. She was going to be going to her chosen university, but for the life of me I can't remember what she was going to study.

Well done young lady.

CHAPTER TWENTY

From ghoulies and ghosties and long-legged beasties and things that go bump in the night, Good Lord deliver us!
Scottish saying

I did promise you all at the beginning of this book that I would tell you lots of different stories, from angel encounters to ghost stories and just about everything in between, so let's have a little break from the healing stories and have a good ghost story instead.

I think you might like this one.

It was a beautiful summer's evening and the sun was still shining when my husband and I set off in our car with the CD player playing my favourite songs and the song that sticks out most in my mind from that evening was Randy Travis singing 'Forever and Ever Amen'. I love that song and I think I must have pressed the replay button at least six times during our journey (probably driving my husband nuts, but he didn't grumble).

We were heading out into the countryside to meet our friends (who I will call Steve and Cath) for a drink and a bar meal. Our destination was over an hour's drive from our home, a lovely old public house steeped in history. Over the previous four or five hundred years it had been a coaching inn set on a road that ran the length of the country from the south to the Scottish borders and I'm sure many a highwayman would have been fed and watered at this inn along with his horse. Then for a hundred years or more it had been a summer residence for an aristocratic family before it became an inn again for the second time. So this very old building had had quite a varied, interesting, chequered past.

Even me at just over five feet felt as if I should duck my head to get through the front door, it was so low. I just made it unscathed without ducking. So you can imagine that there were a lot of men who got caught out and ended up with lumps, bumps and bruises because they didn't duck low enough as they entered the building. Not only was it now a pub but they also provided bar meals and they had acquired a very good reputation. They also had six letting bedrooms and a separate lounge and restaurant on the first floor just for their residents. They served food to non-residents downstairs in the lounge/dining room next to the bar.

I loved this old building because it was so quirky, partly due to its architecture and also because of its age. It had very thick stone walls and most had been left without plaster, with lots of nooks and crannies, just as they would have been hundreds of years earlier.

Now for some reason on this particular summer's evening the pub was very quiet. We found ourselves in the downstairs lounge/dining room all on our own. Steve and David (the boys) got us our drinks from the bar and they also brought Cath and me the menu so that we could choose our food quickly. The boys then went back into the bar to order the food for us all and then they came back into the lounge to join me and Cath, and that's when Cath told us all the local legend of the Grey Lady who was supposed to haunt the pub and apparently a castle about a hundred and fifty miles away. I listened with interest as she explained. The legend said the Grey Lady only haunted the rooms upstairs. She had been seen in the residents' lounge and also in the residents' restaurant upstairs and in one or two of the guest bedrooms, but she had never been seen downstairs. Of course, I found the story fascinating so when the waiter came into the lounge with our food, just after Cath had finished telling her story, I asked him if Cath and I could have permission to go upstairs to the residents' lounge to see if I could pick up on the ghost. And after I had finished speaking Cath piped up, "She's a medium so if the Grey Lady is here tonight she will see her."

I'm sure the fact the pub was quiet that evening helped us enormously because the waiter didn't hesitate, "Yes you can. There are only four people staying with us at the moment so I think you will find the lounge empty. Let me know if you see anything." And that was said with a smile on his face. He turned and left us to our food.

As we were sitting eating and chatting away to each other, as you do when you have loads to catch up with, I had unconsciously been twirling one of my earrings around with my fingers and I hadn't realised that the back had come off one of them. We had finished eating when Steve said to me, "Where's your earring, Isabella? You look daft with just one hoop in your ear. Where's your parrot?"

When I looked down I found my earring resting on my lap but the back to keep it in place was missing. And that's when the hunt began. My earrings were large silver hoops and the backs weren't small but, try as we might, none of us could find it. I didn't want to spoil our night all because I had lost it. I knew I would be able to buy some spare backs to replace it so I suggested we give up the hunt and sit back down and relax and enjoy our evening.

I could see that Cath was edging to go up the stairs to the residents' lounge to see if we could see the Grey Lady and, as neither of the boys were interested, up both Cath and I went. I remember the stairs as being very wide and steep with no carpet on. And I can also clearly remember thinking to myself that the bare stone was not at all inviting or cosy. The stairs led straight to a doorway that was open, leading us into the residents' lounge that was quite a sizable room. There were three doors in the room, the door we came into the room from at the top of the stairs, that apparently was always left open all the time, and the two doors on the right-hand wall.

Now the wall straight in front of us had two huge paintings on. One was of a very fine lady dressed in a dark green crinoline dress, you know the sort, the fairy on the top of the Christmas tree type of dress, and the second portrait was of a very handsome gentleman in his riding gear and underneath the two portraits was a very large old-fashioned sideboard. There were three large sofas arranged around the room, all of them facing the fireplace which was on the same wall as the door through which we had come into the room, and actually the room itself was quite homely.

Cath and I were standing just past the back of one of the settees, looking around the room, when all of a sudden the energy in the room changed and to my amazement I watched as the lady from the picture 'swished' her way into the room. I don't know what other word to use because she made a swishing noise as the huge skirt on her dress passed by the sideboard and almost knocked me off my feet. I could feel the air as it swirled past me, caused by her skirt. I was standing about four feet away from her but the skirt on her dress must have stood out at least three feet. There was a positive wind in the room as she turned and turned again in what seemed like an agitated state. The Grey Lady had made her grand entrance into the room and then she had walked straight towards me, stopping about four feet away with her dress not more than a foot away. Now she wasn't dressed in grey. Her crinoline dress was the most beautiful rich shade of deep-sea green and made of satin. How do I know? Because her dress was almost touching my legs, she was so close to me. I could have put my hand out and touched the skirt of her dress with ease. She was wearing the same dress as the one she had on in her portrait, only it looked so much nicer in 'real life'.

I turned to Cath at this point who was standing looking like a scared rabbit. Her eyes looked very large and very round and she had a glazed look on her face. I knew she couldn't see what I was looking at but, by the look on her face, I knew she had felt the shift in the energy as soon as the Lady had entered the room and the hairs on her arms were standing to attention, as without a word she lifted her sleeves to show me. Then she said, "She's here isn't she?"

"Yes, she's here as large as life."

"My head's gone all woozy Isabella and it's not the drink. What does she look like?"

But at this point our lady was standing staring at me, looking very irate to say the least because I wasn't talking to her, I was listening to Cath.

To this day I don't know what made me say this, but I turned to face the Grey Lady and I came out with, "Please excuse the intrusion into your privacy."

"Hmm."

"But can you please help me? I've lost the back off my earring and, try as we might, none of us can find it. Can you please tell me where it is?"

And in a very grumpy but very clear voice she answered me and said, "It's three rows of chairs back from where you are sitting, behind the fourth chair to the left. You will find it on the floor at the back of the back right leg."

"Thank you," said I.

"Hmm," said she.

And with that she swished herself around twice, took four or five steps forward and disappeared through the wall.

Talk about precise directions!

Now I forgot to mention to you that she didn't come into the room through the door; she came into the room through the wall to the right of the door (as I was looking at it). That was the door in the top corner of the lounge coming from the corridor that led to the bedrooms and she left the very same way, through the wall. It was as if the door we were looking at wasn't there so she used the wall instead, the wall to the right of the door.

As soon as she disappeared Cath said, "She's gone, hasn't she?"

"Yes, she's just walked through the wall."

"The wall?"

"Yes, the wall."

"Why?"

"Don't ask me. I've no idea."

And then I relayed to Cath exactly what she had said to me so that I didn't forget my instructions. I had no doubt in my mind that her directions would prove to be absolutely spot on and lead me to the back off my earring.

Cath and I stood in the room for a few more minutes, looking at each other like a pair of idiots, neither of us quite sure what had just happened.

"I might not have been able to see her, Isabella, but by

heck I could feel her presence it was so strong, and she felt cross."

"You're right, she was."

We both went back down the stairs to join the boys who were sitting having their drinks and as Cath and I joined them, without giving them a word of explanation, I said to them both.

"Watch this."

I followed the instruction our ghost had given me to the letter. I actually counted out loud as I walked to the third row of chairs back from where I had been sitting and then I counted (out loud again) four chairs along and then I bent down beside the back right leg of the chair, and there just where she had told me to look on the floor, just as she had said it would be, was the back off my earring.

I let out a yelp of delight. I picked it up and held it aloft for the boys to see and they both said almost simultaneously, "Woah, how the hell did you do that?" And a few more choice swear words to boot. I just stood there saying, "Thank you, thank you, thank you," over and over.

How it travelled so far across the room was beyond all of us, including me at the time, and it still is.

Needless to say the boys were speechless.

Between Cath and I we told them what had happened and how the Grey Lady had given me the exact instructions as to where the back off my earring was so that was how I was able to go straight to it. And at this point in our storytelling the barman came into the room to collect some glasses, so we told him what had just happened.

"I believe you. I didn't tell you but quite a few people who have seen her have reportedly told staff that she appears to be very grumpy."

I explained to him that I felt she couldn't understand why there were strangers in her home and our presence irritated her. That was the impression she had given me anyway.

I have met quite a few ghosts over the years and it's

amazing how many of them didn't realise that they were dead.

We all had a great night. Good food, good company and a very interesting encounter and Randy Travis singing 'Forever and Ever Amen' all the way there and all the way back home again.

Now you might think that that's the end of the story but it's not.

About a month later I had gone to see my mum to take her out for the afternoon. She couldn't walk very far but she loved to go for a ride in the car out into the countryside. Now mum lived in a little village in the countryside herself, about forty miles away from our home, and on this particular day when I went to collect her I asked her where she would like me to take her and lo and behold she asked me to take her for afternoon tea to the very same country pub where we had met the Grey Lady a few weeks earlier.

Now the pub was a good thirty minutes drive away from mum's home but it was a beautiful sunny afternoon and I knew the drive would be lovely so off we went.

When we arrived it was still lovely and warm and the air was very still and calm so Mum decided she would like to sit outside in the garden to have her tea and cakes rather than sitting indoors. So that's what we did. Afternoon tea in the warm summer's sunshine surrounded by beautiful flowers and the birds singing. What more could anyone want?

Mum loved it.

The gardens at the back of the old inn were lovely.

While mum and I were drinking our tea and eating our scones and cake I explained to her what had happened when David and I had met Cath and Steve a few weeks earlier when we had come to this very pub and, bless her, she was fascinated.

Just as mum and I were finishing our tea I noticed what I thought at the time to be a member of staff come out of one of the outbuildings at the bottom of the garden about fifty yards from where we were sitting and, as he walked nearer towards us, I called out to him, "Excuse me, I wonder if you could help me with something please?"

He stopped walking towards the inn and turned and walked towards where mum and I were sitting.

As he approached us I explained to him how my husband and I had been here the previous month with our friends and then I went on to explain to him what had happened and the reason I had stopped him was to ask if he might know why the ghost or the Grey Lady had walked through the wall instead of the door that evening.

And this is what he said to me.

"I realise that you are not aware but I am the owner of the pub. My wife and I bought it about ten years ago and it's our home as well as our business so I do know a little bit of the history."

I immediately apologised to him for bothering him but he said, "No, that's not a problem. I'm fascinated by the fact that you could see her and that you talked to her and even more fascinated by the fact she spoke to you. I don't know of anyone that she has spoken to and I find that very interesting, let alone the fact she was able to help you. That was amazing. The description of what you saw is intriguing."

By this time he had sat himself down on the spare chair at our table and he continued, "Firstly, you described her as walking through the wall. Well, from what we have been able to find out and from old drawings of the building that we have, we are quite sure that when she lived here in the 1600s the door to the room was not where it is now. For some reason the original door was blocked off. But it would have been exactly where you described that she came into the room through the wall. In other words, she came through the door that she knew to be there, not the door that we can see now, but obviously the door she has always known and has always used."

"Gosh!"

"Yes. You're not the first person to see her walk through the wall but you are the first person that I know of that she's spoken to."

"Have you any idea why she has never been seen

downstairs?"

"Yes, that's quite an easy question to answer. This was the summer residence for the family; they never came here in the winter. We have very harsh winters up here on the moors so for hundreds of years the people living here have only lived in the upstairs of their homes or buildings. They brought as many of their animals indoors (downstairs) out of the severe weather to keep them safe and also to stop them from being stolen. Border raids were rife at the time. I'm sure you can imagine the smell in the rooms downstairs would have been horrendous. Even though there were no animals indoors during the summer months when the family were in residence, the smell would have lingered. But, of course, there weren't any living quarters downstairs only the spaces for the animals. Downstairs for the animals, upstairs for people, so she would never have been downstairs when she was alive. So that's why she has never been seen in the rooms downstairs because they didn't exist when she was in residence."

"Thank you. It was very kind of you to take the time to explain it all to me."

And with that he got up out of his chair, tipped his hat at Mum and me as he said, "Good afternoon, ladies."

He then walked away heading towards the inn and Mum and I finished our afternoon tea.

Questions answered.

I'm feeling a bit sad after finishing writing this story down for quite a few different reasons. Mum's gone now and although I haven't lost touch with Cath and Steve we haven't seen each other for many years. Sad on both counts and also I've never been back to that pub since that day and it is a lovely place to go. The day Mum and I had afternoon tea in the beautiful summer's sunshine in the garden of the pub where the Grey Lady walks through the wall.

One of my lovely memories.

Dad had been gone about eight years when I took Mum out that afternoon. Bless her, she was on her own for many years before it was her time to leave the planet and go home and join him. I have already promised (in my first book) that I will tell the story of her passing sometime in the future, because it was so amazing, but not yet. I still have many more healing stories and adventures to share with you before I get to my mother's departure from earth.

But Dad, God bless him, sent Mum lots and I do mean lots of poems to make her smile and to let her know where he was and that he was never very far away from her. In actual fact, he sent us all lots of words of comfort to help us. He wasn't always helpful though!

It was about seven years after Dad passed over and Christmas was fast approaching. I can remember standing in our lounge at the bottom of my healing bed as I was with a patient and, for some reason, I turned and looked at our mantelpiece above the open fire, when I heard my father say to me, "Mum's going to buy you a clock to put on the mantelpiece for your Christmas present."

"Thanks a bunch, Dad. Now I know what I'm getting for Christmas and you've spoilt my surprise and you know how I love surprises!"

The next time I saw mum I hesitated because I knew she would be cross, but I did tell her what Dad had said to me and she said, "Oh, Isabella, Dad shouldn't have told you."

"Was he right, Mum?"

"Of course he was."

"Wait till I see your father. I'm going to kill him for telling you."

"You can't do that, Mum. He's already dead."

And with that we all burst out laughing.

"Ooh I'm cross with him."

"I know you are Mum, and so am I because that's my Christmas present surprise gone west. Dad better not do that again."

And bless him he never has.

CHAPTER TWENTY-ONE

"If dreams are like movies, then memories are films about ghosts."
Adam Duritz

I think you will like this next story because it's a mixture of a healing story and a story about Spirit people all rolled into one, but I'll just pause to explain my own views on ghosts before I move on.

It's amazing how just a few words can open up a huge topic for discussion.

Ghosts or Spirit people! Is there a difference? And if there is, what is it?

All I can do is be honest with you and tell you my own thoughts on the subject. If you want to know what other people think you will need to do your own research.

In my own mind, all of the Spirit people that I have ever met over the years that I would call a ghost have all been from a time to me that has long been forgotten. In other words, there is no one living here now on earth that can remember them as a living person, so there are no connections left here for them. And, for whatever reason, they have decided not to go into the Spirit world (or Heaven) but they have chosen to stay here on earth instead. Some people might say to you that they are earthbound spirits and I haven't a clue what that is supposed to mean. To me they have either chosen to stay here on earth or they haven't. They are not bound to anything. Choices. Remember we all have them even when we are a Spirit person. Now I also firmly believe that the choice is the person's and I use that word very loosely. A Spirit person might still be here on earth for any number of different reasons. They might choose to stay on earth because they feel they still have unfinished business. But they have yet to learn that once they are in their Spirit body they actually can't do very much to change anything. They might stay here because they feel very safe in familiar surroundings, for example their home.

Unfortunately, in some cases, they still think it is their home which can often cause minor problems for the living. Such as why is my home being haunted? Just because someone dies it doesn't suddenly change them. They are still the same person as they were before they stopped breathing in fresh air.

If my great-great-great grandfather appeared to me I wouldn't know who he was because the connection between us is too far apart for me to recognise him so I would call him a ghost. However, if my Grandfather appeared to me I would call him a Spirit person because I would know who he was; I can still remember him, so we are still connected.

Ghosts tend to haunt old buildings or places where an event has taken place, or the ghost is very strongly connected to, perhaps, even a place they loved.

We have a ghost in our home. Our next-door neighbour has a ghost in her house. I asked her the other month if she would like me to ask her ghost to leave (and I loved her answer). She said to me, "Oh no, I like her being with me. She keeps me company."

Now if I can explain to you that we both live in very old houses in an area where there has been a lot of historic events, then that might help you to understand why we have ghosts all around us. Let's take my ghost first. I first saw her sitting on a window-seat in our front lounge many years ago now. She was wearing a long deep-pink crinoline dress, complete with a large summer's hat covered in pink flowers. She was quite the picture. She was just sitting quietly looking out of the window, doing no harm. I think I saw her about four times over a period of about a year. This was the first year that we moved into our current home. She was obviously a visitor from a few hundred years ago and not connected to me in any way, but connected to the house that we had recently bought. She always smiled at me when I saw her, acknowledging my presence, but she never spoke to me and then she disappeared. After that first year I never saw her again. That to me was a ghost.

About four years after we moved in, our next-door

neighbour told me that she had a ghost living with her. I asked her if she would like me to send her away and her response made me laugh. She told me that she liked her company and she would miss her if she wasn't there. I don't think they ever spoke to each other but it was obvious they both knew of each other's presence and they both liked each other's silent company. And that again to me was a ghost. My neighbour had no idea who the lady was.

Now when any Spirit people come to call, as they do, I can both recognise them and place them. To me they are not ghosts, they are Spirit people. Really, when you think about it, they are actually both the same. They are all Spirit people; it's just that some of them have been walking around here on earth for many years when they should have gone home to the Spirit world. They seem to have got themselves a bit lost for whatever reason, whereas the majority of Spirit people know exactly who they are and they know that they are Spirit, not flesh and blood. I would love to use the word alive, because to me Spirit people are alive, but then it can get confusing. We know and recognise some of them and some of them we don't. I feel sorry for the Spirit people that seem to be lost, for the ones that don't seem to realise that they are dead and don't seem to understand why new people are living in what was their home.

I'm not sure what more I can say to you, ghosts or Spirits. If you know them, call them Spirit people; if you don't, then call them ghosts. At the end of the day, they are actually both the same.

Can you touch a ghost and can you touch a Spirit person? Again I can only give you my own views.

All, and I do mean all, of the Spirit people and ghosts that I have ever met have to me been almost touchable, almost tangible and almost whole and I would also say some more than others. Now what the heck do I mean by that?

Even when I have seen my mother and father they have looked airy or see through or not quite whole to me. If you asked me to describe what they are wearing I could quite easily do that, so I can see them. But I know if I were to try and touch them my hand would go straight through them because I am seeing them here on earth and they are in their Spirit bodies; they are not flesh and blood like us.

The few times that I have been allowed to travel to the Spirit world (Heaven) and please trust me on this, I could feel, I could touch, I could hold, I could cuddle. My father was as solid to me as you are and so were all the other people that I met. But I was in Heaven. I was in the place where my father lived. But, more importantly, I was in the same form as him. I was on the same level of energy as my father. In other words, I was in my Spirit body not my earthly body. I was in Heaven with my father, not my father here on earth with me. And that to me is why I could feel his hand in mine and I could touch him and hold him and cuddle him with ease. Trust me I never wanted to let him go.

That memory for me is very precious and it always will be.

You may have read or heard how some people have seen large groups of what they have termed ghosts. Sometimes the ghosts have been seen as groups of soldiers marching and they have been described as being dressed from both the First and Second World Wars. I honestly feel that when a host of ghosts are all seen together like that, I would describe them as apparitions or almost ghosts. I myself have seen a large number of Roman soldiers marching through a building, along a corridor and then they marched straight through a wall as if it wasn't there and out of my sight. At the time I felt as if I was watching a scene from an old movie and I have often wondered if perhaps what I saw at the time was a very strong memory from the past event that happened, playing itself over and over, just like a film (because other people had reported seeing exactly the same thing in the same place) and we all just happened to catch sight of one of the replays. In other words what I saw and what other people have seen are not actually ghosts or Spirit people at all. We are all seeing the imprint or memory left behind of an event that happened centuries ago.

I'm not sure if I have explained this very well, but for the times I have witnessed groups and happenings, and I have seen quite a few stories being played out, they have all been ghostly apparitions (almost Spirit people). And, interestingly, they were all completely unaware of me. They were not like the ghosts or Spirit people that I have talked to. They were completely unaware of anything going on around them, just like watching a film at the cinema, or on a computer screen. So I am going to put them in a different category or different bracket altogether from anything else that I have described to you to date. Perhaps this is what ghosts really are, just apparitions, memories from an event from long ago, and not Spirit people at all. Anyway that's my thoughts. You, of course, can make your own mind up and have your own thoughts.

Can they manipulate things? Actually, yes they can.

How many of you have watched the film 'Ghost'? I love that film and I was pleasantly surprised when I saw it for the first time because I felt the producers had done their homework really well. They had taken the time to research the subject before they went into production. Patrick Swayze in his role as the ghost learnt how to move objects and he learned how to manipulate the letters on a computer screen and, in actual fact, from my own experience that's exactly what they can do. Ghosts or our Spirit friends are very good at moving things, turning lights on and off and manipulating electric appliances. Your television can go off and on all by itself, and they can also turn your hoover off and on. Light bulbs are very easy for them and don't forget your car alarms. So if you have a loved one in the Spirit world and they should come to call, you will know they are around if your television should suddenly go very loud, or it decides to turn itself off, and don't forget your light bulbs flickering away and not because you need to change the bulb.

There is such a lot more I could talk to you about ghosts but I think I've said enough for now.

Now let's get back to my next story.

The young lady that I'm going to be telling you about

was only nineteen years old when she came to see me for some treatments and I say only because at the time in my ignorance I felt she was very young to be diagnosed with a disease that had such a strange sounding name, but I'm jumping ahead.

I will call this young lady Sandra.

When I answered the telephone to Sandra the first time she rang me she explained to me that she was having difficulty being able to speak clearly and could I make out what she was saying? I said, "Yes," to her and she continued by saying that she had got my phone number from an aunt who had suggested to her that I may be able to help her. And in her rather strange voice she said, "Can I make an appointment to see you please?"

"Yes, of course you can."

"Do I have to tell you over the telephone what's the matter with me?"

"No, not if you don't want to. It makes no difference to me."

"Then I'll tell you when I meet you."

And with that she made an appointment to come and see me the following week.

Her phone call left me intrigued and I spent the next few days wondering what on earth could be the matter that had affected her speech so badly.

When I answered the door to Sandra for her first appointment with me it was almost a case of déjà vu.

She was standing on our doorstep with a very lopsided face and I do mean very. The left hand side of her face and mouth had drooped quite badly which was why she was having difficulty being able to speak clearly. So now I knew why she had struggled on the phone to me the previous week.

It had only been a few weeks earlier when I had waved a very tearful goodbye to Penny for the last and final time and there I was standing in our entrance hall looking at Sandra for the very first time and I couldn't help but think about the very first time that I had set eyes on Penny.

They were two very different girls, with two very

different problems, but two very similar pictures.

I invited Sandra into the room I was working in and asked her to sit down so we could have a chat, as I always do with any new patient.

"What on earth has caused this to happen to you, Sandra?"

You know me. My mouth opened and out my words came.

"I've got Bell's Palsy."

"What on earth is that?"

After she had explained to me what the condition was I asked her if it was normal for someone of her age to be diagnosed with it.

"Apparently, yes. My doctor told me that anyone from about the age of ten can get it."

"Sandra, I would like to explain something to you and I would say this to anyone, no matter what the problem or condition was that they came to me with. To me it doesn't matter what name is given to a person's problem or illness either by the medical profession or by anyone else. Because no matter what name the problem has, to me it's simply an imbalance in the person's aura. So, no matter how complicated or strange or frightening or rare a person's problem sounds, to me it's simply an imbalance in the aura that will have a cause somewhere in the person's past, and that in turn will create the effect, the effect being the illness or disease the person has developed."

I was sitting watching Sandra as I was speaking to her and, as she was listening to me, her head had been nodding in agreement as I was talking.

"Yes, I believe that. I have always thought that there will be reasons for things happening to people. And I think I know what caused this with me. I tripped and fell a few months ago and I knocked my head and I think that's what caused it. I got such a fright. But I also got a very bad infection just a few days after the fall. When my face dropped I got such a shock. I had just got out of bed and I went into the bathroom to wash my face and clean my teeth and that's when I saw my face in the mirror. What a fright I got when I saw myself. I didn't know what was happening to me, my face looked so awful. Mum took me straight to the doctor's that same morning. He took one look at me and said, "You've got Bell's Palsy."

"Mum asked him to explain to us what Bell's Palsy was and he did. My mum was nearly as upset as me when the doctor told us it could last for weeks and even months. He explained to me that, given time, it would clear up but he didn't know how long it would take. I told him about my fall and my infection and he said my fall may have caused it but he felt it would have been the infection I had had. He explained to me that the infection had caused a nerve in my face to become inflamed and that's what had caused the Bell's Palsy. I still think it was the fall when I got such a fright and I hurt myself. I cried all the way home after it happened. I got such a shock."

Sandra's mouth was very lopsided and she had had great difficulty explaining all this to me but she was a very determined young lady. It had taken her quite a while to explain everything, but explain it she did.

I told her that I felt her fall would have caused a shock wave in her aura that could easily have been the trigger for her Bell's Palsy and the infection just after the fall could also have been caused by the shock she had received. They were both very good reasons for her aura to have become out of balance. She had become way out of balance with herself. She was out of ease with herself causing her to unbalance herself, in this case a temporary facial paralysis.

After she had finished telling me her story I asked her to sit on my stool to allow me to work around her head and then I asked her to lie down on my healing bed and that's when the fun began.

I'm never going to forget what happened next. It stands out in my mind from all the other stories I have told you to date, and all the stories I will tell you, because this is the only time in twenty-five years that so many other people have come into my healing space to join a patient. This had never happened before that day and it has not happened since, well not with so many people.

I was standing at the top of my healing bed with Sandra lying on her back with her head resting on a pillow. I had already worked quickly down her spine through her chakra centres. She had just turned over onto her back when her visitors entered my room. At least they came in through the door and not through the wall, albeit a closed door.

Obviously at first glance I didn't know who they were. But I watched in amazement as six Spirit people came through my lounge door one at a time and made their way to my healing bed. As I was watching them all walk towards me they came and stood around the bed beside Sandra, while I tried to work. I say tried because I was gobsmacked. I'd never seen anything like this before. I knew without being told that it was her family and I knew I had a grandmother and possibly her grandfather. Grandma had separated herself from the rest of the visitors and she had come around the bed and stood right beside my left shoulder. The gentleman I felt was her grandfather came and stood on my right-hand side and the rest of the family were all standing down the right-hand side of the bed next to him.

It was as if I was stuck. I couldn't move to my right or my left because there were Spirit people all around me. Now this was a new one on me, I was hemmed in.

Could I walk through them?

Should I walk through them?

I had never been faced with this situation before so what should I do? Obvious really when I thought about it for a few moments.

Just ask!

Grandma came to my rescue and very quickly explained to me that they were all very concerned about Sandra. She was their only granddaughter and they had come today to make sure I wasn't going to harm her in any way. They all wanted to make sure she was in safe hands. I dread to think what might have happened to me if they hadn't liked me. Woe betide anyone who tries to harm this lovely young lady!

I can still picture her grandfather as he stood on my right-hand side with his walking stick in one hand and his pipe in the other. He had used his stick to walk into the room with but he didn't use it to walk out of my room because he didn't actually need it.

When Spirit people first show themselves to me, or to anyone else for that matter, they usually show themselves as they were in this life. That way if I was to see a Spirit person you cared about I would describe them to you as you remember them, when in actual fact they all look very different to when you last saw them, in a fantastically good way.

If they were old and grey when they passed over they are now young and vibrant. If they were disabled they're not now; they are fit and healthy and whole. If they had a leg or arm or hand missing or they were blind or deaf, again they're not now; they are all so wonderfully well. All bits back where they should be and everything working in tip-top condition. My mother had a head of grey hair when she passed over. The next time I saw her she had a head of almost black curls, just as she had when she was in her thirties and I didn't recognise her at first. I mentioned in my first book about my journey to Heaven when I met my father, I described him as 'looking amazing, so well and healthy, just as he had in his prime of his life when I was young'. That's actually how they all really look now. But then if I were to describe them looking like that you wouldn't recognise them, so I see them as you remember them.

So the reason Sandra's grandfather had shown himself to me with his walking stick was so that I could relay that information to Sandra and she could easily recognise who had come to see her and relay the information to her mother.

I wasn't too sure how Sandra would react if I told her she had visitors so I asked her grandmother if it would be okay to tell Sandra that they were all here and she said, "Oh yes. Sandra won't mind, love."

So I did. I said to her, "Sandra, I think you might like to

know that you have some visitors from the Spirit world here for you today."

"Oh, is Gran here?"

"Yes she is."

"And is Grandad here?"

"Yes."

"Wait till I tell my mum. Is there anyone else?"

"Hmm, yes, like crikey Moses, there's six of them!"

"Can you describe them all to me please?"

So I did, each and every one of them.

It seemed that not only did we have her grandparents with us, we also had an uncle who was her grandfather's brother, and a couple of aunts and a cousin of her mother's.

I was able to describe them all to her and she was delighted.

I must admit I was a bit surprised. It was unusual for a young girl to be so accepting of visitors from the Spirit world.

"I can't wait to tell Mum. She will be so happy. She misses grandma so much."

"What I can't quite work out, Sandra, is that your grandmother is such a good communicator and you are so accepting of them all being here."

"Oh, that's easy. Grandma was a medium all her life."

And at that I apologised to her grandmother for my ignorance. She was still standing to the left of me, grinning like a Cheshire cat.

"Now I understand."

Her grandmother was a fantastic communicator because she had been able to see and hear clearly from the Spirit world while she had lived here on earth and now that she was in the Spirit world herself she could communicate equally well back from the other side.

Her grandfather was a lovely, chatty old man. He was white-haired with a lovely twinkle in his eye. He told me all about his love of gardening and how he had grown sweet peas, both to pick and to show, and he said he also kept and flew pigeons. He apparently had won prizes for both his sweet peas and his birds and, of course, I was able to relay all of this to Sandra, who was then going to be able to tell her mother all about her afternoon, the afternoon for her that turned into far more than just a treatment.

Before they all left, Grandma told me they were quite happy for Sandra to come to me for healing because they knew I was going to be able to help her heal far quicker than if she had been left with no treatments. They all now knew she would be safe with me. That was nice for me. Again, I was able to tell Sandra what had been said.

What a story she had to tell her mother when she got home that afternoon.

I wasn't expecting the phone call that I received the following day when Sandra rang me. She told me that her mother had sat and cried nearly all the previous night after she had heard the story of what had happened and Sandra was ringing me with a message from her mother. Her mum wanted to thank me for the wonderful things her daughter had been able to tell her. She apparently had been waiting to hear from her parents for a long time and the messages that Sandra was able to pass onto her had meant the world. They had been an answer to her prayers and she would always be grateful.

It's always nice when someone says thank you. I always get a warm feeling inside when I realise that what I have managed to see and pass on has been accepted with so much love and gratitude. But as I said to Sandra, if it hadn't been for her own spirit family this could never have happened.

Sandra came for about eight treatments with us, by which time her face was completely back to normal.

Grandma and the family never came back to visit, but there was no need for them to. Every member of Sandra's family had got exactly what they wanted or had needed from that one very special visit.

And, as always, I am sending love and blessings to everyone involved in this story and I do mean everyone.

CHAPTER TWENTY-TWO

"Beautiful things can happen in your life when you distance yourself from all things negative."
Source Unknown

I always like to think when someone asks for help I can respond, but this particular week was turning into the twilight zone with no help from me.

Firstly I got a phone call from a stranger asking me to please chase the ghosts out of her house and the second call came from a friend of mine asking me to clear the negative energy or ghost (she wasn't sure which) out of her house before her husband had a nervous breakdown.

Two homes in distress and they were both asking me to help them.

I have been asked to do some strange things over the years but the next two things were probably some of the strangest.

I've always said to my friends and patients when they have asked me if I would ever work from somewhere other than my home, that I wouldn't. I will never work outside of my own home for a very good reason. I don't want to work in someone else's house or from rented premises because I would never know what the energy might be like in the room I would be working in. I have talked about negative energy as being evil (chapter five). Negativity is evil. And because of this someone else's house or rented premises could prove to be a veritable danger zone for negative energy for a hundred and one different everyday reasons: a bad-tempered person in the property who leaves behind their negative energy; an argument having just occurred in the property; a break-up of a relationship; upset or angry people and the list goes on. When anyone opens themselves up to using the Universal energy (including me) it's very important that we are in a positive, safe, loving environment with no negative energy anywhere near us.

And this next story illustrates my point really well.

Just a quick note, this was 1992.

Susan's first contact with me was a telephone call and it went something like this. She asked me if I would please come to her flat and clear away the ghosts that she felt were living in the flat with her. And then she asked me if I had done this sort of thing before and me telling her no, but I had to start somewhere.

When I arrived on Susan's doorstep I rang the bell to her upstairs flat, feeling quite relaxed, all ready to help her.

But as soon as I began to climb the stairs I could feel the oppressive atmosphere. In fairness to her she had the flat beautifully decorated, lovely and light with airy colours but, quite frankly, it could have been painted black the energy felt so heavy.

"Can you feel them?"

"No, I can't feel them. But I can feel it."

"What do you mean?"

"I can't feel or see any ghosts but I can feel the very oppressive negativity. It's so heavy it could almost pin me to a chair."

"Well, that's a ghost isn't it?"

"No, it's not. It's negative energy, not a negative entity and there's a huge difference."

"Is there?"

"Yes there is. If your home had a ghost its presence would be felt wherever it was. In other words, whichever room the ghost was in you would be able to feel a shift in the energy as it came and went. But it could only be in one room at a time. What you have here in your flat is every room filled with the same negative energy. The negativity is oozing out of the walls it's so strong. I think I'd better try and find out for you where this is all coming from."

"So there isn't a ghost?"

"No, but in a way this is more distressing for you. This negativity could make you ill if you were in it for too long. It could have a very detrimental effect on your health and it needs to be cleared. Nine times out of ten a ghost will do you no harm, but negative energy as strong as this will."

Just in case one or two of you are worried, a ghost doing harm is so very rare it doesn't warrant any comment at this time, rare beyond words.

I asked this lady to take me into every room in her flat. I needed to go through each and every room with a fine toothcomb to try and see if I could find where all the negativity was coming from.

We started in her bedroom and there, on two of the walls, were some very large masks, the sort of mask you would find in a shop selling African artefacts. I think you will know the sort I mean. The faces looked evil, never mind the negativity that I could feel coming from each of them.

"Where did you get those from?" as I pointed to the masks on her bedroom wall.

"I was travelling a few years ago and picked them up in a shop just outside Johannesburg. I felt sorry for the shop owner. It was a very poor area and I liked them because they were so different. Is there anything wrong with them?"

"I should coco," came to mind.

"Yes, they are exuding negativity. For all you know they could have been used in black magic ceremonies before you bought them."

"I never thought of that."

"I'm not saying they were, but I wouldn't have them in my home, let alone my bedroom. If it was me they would be out without a thought, but it's up to you what you want to do with them."

I had found my starting point.

"Look, I can point out all the things I can see in your flat that are attracting or emitting evil energy or are giving off negative energy (same thing to me) but it's up to you what you decide to do with the information I'll give you."

"Okay, that's fair enough."

And that's what we did.

Every room in her house, from the piles of Stephen King horror stories on the floor, next to her bed of all places, to the two Alistair Crawley hard-backed books on the coffee table in the lounge. There were two more African masks on the wall in the bathroom and on the bathroom floor were some very strange looking carvings resting up against the skirting boards of all places (again bought in the same shop as the masks) and more horror stories on a shelf in the kitchen next to her cookery books. By the time I had gone into every room I think she had got the idea. She had managed to fill her flat with what to me were items exuding very dark energy indeed.

If she wanted her flat to feel warm and cosy, and light and friendly instead of heavy and oppressive then she needed to get rid of her collections of what to me were very negative possessions.

The choice was now hers.

About two months later Susan rang me and told me that all the negativity had gone. She told me she felt wonderful and her flat felt completely different and with the money she received from selling all of her things she was able to put it towards a holiday. She also told me that when she got home now from work she looked forward to climbing the stairs into her flat, relaxing in a warm bath and snuggling up on her settee to read a book or watch the telly. (But no more Stephen King books.) No more being frightened to climb the stairs and open her front door like she had done before. Susan thanked me for helping her and I've never seen or heard from her again.

With a bit of luck she learnt her lesson the hard way and she will never have any negative possessions in any of her homes in the future, but of course that's her choice.

Now to my friend and her cry for help.

Alice and I had been friends for years. When she rang me on that particular summer's afternoon she was in quite a distressed state. Could I please call in and see her because she desperately needed someone to talk to. Now if you are anything like me, when a friend asks for your help you respond as quickly as you can.

"Oh gosh, Isabella, I don't know where to start. It's Terry. Something's wrong and he's not telling me what it is.

He's not in a good place and he seems very unhappy." (Terry was Alice's husband.)

I was very surprised because Alice and Terry had always seemed to have a really good relationship and he always appeared to be happy whenever I spoke to him. But as soon as Alice had said the problem was Terry my mind went racing away out of control and, I might add, on completely the wrong track as I very quickly found out. But I'm human and as soon as Alice said the problem was her husband I had visions of him having an affair. Sorry, Terry.

"He's so unhappy, Isabella, and I don't know what to do to help him."

"Gosh Alice, I'm sorry."

"I just felt that you might be able to help us."

"I'm not sure what you think I can do."

"I have often thought that we have a ghost in the house because I keep catching a glimpse of a shadow at the bottom of the staircase and I don't like the feeling in that part of the house. But the feeling of heaviness is not just at the bottom of the stairs. Our home feels full of negativity at the moment. I'm not sure if it's Terry causing the problem, or the problem is causing Terry's problem. I just feel, Isabella, that if the negativity or the ghost in the house could be cleared out, if it could be cleared away somehow, then things might improve for Terry and everyone else. What do you think?"

"Now I understand. Yes, I think you might be right. I don't think you have a ghost but I can feel the negative energy. But if I manage to shift the negative energy out of your house and fill your home with light I honestly don't know how this will affect all of you. I don't know if that will be enough to help Terry."

"Anything has to be better than this."

"Okay. When would you like me to try and clear it?"

"Now if you can."

I had to apologise to Alice because I couldn't stop to do it now because I knew it would take at least an hour and I needed to get back home to cook the meal for my family as teatime was fast approaching. So I arranged to go back the following afternoon just after lunch.

Back I went.

Alice and her family lived in a lovely three-storey terraced house.

"Where do you want to start, Isabella?"

"At the top of your house," so that's where we went. Alice and I climbed the three flights of stairs and we both went into the first of the three bedrooms on the top floor of their home.

The best or rather the only way I can describe what I did is to say in my mind's eye I took a large brush, a bit like a witch's broom and I swept the energy out of each and every room. I swept the ceilings, the walls and the floors and I gathered it all up into a pile and then I swept it down the stairs. And I did this in each and every room on each and every floor in their home including the shower room, the bathroom and the separate loo. There wasn't a room or cupboard I didn't sweep clean. I continued into each of the rooms on the ground floor and then I opened the front door and I swept the piles of negativity out of the open door and I also did this at the back of the house. I would describe the negative energy to you by saying it looked like a grey cloud or a thick grey mist, but there definitely wasn't a ghost in sight.

As each room was emptied of the negativity I stood in the room and pictured it being filled with beautiful, golden, loving energy. Once emptied, the space left in each room needed to be filled, but filled with something good, something loving and something positive. And that's what I did with Alice at my side throughout the whole event.

When I had finished Alice made us both a cup of tea and we sat and chatted for a little while about what I hoped I had done and what I had seen in my mind's eye and how we both felt it might affect the household over the coming weeks.

"Do you think it will make a difference, Isabella?"

"I haven't a clue, Alice, but your home does feel a lot lighter."

"Yes, I can feel it. I don't think I'll tell Terry what you've done this afternoon. I'm not sure what he would make of it but thank you for moving the negativity out of our house; it does feel much better. I can feel the difference and I didn't think I would be able to."

And that's how I left Alice that afternoon, much happier about the feeling in her home.

Now what happened next was almost unbelievable.

And this is what Alice told me after the event.

The day after I cleared the house Terry asked Alice to sit down with her so that he could have a talk to her. He explained how he had been feeling over the previous four years. He told her he was very unhappy at work and had been for years, not least because he was having financial problems. He told her he had loved his business when he first started years earlier but it was getting harder and harder for him to keep his head above water. But he had not wanted to tell her what was happening because he hadn't wanted to worry her. Terry, apparently, sat and told her he now hated every minute of trying to run his business. And I think it was at this point in their conversation when Alice said to him, "Enough is enough, Terry. You're far more important to me than a damn business or house or anything else."

From what Alice told me the two of them were up until the early hours of the morning, talking and working out what Terry could do and within twenty-four hours he had closed his business, locked the door on the premises he worked from for years and walked away. And they also put their house up for sale.

Wow!

All done within days of the house being cleared.

Boy had the energy been shifted.

The following week when I saw Alice, after she had explained to me what had happened, she said to me, "There should be a danger notice attached to you so people can be warned."

But she was only half jesting.

Within a very short space of time Alice would tell you it was the best thing that could have happened for all of them.

The outcome?

Their house sold very quickly.

Terry found a new job working for someone else so he had no more money worries or worries about employing people and all that entailed. They were able to buy a much cheaper house which they then renovated and, within a couple of years, they were able to sell it and buy the house of Alice's dreams and that's where they still are to this day.

I will leave this happy ending by sending them all my love.

CHAPTER TWENTY-THREE

"Death leaves a heartache no one can heal, love leaves a memory that no one can steal."
From an Irish headstone

Let's have another ghost/healing story with a bit of a difference and as I'm remembering this particular story it's making me smile.

Do any of you recognise this scenario? You work in the same area and you have heard of another person doing similar work to you.

I had heard about this lady on numerous occasions over the previous three years. She apparently had a very large private therapy practice based not more than five hundred yards from our home. I had heard her name mentioned by both friends and patients but I had never met or spoken to her on the telephone.

Then the day came when a new patient rang me to make an appointment from a recommendation from this very lady (who I had never met) who I will call Marjorie.

Marjorie was to send quite a number of people to see me over the next few years and she even asked me to help her with a problem she was having herself and she was also instrumental in guiding me to do quite a lot of 'light' work for Mother Earth. But that's got to be another book.

So which story do I choose to tell you first?

I started this by saying that this was a strange one but, to be honest with you, the next two stories that I'm going to tell you could both be classed as being strange. But you know what people say, truth is stranger than fiction and this and the next story will prove this beyond a shadow of doubt.

When a new patient rings me I don't expect them to tell me what they want me to do for them, but this lady did exactly that. She didn't hesitate for a moment or miss a beat with her demands. She started our conversation by telling me that Marjorie had given her my telephone number because she thought I would be able to help her. So my immediate thought was that this lady had rung me to make an appointment for a healing treatment from me. Wrong. She had rung me to make an appointment for me to give her a reading and try as I might to explain to her that I didn't do readings for people, and believe me I did try, she was having none of it.

"No, Marjorie says you can."

"But I don't do that."

"But you can dear, and you will."

It would seem that I had met my match with this lady. When I tried to explain to her for the umpteenth time that I didn't do readings for people, I only used my channelling for the healing energy, her response to me was, "Yes you can dear and you will do it for me!"

I gave up and arranged an appointment for her to come and see me the following week.

I spent the next few days picturing in my head what this lady might look like and all of the pictures, without exception, featured her as being a rather large lady. There was no doubt in my mind whatsoever that she was a force to be reckoned with and, I must be honest with you, the more I thought about the way she must look, the taller and wider she became in my mind's eye. So when our doorbell rang on the afternoon of her appointment I opened the door fully expecting to be met by a very large and powerful lady. My hand went straight to my mouth before I had a chance to say or do anything. Thank God I didn't make a sound. I managed to hide my smile behind my hand as I stood in amazement looking at the lady and gentleman that stood before me. All four feet nothing of each of them, although hubby was a good two inches taller than she was.

The most perfect miniature couple I have ever seen in my life! The picture that I had had in my head went out of the window in a flash. They were both immaculately and very expensively dressed from head to toe. Hubby held a small gold-topped walking stick in one hand and she a beautiful bright red leather handbag that matched her red leather shoes perfectly.

I just wanted to fall about laughing at myself for what had been my own thoughts over the past week, because I couldn't have been more wrong with the pictures I had conjured up in my head if I'd tried. For the whole of the previous week I had been picturing a very large, formidable woman who would be able to boss me around with ease. Well guess what, as small as she was, I knew she was still a force to be reckoned with. She may have only been four feet nothing tall but I was about to be putty in her hands.

I invited them both into our home and into our hall and then I asked her, "Would you like your husband to come with you into the room I work in?"

And without missing a beat she said, "Most certainly not! Have you a room you can put him in, because I don't want him with me?"

And me still desperately trying not to laugh.

"Yes, he can go into our television lounge and I'll put the TV on for him. I think the cricket is on at the moment." And that's what he did, much to his delight and relief by the look on his face.

Now this very special little lady deserves a name, so I will call her Hazel. Hazel came into my room, took her coat off and handed it to me as if I was the maid and then sat herself down without any prompting or permission from me. I took her coat and excused myself for a couple of minutes to allow me to go and hang it up in our cloakroom and I also quickly popped into our TV room to check on her husband who was sitting happily watching the cricket. He smiled at me as I popped my head around the door and he thanked me for allowing him to watch the family television. What a very polite, dapper little man.

I went back into our lounge thinking I was going to sit down on our settee so that I could have a comfortable seat while I had a chat with Hazel. But as I walked past the back of the chair she was sitting on I found myself walking around it and I sat myself down on the floor right next to her left foot, just as if I was a young child sitting at the foot of someone very special and I did this without a thought in my head. I then took hold of both of her tiny hands as she had them resting on her lap and I smiled up at her and said, "I told you, Hazel, when you rang me that I don't do readings. I've never done a reading for a stranger in my life and, truth be told, I honestly don't know how to do one. I don't even know how I would start."

And at that exact same moment, within a second of me finishing speaking, the words were no sooner out of my mouth, when I looked up at the closed lounge door behind the chair that Hazel was sitting on and I watched in amazement as two very smart ladies entered my room through the closed door. At least they didn't come in through the wall. They both walked in and stood directly behind the back of the chair Hazel was sitting on, no more than three feet away from where I was sitting on the floor.

"What is it, dear?" Hazel had been watching the expression on my face as the two Spirit people had entered my room.

"I don't believe this, Hazel. Talk about perfect timing. You might just get your reading after all. You're not going to believe what's just happened. I'm sitting looking at two ladies who have just come into the room and they are standing right behind your chair."

"Good. Can you describe them to me?"

"Yes I can. One lady is tall and quite slim and she is wearing a hat. I think the style is called a pillbox; it's sitting perched on the top of her head. She has dark, wavy, shoulder-length hair and the other lady is much shorter and she has much shorter fair hair. They are both very different to look at. Who are they?"

"It's my mother and my sister."

"You're joking."

"No I'm not. Mother was very small but quite plump and my sister was tall and slim, nothing like me. None of us looked alike. It was as if we were from different families, as if we weren't related."

"I'm having trouble believing you, Hazel. Sorry ladies,

but you all look so very different from each other. I would never have known in a million years that you were all related."

I had let go of Hazel's hands as I had been talking to her but I was still sitting on the floor at her feet when I realised that she was beginning to get upset.

"Please tell them I miss them."

I smiled up at her and said, "Hazel, they can hear you. You don't need me to tell them for you, you can tell them yourself."

So she did.

They had a short conversation. Hazel telling them that she missed them both and then me telling her what they said.

Now no one told me that her mother and sister had gone over at roughly the same time. I just had a feeling that they had, so I asked the question.

"What happened, Hazel? Was there an accident? Did something happen to them both at the same time because I have such a strong feeling that they passed over more or less together?"

This is what Hazel told me.

"Mother had been ill for quite a while prior to her passing and my sister and I had taken it in turns to try and be with her as much as we could, so we were both very tired when Mum eventually passed over. We both arranged her funeral. Mother had left quite clear instructions as to what she wanted. We had four funeral cars because there were so many family members that wanted to be included. I was in the first car with my husband and an aunt and uncle. Monica was in the second car with her husband and some more of our cousins and there were other relatives in the other two cars. The service in the church had gone well and we were all on our way to the crematorium when apparently the cars behind us stopped. Our driver had been watching in his rear view mirror and as soon as he realised what was happening he stopped our car and flashed the hearse to let the driver know there was a problem. Our procession was now at a standstill on the roadside but we had no idea why. Our driver backed our car to join the other cars and so did the driver of the hearse with Mother in it. At this point I had no idea what was going on. Our driver got out and went to the second car only to come running back to tell us that Monica had had a heart attack and they had radioed for an ambulance.

I must have looked stunned because Hazel continued, "Yes, my sister had a heart attack on the way to the crematorium for my mother's funeral and she died on the way to the hospital, but of course I didn't find that out until after Mother had been cremated. So in a way they did almost pass over together."

"Good grief."

"The ambulance didn't take long to get to us. They got my sister out of the funeral car and into the ambulance in record time but the undertaker told me that we needed to leave as we were now running late and we might miss our slot at the crematorium. So we left the ambulance men as they worked on Monica. Mother was due to be cremated and we couldn't wait to see how my sister was going to be so we had no choice, we had to almost race to get Mother to the crematorium on time. What a day we were having. How I didn't have a heart attack myself was a miracle. As soon as the service was over and, let's be honest it was all very stressful because none of us had any idea how Monica was at this point, we then all rushed to the hospital. But we were too late. Monica had died in the ambulance on the way to the hospital so no amount of hurrying would have helped me to get to her. We were all in shock and, to be honest, I can't really remember what we did afterwards. I think we all just went home, we were all in such a state."

"When did this happen, Hazel?"

"It happened six months ago and I've wanted to have a reading for the past four months. I wanted to make sure that Mother and my sister were together and that they were both alright."

It was no wonder that Hazel had wanted a reading. She desperately needed to know that both her mother and her sister were together in the Spirit world.

While Hazel had been telling me the story her mum and sister had been listening intently to what she had been saying and I could detect a definite smile on both of their faces. They weren't going to let Hazel leave my home without them both having their say.

And this is when the fun began.

"She loves shoes you know."

"Who does?"

"Mother does, but I must be honest, I rather liked them too."

And that was Monica having the first say.

"Hazel, your sister is telling me your mother loves shoes."

"Loves shoes, that's got to be the understatement of the year."

"Now come on girls, I wasn't that bad."

"Oh yes you were, Mum."

That was Monica again and then Hazel piped up, "Just two weeks ago I went to Mother's house to do some more clearing and I decided to take all the shoe boxes (well I got Alan to get the step ladder and he got them all down for me) from the top of her wardrobe and I got the ones from inside. I counted over eighty pairs and, Isabella, over half of them had never been worn. They were still in their shoe boxes with the price tags still on."

"We used to call Mother Imelda Marcus because she had so many shoe boxes with new shoes in. But it wasn't just Mother; Monica loved her shoes nearly as much."

I wished you could have been in my room with us that afternoon. The three of them were bantering backwards and forwards and they were giggling like schoolgirls. It made my heart sing just listening to them. Even though I was passing on the words that her sister and mother were saying, the conversation still flowed with ease somehow. They were all having such a good girly giggle I'm not sure who was having more fun, them or me.

Then I asked the question, "What are you going to do

with all of Mum's shoes then, Hazel?"

"I'm not sure. Most of them are new and the rest are in such good condition I was wondering if I could sell them to an organisation of some sort. I'm not sure what I'm going to do yet so they will all stay neatly piled up on Mother's bedroom floor until I can decide. But I'm sure someone would like to have them."

"Yes, I'm sure you're right."

"Tell her about the bed."

"What bed?"

And at this point Hazel looked very sheepish and her sister Monica was having difficulty talking to me because she was laughing so much.

"Go on, Hazel, tell Isabella about the bed. You know what I mean."

Now I don't know how this happened but I was given a picture in my mind of a bed being propped up with a pile of books at one of the legs, the sort of thing you would see in a comedy film, so I said to Hazel, "Why am I looking at a picture of a bed being propped up on one leg by a pile of books?"

"Because that's exactly what Alan did to our bed just after we moved house a few years ago. We had been having a problem with one of the bed legs but we hadn't had time to get it fixed so Alan, in his wisdom, propped our bed up with a pile of old books, but he didn't tell me at the time what he had done. I had spent the day doing housework and, without me realising, I must have caught the pile of (unseen by me) books with the hoover and somehow knocked the pile until they almost fell over. It wasn't until we went to bed that night and I gently perched myself onto the corner of the bed just as Alan sat down beside me, that the pile of books gave way and the bed collapsed at one end with us both on it, sending us flying, and we both ended up on the floor in fits of giggles. Mother was horrified when we told her what had happened, weren't you? But the rest of the family thought it was hilarious and they all had a good laugh. We went out and bought a new bed the very next day. And that's the story of the night our bed collapsed."

And it didn't stop there. Her mother and sister brought up two more funny stories for them all to remember and have a good giggle at. One of them was about a pair of curtains hanging at Hazel's kitchen window and another one was about a dog but I can't quite remember what those stories were about. All I can remember was that we were both crying with laughter after the stories were told, along with Hazel's mother and sister and I was still sitting on the floor at Hazel's feet.

I was exhausted by the time their conversations came to a tearful end. They said their goodbyes to each other and Monica and their mother just faded away before my eyes. We had had an afternoon of tears of laughter, lots of giggles and then tears of sorrow as they all said their goodbyes to each other and I have a tear in my eye now as I am writing this, just remembering. But after Hazel had blown her nose in a very ladylike manner, for the umpteenth time, she had a smile on her face.

"You see, dear, I told you you would be able to give me a reading and I was right, you did."

Hazel had wanted me to give her a reading when I was sure I wouldn't be able to.

She got her reading and so much more, and so did I.

I rescued Alan from in front of the television, retrieved their coats for them and I gave them both a parting hug. Just before they left Hazel said to me that she would never forget what had happened that afternoon. It would always be very special for her and, to be honest, it was rather special for me too.

I never saw or heard from Hazel again, but I guess what they all took away from that afternoon was enough, enough for it to last a lifetime for Hazel.

But as always (with a smile on my face for the memory), I would like to send both Hazel, her husband Alan, her mother and sister my love.

Now I may not have heard from Hazel again but I was to both see and hear from Marjorie for many years to come after my afternoon with Hazel and this next story was the beginning of what was to be a long and quite an unusual friendship.

The first time Marjorie rang me (just about four weeks after I had seen Hazel) was to ask me for my help and I was very surprised. I had always assumed that she was far more experienced than me in all things Spiritual. I think because I knew Marjorie was quite a few years older than me and she had been practising as a therapist for a lot longer than I had, I just assumed that she would have far more knowledge and experience but, as is often the case, I was wrong.

Marjorie explained to me over the telephone that she thought she was under psychic attack and she needed my help to stop it. I had to be honest with her and I told her that I had no experience whatsoever with anything remotely like that and I had no idea what should be done, and she said to me, "No dear, you will know exactly what to do when you come and see me."

It was as if she knew me far better than I knew myself or at least she seemed to think she knew my capabilities better than I did and I found her attitude towards me rather disconcerting at the time, to say the least.

As I'm sitting typing this onto my computer screen I can see myself on that day as if it was yesterday, as I left our house and I walked along the road to her place of work for the very first time. It wasn't her home I was going to. That was some twenty miles away from where she worked. Many years earlier she had bought a lovely downstairs flat in what was a nice residential area, the same area that we lived in, and she worked from these premises, building herself a large private practice. People travelled from far and wide to her door and here was me on a summer's afternoon, walking to her premises because she thought I could stop the horrible things that she felt were being directed towards her.

All the time I was walking I kept thinking to myself, "How on earth am I going to be able to help her? How on earth do I stop someone or something from attacking her? I have no experience whatsoever in the strange events or rare occurrences that people call psychic attack. I have no idea what to do, or how to do it, whatever it was. Oh well, she seemed to think I could help her so I'll take today slowly, very slowly. I'll take it one step at a time and see what happens."

I rang her doorbell and when the door opened I was met by a very pleasant, welcoming, older lady and a young man.

"Please come in. We have both been looking forward to meeting you for a very long time."

Well at least she was friendly and very welcoming.

She introduced herself to me and then her son, Nigel, and then she showed me into what she called her waiting room, a lovely sunny room that faced south over her small front garden. It was a very large room. It was furnished as if it was a lounge in someone's home. There was a baby grand piano standing in one corner with lots of photographs displayed on it in an assortment of beautiful frames and I was immediately drawn to one of them. A picture of a pilot from the First World War standing next to his biplane. The room was lovely, it was full of sunlight and not at all what I had been expecting.

"You seem to be drawn to one of my pictures, dear."

"Yes, I have such a funny feeling. I think I know the man in that photo but that's impossible."

"Hmm, perhaps not."

"You're right, perhaps not."

"It's a photo of a distant relative of ours from the First World War. He died when his plane was shot down over enemy territory and his plane and body were never found."

"Gosh, I'm sorry."

"No, that's fine. I didn't actually know him but my parents did. Do you recognise him?"

"Yes, I think I do. He looks very familiar to me, but obviously I can't place him, but I do feel as if I know him. How very strange to find someone I recognise in your home. (The fact this man had been alive before I was born didn't bother me at all.)

"Not so strange when you realise that we are all

connected far more closely than any one of us will ever realise."

And, of course, I knew she was right about that.

"I'm not sure how I can help you because I have no experience of helping anyone that feels they are under psychic attack."

"I know you can help me, dear, because I know you have done this sort of work somewhere in your past and the memory of what to do will come flooding back to you the minute you ask the Universe to help you in your work."

Whoa, how the heck does she think she knows me this well?

And, without missing a beat, Marjorie started explaining to me what had been happening. Apparently she had felt very dark negative energy coming into her reception room through the large bay window and she had also witnessed black shapes, or as she called them dark entities, as they entered her therapy rooms when she had opened the door to some of her patients when they came for their treatments. I was to find out in the weeks, months and years that followed that Marjorie thought that dark entities followed her around everywhere and she was convinced they stuck to her!

I think you will understand when I tell you that Marjorie and I had a strange relationship over the next few years and, let's be honest, I have used the word strange because I could never be what I would call friends with Marjorie because for the life of me I couldn't relate to her. As much as I respected her ability in her chosen therapy, there was no way I could agree with her very negative and strange behaviour.

Now I'm all for live and let live. Everyone has different ideas and beliefs but Marjorie's negativity was to test my patience and then some. It was when she started to tell me that she had been going to bed every night for the past few weeks with tinfoil wrapped around her head to keep the entities from sticking to her that I realised that perhaps this lady had lost her way on the path that we call life and perhaps I needed to point her back onto the right road again, so to speak. And trust me I did try over the next few years, but to no avail. To be honest with you I think Marjorie needed her entities. They were part of her daily ritual and she would have been lost without them.

What I found a bit hard to understand was that her son, Nigel, had fallen hook line and sinker for his mother's negative thoughts and ideas.

Do you recall me telling you Becky's story a few chapters ago and how she had managed to create her own monsters? Marjorie and her son had managed to create their very own world of dark energy and Marjorie's very own dark entities.

Diplomacy was needed this afternoon in a big way. I needed to be very diplomatic and not upset anyone and I needed to keep the laughter that I could feel welling up inside of me from erupting.

Tin foil around her head at bedtime, I'd heard it all now.

"I can just about manage the entities, Isabella, but I'm struggling with the blackness that keeps coming in through the front room windows. Can you please stop it coming in?"

"Yes, Marjorie, I think I can. But have you any idea where it's coming from?"

"Yes, I think so. A few months ago I upset someone I have known for years and I've got a feeling she's the one that is directing black thoughts towards me. She can get very angry when she doesn't get her own way and I'm afraid I stopped her from doing something last year and she's never forgiven me."

"Well, I think I know exactly what I need to do, so I'll do it now for you."

I explained to her and Nigel exactly what I was going to do and why and then I began.

I stood in her bay window looking directly at her beautiful bright white net curtains (and me trying desperately not to laugh because this was a very serious affair for her and her son, albeit mostly brought on by herself) and I stretched out both of my arms. Now I'm not normally that dramatic but the situation seemed to call for a bit of drama for Marjorie and her son's sake. I stretched out both of my arms and closed my eyes. I pictured myself placing a very large mirror against the window so that any dark energy that was being directed towards Margaret and her therapy rooms (if indeed there was) would bounce right back from where it came.

The mirror effect, send it back to the source, don't do anything yourself. No bad thoughts from you being sent out, so no bad karma coming back at you. Just all the bad thoughts being directed to you going straight back to where they originated from.

"Job done, Margaret. No more blackness coming through your windows and you don't have to do anything. It will stop now. But you must make sure you don't send any bad thoughts out yourselves towards the lady you think was causing your problem or anyone else for that matter, because your thoughts will just come back to you."

"No, I realise what you have done and I promise you I won't. Thank you so much. How much do I owe you?"

"Nothing, Marjorie. This has been an afternoon of learning for me and it's been very interesting. You have been sending people to me for healing so I'm more than happy to help you if you think I can. Sending people to me is payment enough. One good deed deserves another, but what about your entities, Marjorie?"

"You've done enough for one day, Isabella. Perhaps another time."

My job seemed to be done for the afternoon so we parted company and I went home, exhausted.

Marjorie was kind enough to contact me about three weeks later to let me know that she was sure the psychic attack she felt she had been under had stopped, and she was ringing me to thank me.

Was it a case of psychic attack?

The honest answer is I don't know.

I don't know if she had brought the problem on herself or if she had been indeed under attack but at the end of the day, whatever it was, it stopped and that's all that actually mattered.

Her entities on the other hand were a different problem entirely but one I was to learn over the next few years she would refuse to let go of. I guess in some ways they were her friends.

I did say at the beginning of this chapter that both the stories I would tell you were a bit strange, but I think Marjorie's story wins hands down for strangeness.

CHAPTER TWENTY-FOUR

"In fifty-one years I have never fought my MS; I have let it teach me."

Me

My feelings are telling me that I'm getting close to the end of this my second book and the only way I can explain the feeling is that the energy of my writing is starting to slow down. So I think now would be a good time for me to give you an update on my MS status before this book comes to an end. So that's what this second-last chapter will be all about. Yes, second-last. I have one more story that I would like to share with you before I finish my writings for now, but before I do let's have the update.

It's been fifty-one years since I had my first MS attack in 1964. It's been thirty-four years since I was first diagnosed in 1980/81 and it's been twenty-four years since I had my MRI head and neck scan in 1991 and I realise that a lot of you reading this might be thinking she was probably misdiagnosed and never had MS in the first place and in a way I wouldn't blame you.

In 2011 I was beginning to doubt my diagnosis myself. I actually said to a doctor at our local surgery, "I'm beginning to think I dreamt the whole thing."

And by the look on his face I think he thought so too.

"Why?" you are going to ask.

Just as I finished writing my first book I had a feeling that I had some of the years wrong that I had been writing about, and it dawned on me that if I could get my hands on my old medical records this would solve my problem. All the dates would be there in writing for me to use as reference points. From 1980 when my then new doctor told me she recognized all my symptoms because her husband specialized in the exact problem she thought I had, and all the appointments and subsequent tests that followed would all be there in my records. Also if I got sight of the dates of my three small operations that happened in the 1960's and 1970's this would also help me. I could make sure I'd got those events and other things that happened to me around those times in the correct years as well.

I had never seen or been given a copy of any letters or reports over the years because that was the rule at the time, you weren't allowed to see your medical records. It wasn't until 1998 when the new Patients Bill of Rights came into force that the law changed and you could request to see your own medical records, but I had no reason to see them at that point in time. Also I never got to see my MRI scan in 1991.

So in 2011, just as I was finishing writing my first book, I made an appointment at our local surgery. As I hardly ever went to the doctors I found myself seeing a doctor that I had never seen before. Our doctor's practice had changed hands a year earlier and I'd never been to the surgery since the handover had taken place. When the takeover had happened all the patients in the practice were sent a detailed list giving us the number of patients in the practice, the area it covered and all the ailments that the patients had, such as the number of diabetics, the number of people with heart problems, but no one had MS. I knew from this that both the previous doctor and our new doctor had no idea that I had it. The reason for this was because in the first thirteen years my husband and I had been registered with them I had never mentioned it (there had been no need to) and I realised that no one had gone back through my old records because again there had been no reason for them to. So what I was about to say to him was going to come as a bit of a surprise.

I explained to him that I wanted to see some of my old medical records from about 1968 through to 1991. He was a bit bemused by my request and asked me why I wanted to do this. I didn't want to tell him that I was writing a book because I didn't know him and I was not about to try and explain myself to a total stranger so I explained that I wanted to check some details relating to the MRI scan that I had in 1991 and a few other things relating to my diagnosis of Multiple Sclerosis from 1981 because we had just become grandparents and I had remembered the professor telling me in 1981 that MS is often found within family groups and as I was asking for my old records I might as well have some of my prior records just out of curiosity.

Trust me, the look on his face was priceless.

He gave himself a couple a seconds before he spoke to me and then he said, "Okay. If you make a list of all the things you want to see I will try and find them for you."

I went home and compiled the list with approximate dates and dropped it in at the surgery the following afternoon. He was as good as his word. He rang me the following week and invited me to come to the surgery to enable him to go over everything with me that he had found.

And this is where the fun started!

He said, "I'm not sure if I've been able to find everything for you, but I've read through everything I've managed to find and I have all the papers that you requested in order by the years, starting with the oldest records first."

So he began. The information from the 1960's and 1970's was all there, with the dates of my operations and the outcomes. I thought we were off to a good start. Then he showed me a hand-written scribbled note on a piece of (what looked like) scrap paper. My mother's name was there, followed by lots of numbers (apparently her blood count). Then below her name was my father's and his blood count and then below that was my name and my blood count, with the words Multiple Sclerosis written next to it. That piece of scrap paper was all there was to show that Professor Branson had ever seen me. There was no letter from my then doctor asking for an appointment with the Professor, there was no letter to my new doctor with the diagnosis of MS from the Professor, just the scribble on a sheet of scrap paper. Fortunately for me, it was headed up with the printed title of the Trust he was being sponsored by in his new private research clinic.

As my then new doctor was the wife of the professor I can only assume all the correspondence that didn't happen happened over their dinner table! And there was nothing in my medical records to show for all the appointments I had with her and her husband, the professor.

Next I had requested the letter that the Head of Neurology had sent to my doctor in 1990, telling her that all patients diagnosed with MS by the professor were to be told they didn't have MS.

But there was no letter.

And my now new doctor, Dr Adam, explained to me that it had probably just been a flyer sent to all GPs in the area at the time and she'd thrown it away.

Great for all of us with MS!

Then I was shown two letters, one from 1990 and one from 1991.

The first was the appointment I had with the new Head of Neurology saying that I didn't have MS and I was wasting his time but that he had made me an appointment for an MRI head scan anyway in his research programme and I would have to wait a year.

Next was the letter from the Head of Neurology, the same doctor, sent to my GP after I had my MRI scan. This is the letter I found very hard to take.

It said I had two very small scars on my brain that might be indicative of MS but again might not be and absolutely no mention of my eye evoked response tests. No mention of the fact he had seen me after this letter had been sent to my doctor at the time and no mention of the conversation that he had with me when he told me I had MS when I asked him. No mention of the results of my eye evoked response test that showed scarring behind both of my eyes and how he had told me he hadn't known how I had walked into his consulting room.

It was as if none of this had ever happened.

Oh and by the way, the letter also informed my doctor that I drank four cans of lager each week and that made me angry. I guess this was the straw that broke the camel's back and I would never have known about any of this unless I'd requested my records, but my records were missing so much and some of what was there was wrong!

I was dumbfounded. At this point I said to Dr Adams, "I'm beginning to think I've dreamt the whole thing." By the look on his face if he had spoken he would have agreed with me!

I've got to be honest and say I was beginning to get upset and not without reason.

There I'd been happily going along thinking everything that had happened to me and had been said to me in 1980/81 and 1990/91 was in my medical records and, within minutes, I felt as if everything might have been in my imagination. I felt as if the floor beneath my feet was moving. I didn't feel as if I was standing on solid ground and it was making me wobble and feel a bit sick.

This was 2011, forty-six years since my first MS attack and I still had nothing concrete in my medical records to say I definitely had MS (other than the scribble on the scrap of paper from the professor).

How would you feel?

I said to Dr Adams, "I don't believe this. Where are my eye evoked response test results?"

"I don't know. There's no mention in any of the letters that you had this test done."

"Wonderful!"

He could see by the expression on my face and the tone in my voice that I was annoyed and upset.

"Would you like me to make an appointment to see the specialist you saw twenty years ago?"

"Yes please."

He told me he would write and arrange an appointment for me and I was to wait to hear from him. I left the surgery with copies of all the letters that he had found. So when I got back home I sat and read through them all a few times to get to grips with what was and wasn't there, and I've got to be honest with you, I sat and cried.

The letter from the MS specialist doctor at the hospital, the one I had seen after my MRI scan in 1991 (the doctor that

Doctor Adams was now trying to get me an appointment with), was the letter that upset me the most. In that letter he informed my doctor that I drank four cans of lager every week. Now this may seem completely reasonable to some of you reading this but when my family read this they will all fall about laughing, because they all know I hate lager. When I had seen the doctor who specialised in MS the year before when he agreed to allow me to have the MRI scan (1990), that was when he told me I didn't have MS and I was wasting his time. He had made some notes and one of the questions that he asked me was did I drink? I had told him that I sometimes drank a can of Guinness or a bottle of stout, as my father-in-law had told me it was good for me (because of the iron content) and he was a doctor remember. That had been translated into me drinking four cans of lager and I've got to be honest with you, the way he had written it down in his letter had made me sound as if I was a lazy lager-lout. I hate the taste of lager and I'm not lazy. Reading his letter had made me feel small and hurt and that wasn't fair.

    This to me was just another simple example of how we as patients are just not listened to by some doctors. Our words fly over the heads of these so-called experts and then they record what they think they have heard us say into our medical records for all time, for other experts to read and rely on. And that's what had made me so cross and upset. He just didn't bother to listen properly to what I said to him that day. I would like to think doctors are a bit more careful now because they know that we can request to see our records at any time, for any reason, and this has got to be a good thing. I honestly wondered as I read through the papers in front of me that night what other untrue things may have been written down about me. I'm sorry if this has sounded like a bit of a rant but it's important to me that I'm honest about what has gone on and how I felt at the time about what I read and was told. I know other people who have asked to see their medical records and they have also been equally upset by what they found and read, and that has got to be food for thought for everyone.

Four weeks passed and I'd heard nothing so I went back to the surgery.

This time I saw a different doctor who introduced himself to me as Dr Mathews. He then went on to explain to me that he had a letter from the MS specialist I had seen in 1991 saying he had now retired. Doctor Mathews then asked me if I would like him to make me an appointment with his replacement. To me this was good news/bad news week. The good news was that I would never have to see that horrid MS doctor at the hospital ever again, because if I had I might not have been responsible for my actions. He had retired, thank goodness. The bad news was that I was going to have to see someone new and explain myself and that was going to be hard for me.

Oh well, one day at a time.

I said yes to Doctor Mathews. Could he please make me an appointment to see the new MS specialist and could I also make a request to see my old MRI scan because I had never seen it? Dr Mathews said he would arrange the appointment and when I received the letter he suggested I rang to speak to the secretary involved and ask her to make sure my old MRI scan was to hand for me to look at when I went for my appointment.

Now I would just have to wait but it in the meantime I could finish my book. Now that I had the correct dates I could alter and change around one or two of the events I had in the wrong years. I think my confusion had arisen because so much had actually happened to me and my family in such a very short space of time it was no wonder I had got a bit confused over some of the years.

About five weeks later I received a letter from the hospital with an appointment date for me to see the new doctor and it wasn't too far away (four months). As the time drew closer I rang to speak to the specialist's secretary. I explained to her that the reason I wanted to see the specialist was to enable me to see my MRI scan from 1991 and also I wanted to get hold of my visual evoked responses test result because they weren't in my medical records even though I had had the test done. She was lovely with me, so friendly and so helpful. She actually rang me back about five days later but the news was not good. She told me that she had tried to locate my scan and my eye tests for me but she was having no luck. Someone in the particular department in charge of old records was going to have one more look in the archive filing department but because it was off-site a few miles from the hospital it was going to take another week before she could categorically tell me my MRI scan and my eye evoke test were missing, possibly destroyed. She told me she was not holding out much hope in finding them. I think she was trying to let me down gently. And then she explained the reason they might have been destroyed was because for the past twenty-odd years I had never been back to the hospital to see anyone.

I thought our medical records were sacrosanct but apparently I have been told that that was very naive of me. I had always thought that my medical records would be left intact and not be destroyed until after I had left this life. But when I asked a friend in the medical world she basically told me to dream on. She said there was a time limit but she wasn't sure what it was now as things had changed over the past few years. But she was fairly sure that a few years ago there was definitely a limit. Some research needs to be done here if any of you are interested. But what that time limit was or is now I have no idea.

So what about mine?

Sure enough, she rang me back a week later and told me my records were gone, apparently shredded along with many others a few years earlier when the hospital had been renovated and modernised. Was this done on purpose or was it a mistake?

I was getting upset again and, let's be honest, who could blame me? ('It could only happen to me' kept going through my mind.) I felt there was no point anymore in me going to see the MS specialist if my MRI scan was not there for me to look at. I would be wasting my time and his and that's what I told his secretary.

"Why don't you come anyway, Isabella, and meet him. He's really nice."

"I can't see the point."

"But he might suggest you have another MRI scan and then you will have your record again in case you need it."

And, to be honest with you, I couldn't really argue with that; she was right.

This lady had been so nice to me. We had chatted away to each other on the telephone about all sorts of things over the previous few weeks and, in the process, I had explained to her that I'd written a book and that was why I had wanted to make sure my records were all there, should anyone in years to come question me or doubt my diagnosis. I wanted to be sure I had the back-up information in the form of my MRI scan and other info in my medical files.

"Come on, Isabella. You already have the appointment so you might as well keep it and see him. Trust me, you won't be disappointed."

"Okay. You've persuaded me."

So I did.

I kept the appointment and this is what happened.

He was lovely, the complete opposite to his predecessor. He listened to a brief story from me as to my previous diagnosis. He also had the letter (the horrible letter) his predecessor had written about me to my previous doctor in 1991 and he had obviously read it. He examined me by looking in my eyes and then he tested my reflexes from both my knees and my feet. And then he touched my face around my eyes by pressing gently onto my skin, and my eyes must have lit up like a beacon as I said to him, "Dear God, I'd completely forgotten; I'd completely forgotten how sore my face used to be to the touch. I had forgotten how I could never wear make-up because I couldn't bear to touch my face."

And he smiled and said, "That's a classic."

And then he asked me to do one or two very simple tasks. One of them was walking on my tip-toes by putting one foot directly in front of the other very closely, with hilarious results. He got me to stop before I fell over and hurt myself.

"With the history you have given me and the tests I have just done I can say without question that you definitely have MS and I'm so sorry this has happened to you. Your MRI scan should have still been on file and I'm more than happy for you to have another one. Would you like to have another one?"

"Yes please."

"Then I'll arrange one for you. It should only take a few weeks for the appointment to come through. I have a feeling we will find that the scars on your brain will have all healed but the scars behind your eyes will still be there, but we will find out soon enough. And I would also like to have your eye evoked potential (EP) study done again."

And with that we all shook hands.

You are all going to have a good laugh at my expense when I tell you what I did next. I turned to my daughter who was sitting next to me at the time and asked her if she thought it would be alright if I gave him a hug (he had been so nice to me) and, let's face it, he had been the only MS doctor that I'd met, other than the Prof, in twenty-odd years that had been nice to me, and she said, "Yes, Mum, of course you can if you'd like to. I'm sure he won't mind."

So I did. Then I thanked him again for being so kind, we all shook hands again, said our goodbyes and left.

Our daughter had accompanied me into the consulting room, leaving David sitting in the waiting room (like most men he doesn't like hospitals) and when we met back up with him our daughter said to her father, "Well she's definitely got MS, Dad."

As if she had also doubted my diagnosis all her life. He just turned to her and said, "But we knew that. We've known that for many years."

This appointment was followed soon after by a letter to my doctor (and a copy to me) confirming my diagnosis of Multiple Sclerosis. This was the first time a diagnosis had reached my medical records and I can't help but write the words 'all things come to she who waits.'

Just thirty years late!

About two months later we were sitting in the waiting room in the same hospital yet again as I awaited my turn to go into the room the scanner was in. That's me, my daughter and my husband. I was not looking forward to the coming event. I had been told that this scanner was much more powerful than the one used in 1991. This was now 2011, twenty years on from my last scan. Bless our daughter who said to me, "Mum, you don't have to have this you know, you don't have to go through with it if you don't want to."

"I know, sweetheart, but I want to. I want to see how my brain actually is now. I need to know for me, not for anyone else, so I do need to have it."

"Okay, Mum, if that's what you want."

Oh my goodness, talk about being noisy, ten times louder than twenty years earlier. So loud in fact that I could hardly hear my father's voice above the din as he came to get me to take me away on another adventure. The machine was making a thumping and whirring noise that was so loud my father had to shout to make himself heard above the racket as I lay there with my eyes tight shut, trying desperately to hear what my father was saying to me. Not only was the noise horrendous, the machine also seemed to dance up and down and swing from side to side. I felt as if I was at the fairground on a merry-go-round and they make me sick. Up, down and then swing to the left and then to the right, this was ridiculous, I was all over the place, and then, and then I was in another world, with my father at my side, looking out over a beautiful pasture surrounded by magnificent trees of every shade of green imaginable.

My father had come to rescue me yet again without me even asking him. He took me away on another wonderful journey just like he did twenty years ago when I had my first MRI scan.

I was only in the scanner about twenty minutes this time, but when I got out I felt as if I'd actually been inside a tumble dryer as it had turned around and around and my brain felt as if it had been fried. I felt disorientated as if I was upside down and hanging from the ceiling. Not a very nice feeling. It almost felt as if my brain had been violated in some way. Blimey, that scanner was so powerful it could have pulled all my teeth out. I had been very aware as my scans were being done that this machine was so much more powerful than the last time. I could feel the pull of the magnets or whatever it was that was taking the images. It felt as if my brain had been invaded by an alien force. But thankfully I had been away on a journey with my father most of the time the machine had been running.

When the two ladies that were operating the machine slowly pulled the tray out that I was lying on, they both said to me, "Now get up very slowly because you might feel a little bit dizzy."

Dizzy. I felt as if my brain had been skewered. It took all of the rest of that afternoon and evening for me to begin to feel anywhere near normal. The very odd feeling did eventually go away but not until the following day.

Next came the appointment for my evoke response test and I felt quite confident in having this test because the last time I had had it done, it hadn't hurt in the slightest. This time there were no sticky plug things to stick onto my head. I just had to sit and watch a flashing screen for about five minutes which I did, but then the nurse said, "We will now do your arms and legs."

I told her I didn't understand and she said, "Oh, the doctor wants the evoke response test done on both your arms and legs."

And she proceeded to attach some wires to my right wrist and this is where it began to feel as if I was being tortured. The pain was horrible and the nurse was not in the least bit bothered that it was hurting me. My husband and daughter were both in the room with me trying to encourage me to continue when I was saying I wanted it to stop. My daughter kept telling me to be brave and my husband said, "Well, you wanted it done." He was not being very kind to me at all and I felt like I was being tortured. First my right arm was tested and I could feel the electric current running right up and into my shoulder and then my left arm and then my right ankle and this is when the pain became excruciating as the current ran up my leg. I was crying with the pain. Then my left ankle and it was at this point that I said I couldn't take it anymore and the nurse said to me she didn't know what I was fussing about because she had tried the machine and she thought it tickled. Tickled! She must have been a sadist.

When it was all over I was very cross with myself. I should have stopped the proceedings as soon as it started to really hurt. My arms and legs were not right for months afterwards and I do mean months.

It took my arms nine months before they fully recovered and felt right again and I could use them without feeling any pain, and it took a full year before I could honestly say my legs were back to normal.

But it only took me a couple of days to realise why the procedure had hurt me so badly.

For thirty-odd years I had worked with and used the healing energy to help myself by helping my own energy field and the flow of my energy to flow down both my arms (not up) and down both my legs (not up). The electric current that had been forced up both my arms and both my legs had forced the energy to flow the wrong way for me, undoing years of the energy flowing the correct way and it took months and months for me to correct it and heal myself again.

I will never allow this test to be done to me again and I'm very cross with myself for not stopping it when it happened. This was yet another lesson I learnt the hard way.

There had actually been no need for me to have that particular test done in the first place. I knew I had MS and so did the specialist so this particular test had been a complete waste of time for me.

I wonder, how many people with MS have had this test done over the years and it's hurt them in the process? Or it has left them with arms and legs hurting for months when they weren't hurting before the test. If I had not been aware of why my arms were hurting and not working properly afterwards or why my legs were hurting so badly I would have been frightened. This was my own fault. I should have stopped the tests before the damage had been done.

It was about six months later before I was able to see the same specialist again to get feedback from my MRI scan.

Again our daughter came with me into his consulting room. After the pleasantries were over and we had sat ourselves down I asked him if I could please see the picture of my brain.

"Of course you can."

He had it ready on his computer screen on his desk for me to look at and he turned the screen slightly around so that my daughter and I could both see it. I watched as he rotated the image on the screen around and, as he tilted the picture of my skull slightly forwards, all the scarring began to appear on the screen. As all the scars came into view, I heard my daughter take an intake of breath as I quickly started to count them all. I lost count as I was reaching thirty and that's when he switched the computer screen off.

"Oh my goodness!" said me.

"Hmm," said he.

"Oh my gosh, I have a lot of scars."

"Yes you have."

"Well that makes a lot of sense to me. I had a lot of MS attacks one after the other for years and it looks as if I have a scar for every attack I ever had and then some."

"Your brain is badly scarred. Some of them are old scars and some of them are more recent and one or two of them are active. You had your first attack when you were fourteen years old and I would have expected you to have been in a wheelchair by the time you were thirty and, let's be honest, at sixty-one you shouldn't be..."

And he left that sentence unfinished.

I know I shouldn't be here now but I am loud and clear and all because of the wonderful healing energy. Anything is possible and I mean anything but, of course, I didn't tell him that.

He then told me that the evoked response tests had shown that the scarring behind my eyes had healed and obviously my MRI scan was showing that the scars on my brain had not healed although there were a lot of older scars that were non–active, which was the opposite to what he had thought would be the case when he first met me.

My visit subsequently warranted another letter to my doctor, confirming my diagnosis yet again and the result of my scan, and the nice thing for me, was that I also got a copy of the letter. But not only that, I had asked the specialist's secretary if I could please have a copy of my MRI scan and she very kindly told me that because of what had happened to me and the fact my first scan had been destroyed by the hospital she would personally make sure I got a copy of my new MRI scan so that the same thing could never happen to me again. I would have my own copy regardless of what happened at the hospital in the future and, true to her word, I received a disc in the post with my scans on. If memory serves I think there are about thirty-seven images, thirty-seven slices of my brain on the disc. So I now have all the records I should have had many years ago. And it wasn't until I had all of this properly recorded that I felt confident to publish my first book. If anyone of any note was now to query my diagnosis, I now have all the back-up information I will ever need.

I have seen the MS doctor once more and he let me see my scan again because I wanted to see if there was any scarring on my brain stem that would perhaps account for the laryngospasms I have had and, sure enough, I have a lot of scarring on my brain stem, but again he switched the screen off very quickly before I had a chance to count them all.

Now I do understand that this doctor and all the other doctors at the hospital only have a very short time allocated for each of their patients so, at some time in the future, I would like to be able to sit down with someone and go over my scan very slowly so that I can sit and count all the scars on my brain and brain stem. I would like to know how many scars I actually have on my brain. We do have a private hospital not too far away from where we live and I know for a fact they have a very up-to-date MRI scanner and the means to be able to read the finished scans so, sometime in the not too distant future when I can afford it, I will arrange an appointment with someone there and take my disc along with my scans on for them to show me. Only this time I will pay for the time for me to be able to sit and count all my scars without the machine being switched off. You might be thinking this is a bit morbid of me, but it's not. In a way, I'm proud of all of them. This is me, brain damaged (damaged being my word because I don't know what other word to use for all the scar tissue on my brain) and I have the scars to prove it. So when I can afford to, that's what I'm going to do. Or perhaps there is some sort of software on the market now for the computer that I can download that would allow me to be able to read my scan in the comfort of my own home. That's got to be worth looking into.

I just think this is all amazing. I am quite badly brain scarred or brain lesion damaged and I now have copies of the scans myself, yet I'm fine. That's how wonderful and amazing the healing energy is and it's there for everyone, not just me.

Miracles do happen, they happen every day, and I'm the living proof.

I'm a walking, talking miracle, wife, mother and grandmother that loves her life. And I'm grateful beyond words for all the help that God has given me over the years and continues to give me.

So from me to you, Lord, a colossal, "Thank You."

CHAPTER TWENTY-FIVE

I cried, I prayed, He listened, I praised.
Psalm 66 -17-20

In Chapter One I told you that I felt as if I was standing in my very own shop of accumulated knowledge with so many different subjects to chose from and share with you. My shop was so full I was overwhelmed at the time and actually I still am! From ghost stories to healing stories to out-of-body adventures and one or two miracles as well.

I also told you that I was going to allow myself the luxury of having a wander from time to time during the writing of this book because there was no need for me to stick to any particular year and I had a feeling as I was writing that my mind would open up a lot of personal spiritual insights. And now that this second book of mine is almost finished, I hope you have enjoyed the journey and my wanderings as much as I have. They have taken us along many different paths, but there is still so much more I have to tell you. In some ways I have only just begun, honestly.

I haven't mentioned one animal healing story in this book and I have many to share. I haven't mentioned any angel encounters and I have some amazing ones. I haven't mentioned any fairy, yes fairy, encounters. I haven't yet talked about healing at a distance, both with people and animals or helping people pass from this life into the next and some of those stories are amazing. Many more out-of-body adventures, visiting other dimensions and other worlds, alien encounters, yes aliens, but to me they are just people (I use that word lightly) from worlds far away from ours, star-born children, master Souls and the list goes on. So there are quite a few more books for me to write if God is willing. But the energy is definitely slowing down on this book, telling me it's time to bring it to a close.

So let's go wandering one more time before this book ends.

From the responses I have had from friends and patients after reading my first book, a lot of people said they enjoyed reading my own personal adventures the most. From my adventure with my father when I was in the MRI scanner for the first time in 1990, to my journey to Heaven when I was blessed to be able to visit, experience and see Heaven and be with and talk to (and cuddle) my father. The positive feedback has given me the confidence that I need to be able to share with you this next very personal out-of-this-world happening. There is also another reason why I want to share this story with you. It's because of what I'm about to tell you that I have never been frightened or fazed by any of the things I have subsequently seen or heard over the years that have been shown to me from the other side of life. Things that would without doubt have frightened me if this next experience had not happened to me when it did. This one amazing event showed me and taught me to absolutely trust God and know, without a shadow of doubt, that anything that I experienced, saw or heard from the Spirit world would always come from a place of love and protection.

There was a right time for this event to happen to me and it happened at the right time, simply because my father was here on earth when it happened, allowing him to be able to help me, by explaining to me what actually happened.

The words below were taken from my father's Holy Bible, The Authorised King James Version. From Ecclesiastes 3:1 "To everything there is a season, and a time to every purpose under Heaven."

Please remember that I honestly don't think that I'm clever or special in any way. The fact I've nearly finished my second book is a miracle to me in itself. My hand has been so well guided (again) and that is why I've made it this far. I'm the one that gets things wrong sometimes and I'm not in the least bit embarrassed by the fact that you should all know. But for some strange and wonderful reason unknown to me I have been very privileged in my life. God has allowed me to see some amazing sights, sights that I realise most people will never get the chance to see.

Do I keep them to myself? Or do I share them with the world?

So from one very humble, thankful woman I would love to share with you one more of my amazing adventures and the only reason it happened was because I simply asked God for help. This is the sort of adventure that only happens once in a lifetime. As much as I would love this to happen to me again I know it won't because the lesson was learnt at the time, and you will see how and why in a few minutes.

Can some of the things that happen to me happen to you? The honest answer is I don't know. That's between your God and you, but I will say to you that to me nothing is impossible if you trust and ask.

I've mentioned before that one of our daughter's favourite sayings is 'shy bairns get nowt', in other words if you don't ask you're not going to get anything and my asking for help was the reason this next amazing event happened to me.

I've mentioned to you a few times that my father was a Methodist lay preacher and he was for over thirty-five years so in a way I have already told you that he believed that he needed to be 'born again in Christ' to allow him to go to Heaven and that's also what my mother believed. In other words, they believed that if you don't believe that Jesus died for you on the cross you are not going to Heaven and that's that. They were both 'born-again' Christians and they had both been all of their adult lives.

Me, I had other ideas.

Ideas I never dared voice when I was young because I would have been shouted down by my parents. I was shouted down on one occasion when I tried to tell them that I could 'hear' voices, so I learnt very early on not to say anything of how I felt. How, from being very young, I was sure I had walked this earth before (dreams, visions and experiences that I have yet to put into a book). I would not have been able to explain myself even if I had thought my parents might listen to me, because at the time I was only a child and I didn't have the correct words to use.

I felt from being little that the earth was a school and we were all here to learn and pupils make mistakes and that's okay. So from a young age I wasn't into the born-again theme; it didn't feel right to me. But because my parents believed it so strongly I did swing from one side of the fence to the other many times over the space of a few years when I was in my teens, and that was fine at the time because that was my way of trying to sort the big picture out in my muddled young mind.

Okay, parents both born-again Christians and me not at all sure if I was or wasn't. So that sets the scene perfectly for what was about to happen to me next.

If I tell you that I wrote this story down in longhand in 1989 and I filed it away with a lot of other writings I think this is telling both you and me, that somewhere in my subconscious I always knew that one day I would be writing my stories down for everyone to read.

I was only eighteen years old when the following story happened. I was thirty-eight when I wrote this story down and I have decided that I'm not going to alter what I wrote down all those years ago. I'm going to more or less copy the original manuscript and let the young woman in her thirties recall the event that changed her life far more than she could ever have imagined.

It all began many years ago now. Something so strange and wonderful happened to me that even to this day the event is still very clear in my mind when I take myself back to that night.

I was living at home with my parents in the big old family home, the one I was married from the first time around. I loved that old house; it had such a wonderful warm friendly feel to it. By modern-day standards it was huge and rambling, yet it always felt very safe to me. Even when the floorboards decided to do a dance at an unearthly hour of the night and the old plumbing joined in the chorus it never bothered or frightened me; it was home. The house was surrounded by beautiful gardens. There was a lawn running from the front bay windows down to a copse of rhododendrons and hidden amongst them was a summerhouse and below that more lawns and an orchard and I could see all of this from my bedroom window.

My bedroom was at the very top of the house in the attic. If you stood in the front garden looking up at the house, my window was perched like a bird's nest four storeys up. I often sat on the window ledge of my bedroom window looking out across the garden and then the valley beyond, frequently having a sly smoke. I freely admit I was no angel. I was a typical rebellious teenager with saints for parents. How they never gave up on me I'll never know. I did all the things teenagers normally do. Boyfriends had been frequent visitors to our home, along with me going to discos, dances and parties. That is until I settled with one particular boy friend just before I turned eighteen, the boyfriend that was to become my first husband. I could go on but if my mother is going to read this I'd better be very careful about the details of my eighteenth year.

How the book got into my possession in the first place? To be honest with you I can't remember, but it did. Little did I know it would have such an impact on me, or begin a journey I would never have thought possible even in a book of fantasy or fairy tales. And as I've said before, truth is often stranger than fiction and this story is stranger than any fantasy or fairy tale that you will ever read and as my story unfolds the telling of it will show you.

As a small child I was taken, sometimes forcibly by the hand, to church each Sunday. It was expected that the family would all turn out in our Sunday best each week whether we wanted to or not. I suppose none of us realised that as small children it is amazing what we actually learn when we are only half listening to grown-ups telling stories. But consciously or unconsciously we do. Even though at the time I didn't realise or appreciate the teaching or the meaning of those early lessons, those stories were all going to play their part in the years to come.

I had always thought that I was a very sophisticated young lady, that nothing could spoil my easy life. Responsibility was a word that had very little meaning for me, especially being responsible for myself.

Mum and Dad were always there to put things right and pick up the pieces when needed. My older brother came in useful if I was short of a lift and I sometimes even got to borrow his car because it was better than mine and more reliable. I should also mention I have a younger sister but when you are eighteen and your sister is just twelve, well, she didn't fit into my life in any way apart from being a pest. Selfish is probably a word that springs to mind in describing me and looking back it fits well.

The book, who gave it to me? I really don't know. I was never one for reading books as a youngster. I was far too busy enjoying my life, but it came from somewhere. I can clearly remember hiding it under my knickers in my underwear drawer in my bedroom just in case my mother found it because at the time I thought that it was full of sex and if Mum found it I would have been in trouble.

It must have taken me at least a week before I got into the story as the only time I could read it was late at night in my bedroom and only for about fifteen minutes at a time just in case Mum came up the stairs, not that she ever bothered me very much once I was in my room. Remember, I was four storeys up and she was convinced that the stairs were growing by the week.

I had been wrong about the contents of the book. It had very little sex in it yet the pictures it was painting in my mind drew me on to finish the story. And finish it I did with absolute horror. The descriptions were so vivid that by the end of the book I was crying because of the sorrow that it made me feel. The words that I had read on the last few pages had touched a part of me that I didn't even know existed. The book was frightening because of its reality and my mind reeled at the implications. That sounds very dramatic but honestly, I was frightened, very frightened.

You see, the story I had read was all about the end of the world and when you are only eighteen years old the last thing on your mind is the oblivion of everything you know and care about, the end of civilisation, the end of all life on earth. The impact the book had on me was very real. For the first time in my life I realised how fragile I was and how fragile everyone around me was. For the next few days after I had finished the book I kept going over in my head the things that I had read and, as each day passed, the pictures of destruction became more vivid by the day. Towns and cities flattened. Mothers giving their babies one last feed with poison in their bottles to send them to sleep forever before they themselves drank from their poisoned cups. As the cloud of radioactivity spread around the globe, countries died, people killed themselves to save themselves from months of agony from radiation poisoning and they killed their children, and this was all done with love so that no one suffered unduly. Horrific! If there was a nuclear war that's what would happen to our world and we would all die. All life on earth would die.

The book had made me stop and think about who I was for the first time in my life but, much more importantly, it had made me question in my mind what would happen to me if I died. It wasn't just the book that I had just read that had me frightened. It was also what was going on in the world around me at the time. There was a lot of unrest. The Vietnam War was in full swing and many people were marching to Ban the Bomb. (They should of course have been marching for peace not against the bomb.) The Arab-Israeli Six Day War had only recently happened and there was a lot of fear in the newspapers and on the television about the possibility of a nuclear war sparking off. I knew this because my boyfriend was actually worried in case a war nearer home kicked off and the British government decided to call up young men and he would have been on the list to be conscripted. It was all just talk, but it was fearful talk. So, between the very negative pictures on the television and the book I'd just finished reading, my mind was in turmoil, full of frightening thoughts and I was going to my bed every night with a very worried mind.

My bed faced the window and I never closed my curtains because it was impossible for anyone to be able to see into my room, I was so high up. I loved the fact I could lie in my bed at night watching the moon and stars pass across the sky. On the night the event happened, about two weeks after I had finished reading the book, I climbed into my bed as usual, but as I lay there my mind was still full of the pictures the book had given me and I was genuinely frightened. I started to cry because I knew if anything happened to end the world my mother and father would definitely go to Heaven. They not only loved their Lord, they practised what Dad preached. They were both what Dad called 'born-again Christians'. Now I had always believed there was a God and I also believed that Jesus had walked the earth but I didn't believe everything that my father and the chapel preached. I had my own thoughts and I kept those to myself because they were different from anything that would have been considered conventional by my parents. So, as my thoughts went running away that night, I knew Mum and Dad would go to Heaven because they were born-again Christians. Would my brother go to Heaven? Well, I honestly didn't know the answer to that. Would my sister go to Heaven? Yes, she was just a child and the Bible makes it very clear that the Lord will protect the children. Would I? That was the big question on my mind that night and I decided definitely not because I wasn't a born-again Christian. There was nothing I could do about that now and, oh boy, that frightened me more than anything. Wherever I went my father and mother wouldn't be. I must be honest and say for all I loved my mother I had never been close to her. Don't get me wrong, she never did anything bad to me but she never showed me or told me that she loved me. She never cuddled me when I was upset, but my father did. I used to think he tried to make up for the fact my mother never gave me the love or attention that he felt she should have. But they were my thoughts and I could have been wrong. As my mind went racing away that night with a multitude of frightening scenarios the most frightening of all was the thought that I would not be with my father, and that for me at eighteen years of age was scary beyond words.

I had never done anything wrong in my life, but I had equally never done anything of any good and I knew it. As a child I always said my prayers at bedtime. As a teenager I had not. But this night I got out of my bed and I knelt down on the floor next to it and I started to pray. I begged God to help me, to help me try and understand why I was who I was and I asked Him if He loved me. And would He keep me safe? And would He allow me to go to Heaven? And I must have asked Him all these questions a hundred times.

I stayed on my knees crying and sobbing and talking to an invisible being for at least an hour. I knew that there was a God because the seeds from many years earlier had been planted very deep. Not only that, even as a very small child, the voice on my shoulder had been very strong with me and I knew as a toddler that there was a force in the world that was around me all the time because I felt it, as young as I was. I couldn't have put a name to it because I was only a child, but I felt it.

I had been out of my bed for quite a while when I realised I was starting to get cold so, reluctantly and still crying, I climbed back into it to get warm, in a very distressed state. Feeling very drained and very tired, I cried myself to sleep.

I woke very suddenly with a jolt.

Something had woken me and I had no idea what and I had no idea why.

I was wide awake within seconds, thinking to myself, "What the heck has just woken me from a very deep sleep?"

That's when I realised that the sky outside of my bedroom window was ablaze with light. It was much brighter than the midday sun yet I was looking at it without it hurting my eyes and everything around me was so still and quiet as if a calming peacefulness had spread from the heavens into my bedroom. I could see everything around me so clearly because my room was full of light as I lay in my bed, looking out of my window into the blaze of brightness in the sky.

Then from nowhere and completely without warning

the whole of my life began to race past my eyes.

Things started to happen so quickly.

I can remember thinking to myself that this sort of thing only happens to people when they're going to die, so I must be dying. I had read in a magazine or I had heard on the television that when you die your life flashes before your eyes and then you are gone, and that's exactly what was happening to me right now, right this second. It was as if I was sitting in a cinema watching a film in full Technicolor, only this film was all about me and no one else. It started from the first memory that I had as a baby in my pram and it ended with what had happened to me that very day. Instead of a soundtrack for every scene I was shown, I felt every emotion imaginable connected to the images I was looking at. I can remember one scene clearly. I watched as I saw myself nipping my sister's leg as she sat on a rug in our back garden at home when we were children. She was only about two years old at the time and she burst into tears. Oh gosh, that was mean of me and the movie kept rolling on. I watched as my life from my earliest memory played out before my eyes and I felt every moment of everything I saw.

Then my thoughts turned to all the things I hadn't yet done and those things went flashing by me. I had always loved children even from being a child myself. I hadn't had any children yet and I had so desperately wanted them and then I felt a pang of sadness as the thought hit the pit of my stomach and I could have cried because I wasn't going to have any as time had run out for me and I hadn't even experienced making love and I had really wanted to try that!

The movie of my life passed before my eyes at an alarming rate and then - and then the most wonderful feeling anyone could ever wish to experience in a thousand lifetimes. I know I can never truly portray the awesomeness of what was happening to me because I don't have the right words to use, but I will do the best I can.

I felt myself beginning to float as if I was the lightest feather in the world. I floated up out of my bed and then I floated towards my bedroom window and the feeling of peace that now filled me from the top of my head to the tips of my toes was so overwhelmingly calming and loving I could have shouted out and cried with joy. And then, to my amazement, I seemed to melt as I floated through my bedroom window with complete ease and I just kept on floating. Up and up I went, travelling higher and higher above the earth as I journeyed skywards towards the amazing beautiful brightness in the heavens.

I felt so completely different, so overwhelmingly calm.

I was at peace, absolute peace.

My thoughts from just moments earlier as I had watched my life race before me had now been completely obliterated, as if my memory banks had been wiped clean and erased for all time as I continued upwards, heading towards the middle of the blaze of light in the sky.

The feeling of calm and of love that surrounded me as I journeyed upwards that night is still something I can remember to this day. The love that I felt seemed to seep into every fibre of my being, filling me with joy. I felt so light. I felt so free.

I found myself floating towards the most beautiful radiance within the light that was all around me, as the peace and love I was feeling soaked into every part of my being and then - nothingness, and I do mean nothing.

The next thing I knew it was morning. To my utter amazement, I was still alive. I really thought that I had died and gone to Heaven so what the heck was I still doing alive? And the amazing thing for me was that I had total recall of everything that had happened a few hours earlier, in the finest of details. One part of me felt very loved and very cared for and at total peace with myself and the other half of me was very troubled.

What the hell happened last night kept running through my mind, or more precisely, what in Heaven just happened?

As I was not one for keeping quiet for more than a few minutes at a time, I think the whole family thought I was ailing for something because I hardly spoke a word for the whole of the following week and the week after that.

About two and a half weeks after my event happened, as I came into our home from work, I walked into the hall in our house and as I passed my father's open study door he called out my name and asked me to come in. At first I thought I must have done something wrong and I was in trouble. But my father asked me to come and sit down beside him because he wanted to talk to me.

So I sat down on the chair on the opposite side of his desk.

"It's not like you, Isabella, to be so quiet. Are you in trouble of some sort? Can I help you?"

Bless Dad; he was always there for me.

Even at eighteen my father still gave me cuddles and I always felt very safe and loved by him. I started to cry. When I think back poor Dad probably thought that I was pregnant or something equally as bad because, as the daughter of a preacher man in the 1960's, you didn't get pregnant. That would have been almost as bad as committing murder. My mother would have died of shame.

"I've had a dream, Daddy, or I think it was a dream."

If you could have seen the look of relief on my father's face as his whole body relaxed when I told him I'd had a dream. You would have thought that he had been on Death Row and he'd just been given a stay of execution. He put his arms out to me to give me a hug and I went to him and sat on his knee and he cuddled me. He asked me to try and tell him what I'd seen so, through my tears, I did. He listened without saying a word as I relayed my story to him. I described all the things that had happened to me and all the feelings that I had felt as the pictures of my life had been shown to me, and the feelings that I felt as I was lifted so gently up and up into the sky. To my amazement, he didn't laugh at me and I will always be grateful for that. After I had finished telling him my story he just sat and gently rocked me to and fro for a good five minutes in perfect silence, and then he asked me, "Do you know what woke you, Isabella?"

"No, Daddy, I don't but it must have been a very loud noise that only lasted for a very short time, just like a short sharp burst of something because I woke from a deep sleep in an instant and as soon as I realised I was awake there was no sound at all. It was the quietest the world has ever seemed to me, so I haven't a clue as to what it could have been."

He gently let go of me and then he said, "Can you get my Bible for me please off the middle shelf of the bookcase and turn to Matthew's Gospel and go to chapter 24, verse 31 and read what it says out loud to me please?"

So I did and as I read the words out loud to him shivers started to run up and down my spine. The words were so amazing and as I read the passage to Dad the realisation of what had happened to me was beginning to sink in and before I had time to say anything to him, Dad then said to me, "Now turn to Mark's Gospel Chapter 13 and read verses 26 and 27 out loud to me please."

And again, I did what he asked. As I was finishing reading the verses to my father I couldn't stop the tears from streaming down my face because the wonder of the words that I was reading to him were rebounding through my mind as I was struggling desperately to try to take in what I was beginning to realise had happened to me.

"It wasn't a dream, Isabella. For some very special reason the Lord above has given you a very special gift. You have experienced and can still feel that 'peace that passeth all understanding.' Perhaps one day you will know the reason why this was given to you."

So, without me trying to preach to you in any way, let me please share the words with you that I read that afternoon out loud to my father from his Bible, as I hold the very same Bible in my hands now, as tears yet again run down my face, yes from the very same Bible. These are the words that I read out loud that day nearly fifty years ago now.

Firstly from Matthew's Gospel Chapter 24 verse 31:

"And he shall send his angels with a great sound of a trumpet, and they shall gather together his elect from the four winds, from one end of Heaven to the other."

And now Mark's Gospel Chapter 13 verses 26 and 27:

26: "And then shall they see the Son of man coming in clouds with great power and glory.

27: And then shall he send his angels, and shall gather together his elect from the four winds, from the uttermost part of earth to the uttermost part of heaven."

These quotes were taken from my father's King James Bible. His Bible, the Bible he used to preach from for many years, the Bible my father loved to hold and read from, the Bible that was given to me after he left us all here on earth in 1988.

Now after I had read from my father's Bible I was visibly shaken. This had been a monumental event for me. Please remember I was only eighteen years old when this happened to me and I certainly wasn't capable of turning into a saint then or now. But I do remember, from that moment on, I knew for whatever reason that God did love me, truly loved me even though I wasn't what conventional Christians would call a born-again Christian and I felt so safe, really truly safe and my saying that is going to rock a few boats. The fears I had had about dying completely left me, never to return.

My lesson that night had been huge and that word is much too small.

God loves me.

I know that when it's my time to leave the planet I know, without a shadow of doubt, that I'm Heaven-bound. But you all need to realise He doesn't just love me, He loves all of us.

Now my story doesn't quite end there. A few weeks after my event my parents had a very special friend come to stay with us for a few days. We all called him Uncle James. He wasn't a real uncle, he was a very good friend of both my grandparents and my parents, but we had all known him since we were born and we occasionally went to stay with Uncle James and Aunt May and their five children for a holiday in their home in Scotland, a very large home. Now Uncle James was a very well respected preacher in his own right in Scotland and he was also a very astute businessman.

Uncle James had had a very strong influence on my father. It was he who sponsored my father to become a preacher. Now I'm telling you this because on the second night of his visit my father asked me to join him and Uncle James as they both wanted to talk to me but, bless Dad, he knew I would be nervous so as I entered the lounge they were both sitting in he stretched out both his arms to me and beckoned me to sit down on the settee right next to him so he could put his arm around me and cuddle me, where he knew I would feel safe.

Uncle James began to question me about my experience and by the time my story was finished he also sat very quietly for what seemed like an age before he spoke. I can't remember his exact words but as near as I can remember, and may he forgive me if I get a bit of it not quite right, "I don't know why this happened to you, Isabella. I have not heard of anything like this happening to anyone. How wonderful for you. God must have a plan for you that none of us yet knows. You must be going to do something very special with your life and one day you will know what it is. You will remember back to the night your event took place and you will smile. Because no matter what the task is that lies ahead for you, and how difficult it might be at times, the memory of that special night will always be with you; nothing can take it away from you. The memory of how much God loves you, and how well protected you are, will always be with you."

I can still see Uncle James sitting on the settee next to my father all those years ago and, as I stood up to leave the room, he had a kindly smile on his face and as he looked at me he was slowly nodding his head up and down in agreement and wonder at what he had just been told. I left them both discussing what had happened to me and I went upstairs to my room. Apparently my event took over the conversations for the rest of his stay with my parents.

I'm never going to forget my special event so that's why I know I'll never have the same experience again, because I don't need it.

Lesson learnt.

In fact, that night taught me more than I will ever be able to truly comprehend. It set me up well for the things that have transpired and followed in my life.

It was wonderful for me to have been able to share this experience with my father and it was very reassuring for me that both my father and Uncle James never doubted me for a moment and, of course, as the years have gone by, my event has been the prop I have lent on many times when strange and wonderful things have happened to me.

What an amazing experience. And the book that sparked my amazing event was 'On the Beach' by Nevil Shute.

It was a very long time ago now that it happened but, as I'm sitting here typing away on my little laptop, that night is as clear as if it was yesterday, as is the clarity of the day my father called me into his study and sat and cuddled me.

I guess the very important things that happen to us all in this life are recorded in such a way that we can have clear recall if needed, and this story was needed by me in my storytelling. The fact I had scribed it all down in a note book in 1989 was a huge help to me, but I wonder if you all realise that I have just enjoyed an afternoon with my father that I would otherwise not have had if I had not just scribed it all down again for you to read, so thank you.

For those of you that may not be sure what I mean, my precious father has been by my side this afternoon as I have been writing this.

So I leave you all now (for a little while) with a tear in my eye and a very big smile on my face.

Printed in Great Britain
by Amazon